IDAHO unBOUND

A Scrapbook & Guide

IDAHO *un*BOUND

A Scrapbook & Guide

Clay Morgan, writer
     McCall, Idaho

Steve Mitchell, editor
     Hailey, Idaho

Don Gill, illustrated maps
     Gooding Idaho

Clark Heglar, "Oldest Man in Idaho Series"
     Ketchum, Idaho

West Bound Books
PO Box 753
Ketchum, Idaho 83340

1 2 3 4 5 6 7 8 9   95 96 97 98 99

Library of Congress 95-061185
ISBN 1-887504-00-3

Credits

Writer	Clay Morgan
Editor & Publisher	Steve Mitchell
Illustrated Maps	Don Gill
Oldest Man in Idaho Tales	Clark Heglar
Designer	Mark Kashino
Production	Peak Media, Hailey, Idaho
Enhanced Topo Maps	Raven Maps, Portland, OR
Editorial Research	Ryan Fanzone, Scott Mitchell

Special Thanks to

Mark Kashino, friend and creative talent-supreme, for his book design, enthusiasm and support for the project.
Steve Bly and Steven Snyder for their outstanding current photographic portrayals of Idaho land and life. Clarence Stilwill and Tina, Brad, Steve, & Michael of Peak Media for their ideas, encouragement, and professionalism.
Steve Giacobbi, advisor, friend and supporter for the project.

And....
Clarence Bisbee, whose original turn-of-the-century silver print photographs set the standard, and Vardis Fisher, who set some writing standards while breaking many rules.

... and the many Idaho writers for generously sharing their work for reprint, and showing us glimpses of Idaho we might not have experienced ourselves.

... and to Teddy Roosevelt -for making us believe there is a Sasquatch.

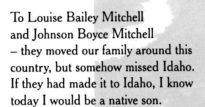

To Louise Bailey Mitchell
and Johnson Boyce Mitchell
– they moved our family around this
country, but somehow missed Idaho.
If they had made it to Idaho, I know
today I would be a native son.

– SM

For Adam and Ryan Morgan
– wide-eyed boys who help their
Dad live Idaho twice.

– CM

MAPS

Four types of maps have been provided.

—Artist & cartoonist Don Gill has created illustrated maps of the
state and its seven regions. Idaho history, its landmarks and
legends, are included in Don's unique style. His maps are
available in poster size from the publisher.
**** located: at the beginning of each region chapter, and as the
foldout page for the state map.

—Raven Maps of Portland, Oregon is the leader in creating
enhanced topographic maps that allow the viewer to easily
envision the terrain of a specific area. Raven provides a more
official mirror of the Gill illustrated maps.
**** located: at the beginning of each region chapter, and as the
foldout page for the state map.

—Abbreviated regional maps are placed at the end of each
regional chapter as handy references to the stories, towns, events,
restaurants, and attractions within that region.
**** located: at the end of each regional chapter.

—Special interest maps are included periodically that illustrate the
rivers of Idaho, the recent release of wolves into the state, Idaho
ski areas, Chief Joseph's flight, etc.
**** located: scattered throughout the book.

CONTENTS

FORWARD

Idaho Unbound: A Scrapbook & Guide is intended to provide a lively and interesting look at this fabulous state. This is a book for those who plan to come to Idaho, and for those families who came and stayed.

Both historic and current writers have been selected to provide a number of different glimpses at the various geographic regions of Idaho, and also Idaho history, heritage, culture, and the fabled Idaho outdoor recreation and lifestyle.

Both historic and current photographers have been selected to show the widest range of striking graphic impressions of this land, its people, flora, and fauna.

No Idaho history nor guide book in the past has had maps like you will find in *Idaho Unbound:* Sixteen color maps, eight by illustrator Don Gill, and

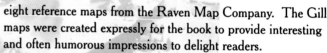

eight reference maps from the Raven Map Company. The Gill maps were created expressly for the book to provide interesting and often humorous impressions to delight readers.

Idaho lore and tall tales, as told by Clark Heglar (aka "The Oldest Man in Idaho") are scattered throughout the book.

The original text for the book is written by award-winning fiction writer Clay Morgan, and flows through the book at the bottom of most chapters.

Today, in-migrants from other states and tourists flock to Idaho. A friend of Ansel Adams, an engineer and inventor, who along with his brother acquired great wealth from technology, offered words of reflection that today bear sharing:

"A rich man went into the wilderness and saw all save the essence.
He brought with him all the luxury that wealth could buy.
And with it his own enslavement, and his own blindfold.
He went away having seen everything
but having realized nothing."
— Russell Harrison Varian

Idaho Unbound provides tall tales and stories for your amusement, wonderful photographs for your enrichment, history and information for your education, ...and a few thoughts for our reflection.

— Steve Mitchell
June, 1995

IDAHO

Base Map (C) 1987 Raven Maps & Images Revised 1992

Land Area: 82,700 square miles.

Designated forest and wilderness,
2.4 million acres, the most in the lower 48 states.

200 mountain peaks over 8,000 feet.

2,000 plus lakes. 16,000 miles of rivers and streams.

The most whitewater in the U.S.

America's deepest gorge, Hell's Canyon,
is half a mile deeper than the Grand Canyon.

Bruneau sand dunes tallest in North America.

Shoshone Falls is higher than Niagara.

Chapter I
INTRODUCTION

INTRODUCTION TO IDAHO
by Clay Morgan

"Idaho Unbound," says it as well. Idaho is not easily tied up in a package. And anyone looking for a precise definition of Idaho embarks on a Gordian quest. But that seems appropriate, because the way of the quest has long been the Idaho way. This is still the land of the pioneer and the starter-over. The wanderer, the lover, and the dream.

"A scrapbook . . ." Well, that suggests Idaho, too. This state often seems to have been cobbled together — by nature and by people — into an incongruous marvel that is more than the sum of its parts. "Scrapbook" suggests the project isn't finished, and one look at Idaho confirms that notion.

". . . and Guide." Now, here the publisher may be pressing his point. But as any backcountry veteran will tell you: the definition of an Idaho guide is anyone who has gotten lost here, before.

Idaho – known for it's mountains, rivers, plains, and lakes – sometimes in combination. Little Redfish Lake and the Sawtooths.

"Have you been to the high mountains? Have you seen great masses of bear rock, great waterfalls, and turbulent rivers? ... One who knows this world, must know more than mountains and rock and rivers." – Russell Varian.

An Idaho saying goes, "You can't get here from there."

The *here* in question is Idaho itself.

Sometimes it seems you can't get here from *here*. . . And yet here you are, happy and surprised — and usually out of breath.

Rugged, rangy, elusive, ever-changing, Idaho presents a challenging vision. "It's the light," someone might say. "The way the light doesn't fall or shine or even glow like it does in other places. You know what I mean? Here, the light . . . Oh, what can I say? The clarity tricked me. It magnified my ambitions. I thought that's where I was going was closer. . .

"I mean, just look," our someone might say, "at that tall pine on that near — er, I mean that *distant* — ridge. How far is that? Five? Ten? (Our someone's voice is rising.) Twenty-five miles? Good gawd! (Our someone is shouting now.) It might be two days and a half! (He's screaming now.) Without the benefit of helicopter! (Whispering, now) Oh, well, I'd go back where I started, if I only knew how to get back there."

Idaho is that way. Both geographically and historically. You think you've got it figured. Then you learn more. Many an Idaho river boatman have floated by a wild-eyed hiker, shouting at the river in dismay or delight. Or in both dismay and delight, at the same time. And if the boatman is like Wally Beamer of Lewiston, he turns to his passengers and says, "Remember now, that's just one Idahoan's opinion . . . today."

Just one person's Idaho. Every angle is new. The light on the land, the land in the light. Our someone might say, "I was enjoying the scenery and then I fell off the cliff." There's an Idaho moment that has been shared by many. People often come to Idaho the way philosophers come to a realization — by felicitous serendipity. Idaho was something wonderful they found when they didn't even know they were looking.

"I was on my way from Louisiana to Alaska," Lilbyrn Helmich of McCall once said, "until I got high-centered in Idaho." Both physically and spiritually, many people have high-centered — quite happily — in Idaho.

The mighty and mysterious Snake River touches five of Idaho's seven regions before emptying into the Columbia on its run to the Pacific, and the legends of the River of No Return are as numerous as its rapids.

* * * * *

An Idaho too hard to figure.

An Idaho too hard to traverse.

An Idaho too surprising to define.

As Idaho backcountry pilots say, "Even the clouds have rocks in them."

And so do Idaho dreams.

But that is all for the better. Once a place is defined and smoothed out and paved, in many ways it is dead in the mind. Luckily, contradictory Idaho is more than alive. In many ways, it is fresh born.

* * * * *

Some people say that Idaho is what America was. Of course, what America was, was a vehicle for self expression, greased with sweat and fired by the fuel of opportunity. What America was: That is Idaho now. Earnest, energetic, sometimes foolish, always kind.

And remember that America was also funny. Funny in an innocent, kidding, laugh-at-itself way. America could kid, grin, and still get its work done, taking everything seriously but itself. True grit and ready grin. Those were American qualities. That is Idaho today.

* * * * *

"Idaho Unbound — a Scrapbook and Guide" attempts to unbind a few misperceptions. It also hopes to scrap a few illusions. And it offers to guide the intrepid reader through a marvelous place.

Upper Left: "Salmon River near Buckskin Bill's. Wild water, wild elk, wild sheep, wild bear, wild wild." – Steve Snyder

Lower Left: Another pristine backcountry Idaho mountain lake.

IDAHO AGRICULTURE

Although mining, forest products and food processing play a role in Idaho's business scene, a major portion of Idaho's economy is geared to agricultural production and related agriculture service industries. The state's agriculture is highly diverse, a fact that insulates its economy from many of the ups and downs that affect the prices of individual commodities. Major crops include potatoes, wheat, barley, sugar beets, hay, dry peas and beans, hops and onions. The state also has a large livestock industry, raising dairy cows, beef cattle, hogs and sheep. Idaho is ranked first nationally in the production of potatoes, barley and trout.

NATURAL FEATURES

Idaho has more than 200 mountain peaks of 8,000 feet or higher. The nation's deepest gorge, Hell's Canyon is also found in Idaho. There are more than 2,000 natural lakes. It is the most heavily forested of the Rocky Mountain States with over 40% of its acreage covered by trees.

HEMINGWAY IN SUN VALLEY

The celebrated author Ernest Hemingway first traveled to the area in 1939, one of many celebrities Union Pacific Railroad chairman Averell Harriman invited to Sun Valley. Like many of the others who visited, Hemingway found something here that drew him back many times over the years. While in the resort, Hemingway enjoyed hunting birds and big game. In the fall of 1939, he finished one of his most well-known novels, *For Whom the Bell Tolls*, while staying at the Sun Valley Lodge.

OLDEST MAN SERIES
THE SHAPE OF IDAHO

A lot of people think the shape of Idaho is strange, but a lot of people just think Idaho is strange any how.

The old timers always said when they carved Montana Territory out of the Idaho Territory in 1864, that the border was supposed to have been the continental divide. If so, the border would have been just west of Helena,

Montana and Idaho wouldn't have it's distinctive panhandle. The story was that the surveyors started up the continental divide OK, but when they got to the Lost Trail Pass the surveyors got drunk and followed the wrong mountain range on up to Canada.

Well, that's a good story, but that's all it is, just a story, because the border was surveyed from the north to the south, so the surveyors followed the right mountain range. Now they may or may not have been drunk, but they followed the right range.

NOTE: Even though the continental divide is a natural boundary that crosses the width of the United States. (It goes through five states, New Mexico, Colorado, Wyoming, Idaho and Montana.) The continental divide is used as a state line just once on a small segment between Idaho and Montana.

Left:
Malad Falls.
Top right:
shadows still
creep across
the Snake
River canyon

FAR CREEPS THE SHADOW
CASDEC-832.

"Pioneer Mountains Moon.
Sunset – balances – Moonrise."
Photo below: Steve Snyder

WHERE IS IDAHO?

It seems like a lot of people don't know where Idaho is. They think that they do, but when they find out that you're from Idaho, they start telling you about an Uncle of theirs that works in the mills back in Ohio, or a cousin that farms in Iowa. I think I know what happened. Idaho is the only state settled from the west. All the people that came to Idaho after gold and silver was discovered, came from Oregon and the gold fields of California, so when they wrote their folk back home about Idaho, there wasn't anybody back east that they were writing to. Of course they weren't confused to start with when they made Grangeville the county seat of Idaho County and Idaho Falls the county seat of Bonneville County and Idaho City the seat of Boise County and the town of Boise the seat of Ada County. Of course Lewiston is the county seat of Nez Perce County and Nez Perce is the seat of Lewis County. Shoshone is the seat of Lincoln County, and Wallace is the Seat of Shoshone County, over 300 miles away.

A Sixteen Horse String Team, Freighting Supplies to the Mountains

NOTHING LIKE IDAHO

Talk not to me of Eastern States, their cities large and grand;
With operas and seaside joys way down by Jersey's sand;
Of cafes fine and swell resorts, and functions up in G,
Idaho, perched up near the sky, is good enough for me.

I've hit the trail to Iowa, and examined Kansas, too;
I've touched the highest spots they've got in far-famed old Mizzoo;
I've wintered in Los Angeles, also in Washington, D. C.;
But none of these can get my game—they're all too slow for me.

A. K. YERKES, *Sour Dough Creek, Ida*

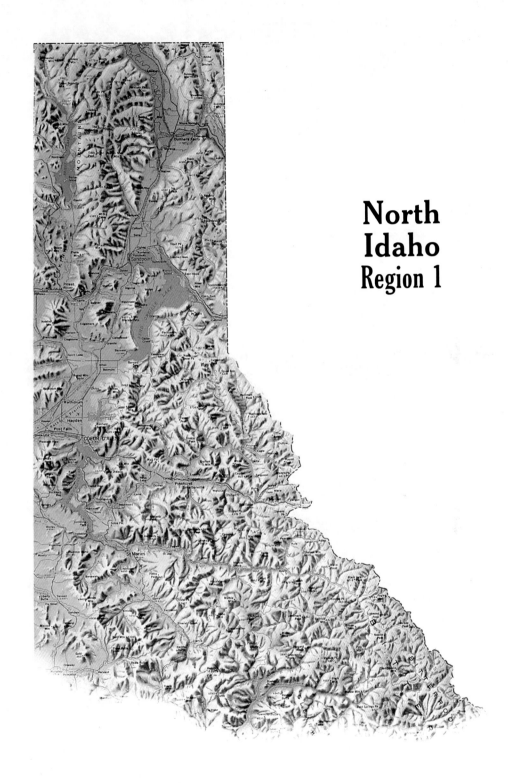

North
Idaho
Region 1

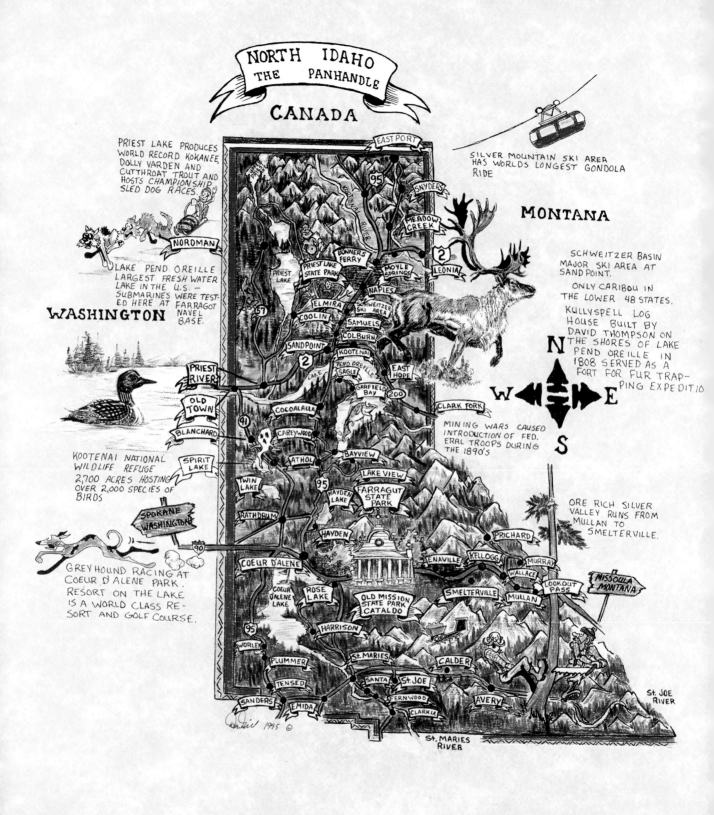

NORTH IDAHO
THE PANHANDLE

CANADA

MONTANA

WASHINGTON

PRIEST LAKE PRODUCES WORLD RECORD KOKANEE, DOLLY VARDEN AND CUTTHROAT TROUT AND HOSTS CHAMPIONSHIP SLED DOG RACES.

LAKE PEND OREILLE LARGEST FRESH WATER LAKE IN THE U.S.— SUBMARINES WERE TESTED HERE AT FARRAGUT NAVEL BASE.

KOOTENAI NATIONAL WILDLIFE REFUGE 2,700 ACRES HOSTING OVER 2,000 SPECIES OF BIRDS

GREYHOUND RACING AT COEUR D'ALENE PARK. RESORT ON THE LAKE IS A WORLD CLASS RESORT AND GOLF COURSE.

SILVER MOUNTAIN SKI AREA HAS WORLDS LONGEST GONDOLA RIDE

SCHWEITZER BASIN MAJOR SKI AREA AT SAND POINT.

ONLY CARIBOU IN THE LOWER 48 STATES.

KULLYSPELL LOG HOUSE BUILT BY DAVID THOMPSON ON THE SHORES OF LAKE PEND OREILLE IN 1808 SERVED AS A FORT FOR FUR TRAPPING EXPEDITIO

MINING WARS CAUSED INTRODUCTION OF FEDERAL TROOPS DURING THE 1890's

ORE RICH SILVER VALLEY RUNS FROM MULLAN TO SMELTERVILLE.

N W E S

EAST PORT
SNYDERS
MEADOW CREEK
BONNERS FERRY
PRIEST LAKE STATE PARK
PRIEST LAKE
MOYLE SPRINGS
LEONIA
NAPLES
ELMIRA
SCHWEITZER SKI AREA
COOLIN
SAMUELS
COLBURN
SANDPOINT
KOOTENAI
PEND OREILLE
SAGLE
EAST HOPE
GARFIELD BAY
PRIEST RIVER
CLARK FORK
OLD TOWN
COCOALALLA
BLANCHARD
CAREYWOOD
ATHOL
BAYVIEW
SPIRIT LAKE
TWIN LAKE
LAKE VIEW
HAYDEN LAKE
FARRAGUT STATE PARK
RATHDRUM
SPOKANE WASHINGTON
HAYDEN
PRICHARD
ENAVILLE
KELLOGG
MURRAY
WALLACE
LOOKOUT PASS
MISSOULA MONTANA
COEUR D'ALENE
COEUR D'ALENE LAKE
ROSE LAKE
SMELTERVILLE
MULLAN
OLD MISSION STATE PARK CATALDO
HARRISON
WORLEY
PLUMMER
St. MARIES
CALDER
TENSED
SANTA
St. JOE
SANDERS
EMIDA
FERNWOOD
AVERY
CLARKIA
St. JOE RIVER
St. MARIES RIVER

95
2
57
41
90
200

Chapter II
NORTH IDAHO
Region I

"What you notice first in northern Idaho are the noble stands of timber, of white and yellow pine, of larch and fir, of cedar and hemlock and spruce. They rise majestically, even awesomely, and you find yourself speaking quietly in the felt presence of the forest gods.

Here and there arc mills, and now and again big trucks come rolling by laden high with fine, clean logs, and the air tastes of pitch and needle and sawn wood, and you feel humble and exhilarated and altogether good."

—A.B. (Bud) Guthrie

Astonishing North Idaho presents an unexpected paradise.

Here, hard scrabble independents live amid loveliness. Artists, loggers, miners and singular individualists co-exist on a stage of geographic grandeur. Deep summer greens change to wide winter whites against an amazing backdrop of the past.

North Idaho's 46 mile-wide strip between Washington and Montana contains a welter of wonders, natural and man-made. Mountains soar above three of the Northwest's greatest lakes. Blue-green forests stretch northward through Canada. Some rivers plummet; other rivers loaf. Caribou, wolf and grizzly roam.

IDAHO'S HISTORIED GATEWAY TO CANADA

by Frances Sleep

As an elaborate antimaccasar on the chair back of Scenic Idaho, Boundary county at the extreme northern boundary of the state is a richly embroidered "tidy" of natural beauty.

Having the distinction of being the only county in the nation to be bounded on three sides, not by sister counties, but by two states and a foreign country, Boundary county has an area of 1276 square miles and ranks 23rd in size among the state's divisions. Neighbors to the north are the Province of British Columbia, Canada; while Boundary county's western limits are shared with Washington and on the east by Montana. Origin of its name is obvious, since it lays along the northern boundary of the United States and Canada.

Bonners Ferry, on a natural waterway to the south of these diggings, provided one outlet from the Canadian gold region. Some traces of the old Wild Horse trail that wound over the Selkirk Mountains to the west have been preserved and marked through the interest and efforts of Boundary county Boy Scouts.

More than 15 creeks of varying size drain the Selkirk mountains to the west and empty into the Kootenai river in Boundary county. The roaring Moyie river, fed by half as many tributaries, dashes down from Canada through the Purcell mountains on the east to join the Kootenai a few miles out of Bonners Ferry.

This rugged terrain provides some of the most bountiful and primitive hunting in the Gem State. A wide variety of wild life awaits the sportsman ranging from

History haunts the hills and hangs out on the street corners. Pioneer and mining vestiges abound. Small towns grow larger as newcomers move in and Indians continue to press for their rights as stewards of a great land. Tourism, industry and recreation attempt to dance with a delicate nature. A paradise stands in the balance; the scales tip and wobble.

Idahoans have a saying: Idaho is what America was. But there probably was never an America quite like North Idaho. Not all as one small, sweet vision, anyway. North Idaho is a heaven for the eye.

If Idaho is a young state, North Idaho feels old. Not timeless or ageless, but ancient and wise. All the ages exist here, all at once. It seems appropriate that in North Idaho scientists discovered a one-and-only

the tricky whitetail deer, which frequently in the fall is found feeding placidly with highland farmers cattle, to the majestic elk and big gray mule deer in the far mountain reaches of the county to the northwest. Bear are plentiful, both brown and black species.

Water fowl have a fly-way through the Kootenai river valley from Canada on their way south to winter feeding grounds. They stop the length of Boundary county to feed in the stubble fields of the wheat land which occupies approximately 36,000 acres of rich soil reclaimed from the Kootenai river by dikes. Canadian geese are included in this fall sport hunting as well as pheasant.

The quality and quantity of fishing in Idaho's northern-most county is only now coming to the attention of out-of-state nimrods. The Moyie river is one of the finest trout streams in the state.

Boundary county streams and Lakes, many of them in the mountain fastness of virgin timber, produce game fish of several descriptions, with trout far in the majority . . . Dolly Varden, rainbow, cutthroat, and eastern brook. And it is no fish story that from the icy depths of the glacial fed Kootenai it is possible to catch a fish so large a horse is needed to pull it ashore . . . the mighty sturgeon.

In all the grandeur of its many scenic points perhaps Boundary county is most proud of its Chimney Rock. Nearby is Harrison lake, a blue-green gem nestled in a setting of timbered beauty. Other landmarks here, Roman nose mountain, 7264 feet in elevation; and Gunsight peak, 7357 feet, provide homes for mountain goat.

Chimney Rock, while not so high (its elevation is but 7136 feet) is by far the most challenging. Looming gaunt and bleak, a chimney-like pinacle of barren, precipitous rock pointing heavenward more than 300 feet above its surroundings, Chimney Rock stands silhouetted against the skyline above its neighbors, the Selkirk mountains. ⌁

Today skiers from all over the West have discovered Schweitzer Basin, but many are unaware of the colorful history that has unfolded below. Nearby Coeur d'Alene Lake boasts both a town history and a world class resort – "The Coeur d'Alene.

remnant of a millions-year-old magnolia, with some of its DNA still intact.

To get a feeling for this place, stand among the great cedars at Hanna Flat Cedar Grove, just past dusk, as they exhale their aromatic sighs. That ginny old oxygen brings a sense of long life — perhaps the oldest breath of eternity that one can experience on earth.

Of course, North Idaho's mountains and lakes are older than the cedars and magnolia. The rugged Selkirk Range reaches north from Coeur d'Alene along Washington into Canada. The Selkirks are mainly granite while north Idaho's other great ranges, the Purcells, the Cabinets and the Coeur d'Alenes, are mainly folded from sedimentary rock. The tops of these mountains shoulder beautiful glacial valleys. Their feet

THE HOUSE OF THE GREAT SPIRIT

By: Fran Bahr

As I-90 drops down from 4th of July pass headed east toward Kellogg, it threads its way across the boggy flats bordering the North Fork of the Coeur d'Alene River. On a knoll lifting out of the flats sits a columned building, reminiscent of Greek architecture, whose off-white clapboard siding turns bright yellow in the evening sun. The oldest building in Idaho, the Cataldo Mission at Old Mission State Park, draws worshippers and travelers as it did 140 years ago.

The mission owes its existence to the desire of the Shee-chue-umsch, or Coeur d'Alene Indians, to worship a god more powerful than any other. These Indians hunted each year with the Flat-heads in Montana and heard stories about the Blackrobes (Jesuits) who taught a new way. DeSmet taught the Schee-chue-umsch sacraments like the Lord's Prayer and promised them that he would send teachers. He dispatched Father Nicholas Point and brother Charles Huet to establish a mission at the south end of Lake Coeur d'Alene, but they soon moved the mission north to a more desirable hill on the Missouri/Oregon trail, 16 miles east of Lake Coeur d'Alene.

The Old Mission slowly fell into disrepair until 1924 when the Jesuits deeded the church and grounds to the Diocese of Boise. That next year 2000 visitors joined in an automobile pilgrimage to the mission to "remember" and celebrate a High Mass offered by Father Cataldo, then 90 years old. Some of these celebrants were elderly tribal members who built the church and had not returned since they left 48 years earlier. The depth of the people's love for the Old Mission inspired a partial restoration in 1925. Thirty-seven years later, in 1962, the U.S. Department of the Interior designated the Cataldo Mission a National Historic Landmark, and in 1973 the Idaho Bicentennial Commission restored the building and grounds to their present condition.

Now one of Idaho's six state parks, a goal is to keep the mission alive and well with events where participants practice and demonstrate skills that would have been used in daily life. back during the heyday of the Mission."

One such event is the Historic Skills Fair, the second week in July. Blacksmiths, gold panners, spinners, quilters, pine needle basket-makers and even a crafts-woman who makes cedar hark dresses, ply their trades on the spacious, rolling lawns surrounding the church. Visitors take in the sights and then enjoy a home-cooked meal while listening to fiddlers for entertainment.

Another event, is the Mountain Men Rendezvous the third week in August. Taking painstaking care to replicate the lifestyle of mountain men, the participants put up lodges below the visitor center in a grove of cotton-woods. There they set about living as men and women did 100 years ago, building teepees and lean-tos, doing leatherwork, drying jerky and cooking those ever-present staples, beans and fried bread.

The most popular event, and appropriately so, comes mid-August when the Coeur d'Alene Indians return for The Feast of Assumption as they have for many years.

Coeur d'Alenes don their handsome ceremonial dress to re-enact the story of The Coming of the Black Robes.

The Coeur d'Alenes' ties to the Old Mission, even after 100 years, may become more firmly knotted. The Catholic Diocese still owns the mission, but in 1975 it deeded the mission and grounds to the Bureau of Indian Affairs to

bathe in deep waters of enormous blue lakes. Their hearts are shot through with valuable minerals, which have underwritten the area's rich history.

The glaciers scoured North Idaho for tens of millions of years, often filling the Purcell Trench with ice from way up in Canada. Sometimes the ice did more than laden the valleys. At least 41 times at the site of Lake Pend Oreille, a great glacial ice dam would first float free and then burst, loosing a wall of water 2000 feet high which lead hundreds of cubic miles of unstoppable water tumbling Idaho boulders to the Pacific. These glaciers left North Idaho with its three great lakes, so enormous that they look like ocean bays.

The Great Age of mammals still exists in North Idaho. Elk, deer, moose, black bear and cougar are

be held in trust for the Coeur d'Alenes. If the Indians wish to become the operating agency in 2015, they may step forward.

To see the grandchildren and great grandchildren of these who built the mission manage Old Mission State Park would seem the appropriate ending to a long saga of change for the Shee-chue-umsch. It would close the circle those old black robes started so many years ago.⏴

The Mission of the Sacred Heart at Cataldo hosts a reenactment by the Coeur d'Alene Indians of the "Coming of the Black Robes" each year during August.

Wyatt Earp in Murray

Have you ever heard of a little Idaho town called Murray? Maybe not, but I bet you've heard of a couple of Western characters called Wyatt Earp and Calamity Jane. They knew all about Murray, Idaho.

Murray, Idaho, located in the mountains just north of Wallace, has about 100 residents nowadays, but in the mid-1880s it was a thriving boomtown. A gold rush came to Murray in 1883. Gold meant miners, and miners meant saloons, supply stores, and a red light district. The latter attracted some colorful ladies like Terrible Edith, Molly B. Dam, and Calamity Jane.

Virgil and Wyatt Earp had some mining claims in the area, and they ran a saloon in nearby Eagle City. An 18 newspaper ad for their saloon called it the "finest appointed saloon in the Coeur d'Alenes... with the finest brand of foreign and domestic liquors to be found in the United States." The ad also suggested that customers of the Earp brothers' White Elephant Saloon, should come "and see the Elephant.".

Virgil and Wyatt Earp didn't stick around long, though. Murray boomed for about a year and a half, then just hung on for another 25 or 30 years. During its life as a mining center, about $1 million worth of gold came out of Murray, though the little town is still worth visiting. The Sprag Pole museum has a fascinating collection of mining tools, whiskey decanters, and guns. It also claims to have the world's longest wooden chain. It's 120 feet in length. Can your wooden chain beat that?

Murray, Idaho... just one of hundreds of fascinating places to visit around the State.⏴

common. Mountain goats can be watched from boats on Lake Pend Oreille. More rarely seen, but more significant in their presence are the ghostly gray wolves and fearsome grizzly, and the only herd of caribou in the contiguous United States.

Human time began in North Idaho as "Indian Time." Imagine calendars with no numbers. Then imagine no calendars. Then go stand among cedars, at dusk. EuroAmerican time began in North Idaho in 1808, when David Thompson reached Bonners Ferry from the North and began his scientific surveys.

Thompson established Kullyspell House on Lake Pend Oreille, near Hope, only two years after Lewis and Clark had passed through Idaho to the south. Thompson's "strong Log building" was the first fort

OLDEST MAN IN IDAHO SAYS

CATALDO MISSION

The Cataldo mission is the oldest standing building in Idaho. The Belgium Jesuit missionary, Pierre-Jean De Smet and his fellow missionaries, Anthony Ravalli and Nicholas Point established several missions in the Rocky Mountains. One of them was the Mission of the Sacred Heart for the Couerd'Alene Indians on the banks of the St. Joseph River, now called the St. Joe river, late in 1842. Because of flooding and mosquitoes they moved to higher ground in '46. The site, they chose was on the Coeur d'Alene River. It was at this site that Father Ravalli, an Italian, started building the church in 1847. He must have been pretty handy, because he built that church using only a broadax, an auger, a penknife, pulleys and ropes, whipsaw and the unskilled labor of the Indians. They started using the building in '54, but it wasn't finished until 1868.

In 1865 Father Joseph M. Cataldo, a Sicilian, was placed in charge of the mission. People thought he was a frail man, the Indians called him "Dried Salmon", but he lived over 90 years, and they named the church and a town for him. Caltaldo, not Dried Salmon.

In 1877 they surveyed the boundaries for the new Coeur d'Alene Reservation and found that the church and the Scared Heart Mission was outside the reservation. So they moved the mission, not the church building, south to De Smet, Idaho, that was named for the Jesuit that had started the mission in the first place. The town just north of De Smet had wanted that name, but the post office said they were too late, but they could spell the name backwards and that would be all right. The citizens of that community thought that was a good idea, so that is how Idaho got the town of Tensed, even though it was misspelled by the post office. It's no wonder we can't get our mail.

Larger than Lake Tahoe, Lake Pend d'Oreille is the largest of the northern lakes, used for testing submarines by the Navy. Ferry boats and trains provided the popular transportation to and from the town and lake of Coeur d'Alene for years.

established in the Pacific Northwest and the first cabin built in Idaho. Although a marker stands near Hope, no ruins remain but the scenery endures much as Thompson saw it.

David Thompson was much impressed with the Indians he met here, noting they seemed, "a very different race of people than those on the east side. [These Indians] pride themselves in their industry, and their skill in doing anything."

The Couer d'Alene Indians had become horse people before Thompson arrived. They rode on buffalo hunts with the Nez Perce, their neighbors to the south. The Kutenai were canoe people, taking much of their sustenance from the lakes. The lifestyle for both tribes was fundamental and wonderful.

A SUNKEN TREASURE

Today the tale is about a sunken treasure, but no pirates were involved. In the late 1880's many thousands of tons of ore were floated across Lake Coeur d'Alene from the Silver Valley mines in the Wallace and Kellogg area. The ore was loaded onto barges at Mission Landing near the Cataldo Mission, and towed by steamer down the Coeur d'Alene River and across the lake. In the winter the ice breaker Kootenai assisted with the job of transporting the ore.

Late in the fall of 1889, the captain of the Kootenai received orders to bring two barges, each loaded with 150 tons of ore, down from Mission Landing. The Kootenai pushed one barge and towed the other for a while, but the captain had trouble breaking through the ice, that way. He decided to tie up the front barge, leaving it behind, and tow the second barge on down to the ice free lake.

The icebreaker and its barge slipped quietly into the the lake about midnight. Most of the crew was asleep, thinking they had left potential problems behind them in the icy river.

Near McDonald's Point, on Lake Coeur d'Alene, something happened that caused the loose ore on the barge to shift. The barge tipped first one way, then the other, and 135 tons of high grade silver ore poured into the lake. That was about $15,000 worth in 1889.

Over the years at least two efforts to recover the ore have failed. It would be expensive to bring up 135 tons of rock from a depth of 100 feet. Perhaps if the price of silver goes up enough, someone will try again.⤥

...from A. B. Guthrie

If gold has petered out, silver hasn't, or lead, or zinc. The Coeur d' Alene mining district in the north, though almost the only hard-metal district in the state, is one of but eight in the world that have produced more than a billion dollars in gross value, and it is still a-goin'. It lies along the south fork of the Coeur d 'Alene River and is about twenty-five miles long and four or five wide and supports the towns of Mullan, Kellogg and Wallace. Once a brawling community where labor and capital toughed it out, the district appears ordered and steady these days, and men vote bonds whose pre-decessors voted with bullets.

But for a runaway, three-dollar jackass the Coeur d' Alene strike wouldn't have been made when it was. One night the animal took leave of N.S. Kellogg, a destitute carpenter turned prospector. Exhausted after he had tracked it down next morning, Kellogg sat down to rest and listlessly picked up a loose rock. Beneath it he found galena, the outcrop of silver-lead vein, and still more galena. He was in.

The jackass, once-because of its hellish bray-regarded as a nuisance in the town of Murray, became a privileged character after the strike. But only for a time. After its hour of glory someone tied a few sticks of dynamite to it, lighted a long fuse and sent it on its way.

Years later some joker or jokers erected a sign:

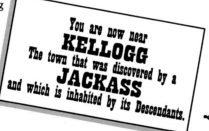

You are now near **KELLOGG** The town that was discovered by a **JACKASS** and which is inhabited by its Descendants. ⤥

The Coeur d'Alenes now have a reservation, stretching south from Lake Coeur d'Alene. The Kutenai never signed a peace treaty with the U.S. They live on their 12.5-acre "mission," near Bonners Ferry. In 1974, out of frustration, the Kutenai declared war against the United States, and charged anyone who drove across their land the token — but symbolic — toll of ten cents.

After European missionaries arrived in 1842, they found the Indians' many skills came in handy. The Coeur d'Alenes helped Father Ravalli build the magnificent Cataldo mission— the House of the Spirit and the oldest building in Idaho — using almost solely native materials, including grass and mud.

SEARCHING FOR THE SILVER LINING

by Earl Bennett

FLASH: May 2, 1884-Rich lead and silver ore discovered at the surface near the future townsite of Burke. Tiger and Poorman mines quickly staked.

FLASH: September 9, 1885-Bunker Hill Mine discovered by Noah Kellogg. Claims jack-ass actually found the mine. (Will become largest lead/zinc mine in the United States.)

FLASH: July 11, 1892-The Frisco Mill has been blown up by miners's union activists at Gem in northern Idaho. Governor Willey asks for federal troops. Charles Sirringo, a spy for the mine owners, has a harrowing escape from the miners. New union formed called Western Federation of Miners.

FLASH: April 29, 1899-The Bunker Hill and Sullivan mill at Kellogg has been blown up by union radicals. Governor Steunenberg calls on federal troops for assistance. Wallace under martial law.

FLASH: June 2, 1901-Fabulous silver-bearing ore found in the No. 2 tunnel of the Hercules Mine. Day family and other investors guaranteed millions.

FLASH: 1903-Charles Sweeney and John D. Rockefeller form the Federal Mining and Smelting Company and launch audacious plans to take over all of the mines in the in the Coeur d'Alene.

FLASH: December 30, 1905- Former governor Frank Steunenberg assassinated at his home in Caldwell by Harry Orchard, paid assassin of the Western Federation of Miners. Orchard implicates top union officials. Clarence Darrow gets union big-wigs off. Orchard serves life in Boise pen.

FLASH: 1906-James F. Callahan ships ore from rocks believed barren by mining experts. Callahan rich. (Company will eventually become today's Callahan Mining Corporation.

FLASH: 1931-Fabulous ore discovered in the Sunshine Mine on the 1700-level. (Mine will eventually produce over 350 million ounces of silver.)

FLASH: 1938-John Sekulic, a garage mechanic from Mullan, buys the Lucky Friday Mine, thought worthless, for $ 15,000. (Mine turns out to be one of the giants in the district. In 1958 Hecla buys in, eventually gains control.)

FLASH: January 1, 1955 - The Galena Mine, another huge silver mine, placed in production by Asarco. (In 1974, the company opens the Coeur Mine, the newest digs in the district.)

FLASH: August 25,1981-Giant Bunker Hill Mine complex closes. Silver Valley loses 2100 jobs.

FLASH: February, 1985-Billionth ounce of silver mined in the Coeur d'Alene. District claims largest recorded silver production in the world.

Sound like chapters from a Louis L'Amour adventure yarn, or a fast-paced western at the Bijou? Not so! These news items are part of the true story of the richest silver mining district in the world, located in the Silver Valley of northern Idaho. Is this a tale of harlots, villains, millionaires, scalawags and vagabonds who became rich beyond their wildest dreams? Yes, indeed, but it is also the story of Cousin Jacks (Cornish miners) and Dagos (Italian immigrants) who came to America in search of streets paved with gold and found in-stead the black depths of the Coeur d'Alene mines.

The story of the Coeur d'Alene is integral to Idaho's history, the history of the labor movement in the United States, and the development of our domestic mining industry. Where is the excitement of this bygone era in the Silver Valley

---

Soon mass immigration by EuroAmericans changed the Indian life forever. In 1861 a young muttonchopped Army lieutenant named John Mullan engineered the Mullan Road, between the Missouri and the Columbia Rivers, right past the front door of the mission.

The Mullan Road brought settlers — farmers, miners, loggers and merchants. North Idaho's lowlands still produce wheat grass seed, and specialty crops. Anheuser-Busch operates an important hop farm near Bonners Ferry.

Timber is still the king "crop" in North Idaho. Nearly every tree species that grows anywhere in the Northwest — Rocky Mountain or Coast — grows well in North Idaho: fir, hemlock, cedar, pine, spruce and

today? Stuffy boardrooms and boring stock-holders meetings sound dull. Give us the good old days.

Well, folks, the good old days never left. In 1979, maverick officers seized control of Sunshine Mining Company in a corporate move that would make a Harvard MBA or the "good old boys" in the Mine Owners Association smile with pleasure.

Or how about when the Hunt Brothers of Dallas, Texas, ran up the price of silver from $3 per ounce to over $50 an ounce in 1979-80? At that price, everybody raced out to melt down Grandma's tea set or silverware and cash in on the bonanza. Hecla Mining Company used the price swing to wipe out over $90 million in debt and become a major player in the industry.

And don't forget Coeur d'Alene Mines Corporation, who just a few years ago was a tiny company with only the Coeur Mine as an asset. Today, Coeur d'Alene Mines is a major silver producer. They operate the Rochester Mine in Nevada, the largest heap-leach silver mine in the world, and a new gold mine in central Idaho.

Action in the Coeur d'Alene continues fast and furious, and the end of our story is nowhere in sight.

Over 100 separate mines in the Coeur d'Alene district are hosted in rocks of the Belt Supergroup, a five-mile-thick pile of sedimentary rocks laid down in a long-forgotten ocean that existed from 800 million to 1.5 billion years ago. Millions of years after the sea disappeared, huge fractures or faults cut these rocks. Metal-bearing fluids migrated along the faults to produce the rich ore-veins that are mined today.

This 1884 Coeur d'Alene placer mine brought ore out of the mountains, and tunnels brought people through mountains to and from other states.

THE SUNSHINE MINE DISASTER

Just off Interstate 90, near the Big Creek exit, stands a 12-foot high steel statue of a miner at work. A dim lamp glows on the miner's hard hat, in memory of Idaho's worst mine disaster.

At about noon on May 2nd, 1972 miners noticed smoke inside the Sunshine Silver Mine near Kellogg. The mine is a labyrinth of tunnels and shafts a mile deep and more. It was almost impossible to tell just where the smoke was coming from.

One hundred seventy-three men were in the mine on that fateful day. At the first hint of smoke they began to evacuate. There are tales of bravery and tragedy too lengthy to recount. A hoistman ran his elevator-like hoist, lifting men through the toxic smoke to safety—until he died at the controls. One rescuer gave up his oxygen mask to an escaping miner, and in turn gave up his life. Heroism was the rule of the day with so many lives at stake.

Rescue efforts went on for a week, with nearly 100 men brought in from surrounding states and Canada. Then, on May 9th, two miners were found alive. Hopes soared with the discovery of the men, and rescuers redoubled their attempts. But that night workers began to recover bodies. The grim task continued until May 13th, eleven days after the fire began. There were no more survivors to be found.

Ninety-one men died from carbon monoxide poisoning inside the Sunshine Mine. The fire, with its deadly smoke, apparently started by spontaneous combustion in a junk pile deep within the mine. The Sunshine Mine disaster remains one of the deadliest in U.S. history.

larch. Here stood the greatest stands of white pine in North America, until overharvest and disease devastated the stands.

A much quicker catastrophe struck timber stands with the "Big Blow Up" wild fires of 1910. After a horribly dry spring, the citizens' worst fears came to pass when a monstrous wind blew in from the southwest. The approaching smoke clouds became so black that people argued whether they meant fire or rain. That is, they argued until the clouds began to rain fire. Three million acres burned, scores of people perished, several towns in the fires' paths vanished. In Wallace, they ran out of water and had to fight fire with beer.

Mining did most to change North Idaho. It brought people, created wealth, and changed the environment.

HARDHAT

Nineteen men and one woman reached the scene of a gold strike in the Coeur d'Alenes. A tent served as a saloon, the one log house being reserved for the woman. One evening she lifted the flap of the saloon tent and announced that she had shot Hardhat. There was no excitement. The men strolled over and observed that Hardhat was dead all right; had been too drunkenly amorous, apparently, and had reached the end of his trail. A committee was appointed to serve in the capacity of a coroner. Its report of the circumstances did not mention Hardhat at all; but it did express regret that the cleaning up of the new camp had been left to a lady, and extended thanks to her for a job well done.

Mullan, Idaho in 1909, the year before the fire.

THE CAVE IN
By: Helen Blume

It was early in the morning
when the sirens started their din
The graveyard shift had gone home to bed
The day shift had just gone in.

The town, as with one mind one heart
froze in its tracks at the sound
then moved as one to the tunnel
Loved ones were underground.

In minutes the yard was crowded
Not a word was said
They waited in abject silence
not knowing how many were dead.

The rescue squad went into action
and in less time than it takes to tell
miners were pouring from the pit,
jerked from the jaws of hell.

Then when the roll had been taken
all were there but three
No one knew what their fate was
No one knew where they might be.

A hundred women waited
silent, bewildered, numb
Two had husbands in the pit
One of them had a son.

For comfort they huddled together
to share the grief of the three
Each holding the silent knowledge
"Tomorrow, it may be me! "

On the fourth day deep in the tunnel
the workers silent and grim
suddenly stopped the digging
A cry came for help, weak and thin.

In a frenzy they dug through the rubble,
Through the trap where the tunnel had caved
One man was crushed by massive rocks
the other two were saved.

Waiting outside the tunnel
three women bewildered, numb,
Two had husbands returned to their arms
One of them lost a son.

As usual gold held the gleam that started the rush, but in North Idaho silver sustained the flow. Legend says that Noah Kellogg's jackass found the celebrated Bunker Hill road while sniffing at something shiny.

In 100 years North Idaho produced one-half million ounces of gold and one billion ounces of silver, from mine shafts reaching more than a mile underground. The Coeur d'Alene mines account for 80 percent of all the color ever mined in Idaho, making them one of the most productive mining districts on earth.

The Coeur d'Alenes also account much color in Idaho's history. On the gilded side glimmers the story of one Molly b'Damm, a "working" lady whom miners often sprinkled with gold dust, while she took her bath.

THE FIRE OF 1910

by Paul Mather

The fires of Northern Idaho and Western Montana, which on Saturday and Sunday, August 20 and 21, 1910, burned together into one huge conflagration, burning over an area of more than two million acres, destroying approximately two billion feet of timber taking 85 human lives, 30 horses, and thousands of fish, birds and wild animals, may well be classified as one of the world's greatest fires.

Forest fires began burning on the lower slopes early in May, which was two months in advance of the usual dry season, and their number rapidly increased through May and June. There were no lookouts at this time and detection of new fires depending on intermittent patrols. But forest rangers with a small amount of help succeeded in extinguishing all of the fires up to the latter part of July During July however, the fires became so numerous that it was difficult to man them and watch them after they were placed under control. On the evening of July 26, a sever electric storm, unaccompanied by rain, passed over the Coeur d' Alene Forest. Fire fighting crews were immediately busy looking for lightning fires, and during the next three days after the storm, fifty-two lightning fires were extinguished and may others that were discovered could not be reached in time to keep them from spreading. By August 1st there were men working on twenty-two large fires on the Coeur d' Alene Forest alone.

It should be noted at this time that there was no reserve of fire equipment in the Region. As new crews were put out, new equipment was purchased from the hardware stores. Axes, mattocks, shovels, cross-cut saws, wash boilers, tubs, coffee pots and frying pans were bought as needed until the supply in most of the local stores was exhausted.

Not only was equipment lacking but man power was also desperately needed. Men were shipped from Missoula, Spokane, and Butte, until the supply of floating labor was exhausted. A fifty-man crew was considered to be a big crew. And it was this size crew that was put on a "large" fire when in reality a five-hundred man crew would be necessary. In many cases five or ten men were fight-ing fires which would require a hundred to do effective work.

SNOW SCENE NEAR WALLACE IDAHO.

To remedy this lack of man-power, President Taft, on August 8th, authorized the use of regular Army units for fire fighting duty. Thus, about eight or ten companies were assigned to Region One on the Coeur d' Alene, Lolo and Flathead Forests. But most of them had arrived just before the big blow-up to be of any significant help, though they proved to be of value for police purposes during the general disorganization after the big fire.

On practically every one of the fires on the Coeur d' Alene Forest as well as other forests in the northwest, long trails had to be cut through the dense forests before they could reach the fires, this quite often delaying the firefighters to such an extent that the fires were beyond control before any work could be done upon them. In many instances it was necessary to cut 25-30 miles of trail through a heavily timbered and rough mountainous country before it was possible to get a pack train with provisions and tools to the locality where the fire was burning.

Nevertheless, in spite of the problems of equipment, men and logistics, by August 1st, it

---

On the scarlet side of history bleed the North Idaho mining wars, at the turn of the century, when the mining companies hired private armies and the miners marched into Wallace and Kellogg, 2000 strong, with pounds of dynamite to blow up an ore concentrator. Idaho's governor imposed martial law and called in federal troops.

Tourism now best exploits North Idaho's color. Natural beauty, historic interest and recreational opportunities abound in every corner of the region.

Wallace offers history in every dimension. Its elegant brick and wood buildings, its windows leaded and beveled and its wooden staircases stepping up mountainsides. Wallace is so "timely" that by merely

was estimated that throughout the region more than three thousand small fires and ninety rated as "large" had been controlled. Moreover, by the end of the first week in August things in the Region began to look better. On the 9th of August, Elers Koch, supervisor of the Lolo

Forest, whose forest had been particularly hard hit, made the statement to the press that every fire on his Forest was out or practically under control. In addition, Regional Forester William Greely, asserted on the same day, that the general was greatly improved.

However, once again this optimism was dashed, for on the morning of August 20th the wind began to blow. It was a heavy wind blowing out of the Southwest and all along the lines, from the Canadian boundary, south to the Salmon River, the gale blew. Little fires turned into big fires and fire lines which had been held for days were soon lost.

The town of Wallace had laid in a state of pending doom, so to speak, since the latter part of July, with numerous fires to the south, just across the St. Joe divide. The people of Wallace were extremely concerned. This can be borne out by the fact that a newspaper reporter

stated on August 14th that all insurance men had their clerks busy writing fire insurance, policies, and were not refusing any business. On August 20th, when the sky turned that "ghastly yellow," it was apparent to everyone that the flames were on there way.

The fire broke into Wallace at approximately 9:00 p.m. That night before it was brought under control, the whole east side or roughly one-third of the town, had burned. The costs of the fire in Wallace were estimated at one million dollars with over one-hundred buildings being burned and two townspeople losing their lives. Fortunately, the women and children were evacuated by a special train that Weigle had ordered earlier in the day.

For those out in the woods, things were worse, as many crews were trapped in the onrush of the fire. Emery Wilson wrote in his notebook that the firefighters had, absolutely lost control and being unable to longer battle with this terrible element of destruction, the men who were fighting these fires began a mad race before the leaping flames for safety. Some fled to bare mountain peaks, others crept into prospect tunnels, while a few more fortunate, buried themselves in the mud and water in the creek beds.

In area, the fire covered more than three million acres, of which 2,595,635 acres were on national forest lands.

Reports of property damage were also incomplete. However, one-third of Wallace was burned, and the little towns of Taft, DeBorgia, Haugan and Tuscor were all entirely destroyed.

Left: Wallace after the worst fire in North Idaho's history –1910.

Right: Down at Coeur d'Alene Lake, bathers enjoyed the water then as now.

changing the years and makes of automobiles (or wagons) parked along its streets, one can imagine his or her way through the decades. Wallace often receives the most rainfall in Idaho and the mountains above town are darkest green.

Just downstream from Wallace, Kellogg presents other faces of the past and the future. Here stands the memorial to the 70 miners who died in Sunshine Mine disaster. From here rises the world's longest single-stage gondola, which carries skiers to the Silver Mountain ski area and mountain bikers to many miles of free-wheeling.

West of Kellogg, past the old Mission, begin the waters of Lake Coeur d'Alene, one of the three North

From Ivan Doig's "ENGLISH CREEK"

"It was a fact that the legendary fires occurred over there west of the Continental Divide. The Bitterroot blaze of 1910 was an absolute hurricane of flame. Into smoke went three million acres of standing trees, a lot of it the finest white pine in the world. And about half the town of Wallace, Idaho, burned. And this too: the Bitterroot fire killed eighty-five persons, eighty-four of them done in directly by the flames and the other one walked of a little from a hotshot crew on Setzer Creek and put a pistol to himself. The Forest Service, which was only a few years old at the time, was bloodied badly by the Bitterroot fire. And as recently as 1934 there had been the fiasco of the Selway fires along the Idaho-Montana line. That August, the Selway National Forest became the Alamo of Region One. Into those back-country fires the regional forester, Major Kelley, and his head-quarters staff poured fifty-four hundred men, and they never did get the flames under control. The Pete King Creek fire and the McLendon Butte fire and about fifteen smaller ones all were roaring at once. The worst afternoon, ten square miles of the Selway forest were bursting into flame every hour. And when the fire at Fish Butte blew up, a couple of hundred

CCC guys had to run like jackrabbits. Five fire camps eventually went up in smoke, both the Pete King and Lochsa ranger stations damn near did. Nothing the Forest Service tried on the Selway worked. Nothing could work, really. An inferno has no thermostat. The rains of late September finally slowed the Selway fires, and only weeks after that Major Kelley killed off the Selway National Forest, parceled out its land to the neighboring forests and scattered its staff like the tribes of Israel. The Selway summer sobered everybody working in Region One - that total defeat by fire and the Major's obliteration of a National Forest unit - and for damn sure no ranger wanted any similar nightmare erupting in his own district."

Idaho great lakes. All are great sport fisheries, producing trophy mackinaw, kokanee, kamloops, cutthroat and Chinook. All are beauties, presenting differing vistas at each bend in their many-bended shorelines.

Lake Coeur d'Alene and city of Coeur d'Alene have been North Idaho's main watering holes for more than a century. Steamers, mail packets and log-boom tugs plied its waters for years. Tour boats now cruise the lake and the shadowy St. Joe River. In 1878 the U.S. Army established a fort where the river leaves the lake and later named it Fort Sherman for General William Tecumseh Sherman (who, ironically, once suggested draining the lake). North Idaho College now occupies the Fort Grounds. Up the beach from the college rises the Coeur d'Alene Resort, one of the finest recreational resorts in the world, which offers its

OUR OLDEST STATE PARK

Probably the first thing you should know about Heyburn State Park is that it is nowhere near Heyburn Idaho. Heyburn—the town—is in southern Idaho, near Rupert. Heyburn—the park—is in northern Idaho, near St. Maries. Both places were named after Senator Weldon Heyburn, who served in Congress from 1903 until he died in office in 1912 .

Senator Heyburn would probably not be completely pleased to have a state park named after him. Although he was responsible for getting the US government to aside the land that is now Heyburn State Park, he wanted the site to be a national park. He didn't think the state was capable of running a park.

But the state successfully runs the Pacific Northwest's oldest park, which was set aside in 1908. The park has a total of 7,800 acres, 2,300 acres of that is water. It's most famous feature is a river that runs through that water. The "river between the lakes" is where the shadowy Saint Joe meanders through Chatcolet; Hidden, Round and Benewah Lakes, keeping a thin strip of bank on either side.

Heyburn State Park is a haven for wildlife, especially waterfowl. Blue heron and osprey are common in the park.

One unusual feature is the wild rice growing in the park's lakes. There's enough there to commercially harvest, and they celebrate the rice harvest each year at Heyburn State Park during the August Wild Rice Festival.◅

LAKES OF THE NORTH

The rivers of Idaho provide extraordinary fishing for salmon and steelhead and other varieties of trout, but it is the lakes of the north that are really sensational both in size and number of fish and fishing records. Lake Pend Oreille has yielded the world's record rainbow- thirty-seven pounds -and the world's record Dolly Varden or bull trout- thirty-two pounds. Priest

Lake set the American record for Mackinaw or lake trout with a specimen weighing fifty-one pounds. An innumerable concentration of Kokanee or bluebacks inhabit the waters of Lake Pend Oreille. They are a tasty, smallish, up-to-fourteen-inch salmon, and a million were caught in the first six months of one season. Once there was no limit on the catch. Nowadays you're risking trouble if you yank out more than fifty in one day. For all these blessed opportunities, the state license costs the outsider only three dollars for five days, or ten dollars for a year.

The story of the Kamloops is a story of private enterprise and public astonishment. The fish, a rainbow in everything but size, is a native of British Columbia. In 1941, a group of Sandpoint citizens brought in some eggs. For four years thereafter nothing outward happened, and then one day in 1945 a man came into town lugging a thirty-two pounder. It was a sensation, and no wonder. For twenty-nine years the world's record for rainbow had stood at twenty-six pounds. Since then, the record has risen , and each year at the opening of the season there's a big to-do at which the taker of the biggest trout is duly honored.

One of these honorees won additional distinction in the spring of 1947. Here he was ashore with the record fish, and photographers were popping bulbs around him, and for a final shot it was suggested that he stand holding his prize in the stern of his boat. He was an obliging man. He did so. And somehow the trout slipped from his grasp. Somehow, though dead, it sank like a stone, and in deep water. There was a moment of paralyzed incredulity. Then the man, Lord love him, shrugged and turned away and said, "I always heard they threw 'em back unless they weighed forty pounds." p.s. They dredged the fish out later.◅

---

beautiful golf course with the famous floating green — another example of how often this lake has floated people's dreams.

Lake Pend Oreille is Idaho's deep giant, so profound and mysterious that the U.S. Navy has used it to test secret submarines. The town of Sandpoint graces the lake's north shore. Sandpoint and Hope, to the east, have become artists' havens. A few miles above Sandpoint, the Schweitzer Basin ski area offers premium skiing and grand views of the lake.

Priest Lake is the smallest great lake, at a mere 17 miles long, but it figures as the big favorite of many. Above Priest's fish-filled waters, the surrounding Selkirks rise majestically 5000 feet skyward.

North Idaho's lakes are idyllic, but this clearing of the 1910 fire, and the stands of heroic timber gave Idahoans a constant reminder of nature's fragile balance.

CALENDAR NORTH IDAHO

January
Sandpoint Winter Carnival, Sandpoint
Sled Dog Races, Priest Lake

May
Pioneer Days, Coeur d'Alene
Depot Days, Wallace

June
Post Falls Days Bluegrass Festival, Post Falls

July
Historic Skills Fair, Cataldo Mission

August
Salmon Fishing Derby, Coeur d'Alene
North Idaho Fair & Rodeo, Coeur d'Alene
Hukleberry Festival, Wallace
Mountain Man Rendezvous, Cataldo Mission
Sandpoint Arts & Crafts Festival, Sandpoint

December
Christmas Concert & Performances, North Idaho College, Coeur d'Alene

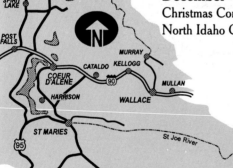

TIPS: FOOD & SHELTER IN NORTH IDAHO

The Coeur d'Alene Resort: World class resort on the lake. Golf course labeled "America's most beautiful resort course" by Golf Digest. Even locals spring for their famous Sunday brunch for occasions.

Connie's: A Sandpoint favorite for breakfast, downtown motel is recommended as well.

The Blackwell House: Moderately priced B&B in Coeur d'Alene in restored 1910 Victorian.

Hill's Resort: Family resort award winner on Spirit Lake.

Hudson's Hamburgers in Coeur d'Alene. Since 1907! Featured in USA Today as one of top hamburgers in the country.

The Hydra Restaurant: Favorite of locals for years, attractive reasonably priced garden setting.

Papino's: In Coeur d'Alene. Excellent Italian has been a Coeur d'Alene tradition for years.

Pines Resort: In Coeur d'Alene. Variety of accommodations and rates, lounge, pets allowed.

Rustler's Roost: In Coeur d'Alene or Hayden Lake is the local's favorite breakfast spot.

The Shore Lodge: In Sandpoint. Moderately priced, attractive on the lake; special ski packages during winter.

Wolf Lodge: Best steaks and prime rib a few miles outside of Coeur d'Alene.

From deep underground its historied mines, across its big waters and forests and up its steep mountainsides, North Idaho presents its residents and visitors with a feeling of one-and-only. Perhaps this is why its inhabitants so well represent that only-in-Idaho personality mix — fierce individualism and almost libertarian tolerance.

North Central Idaho
Region 2

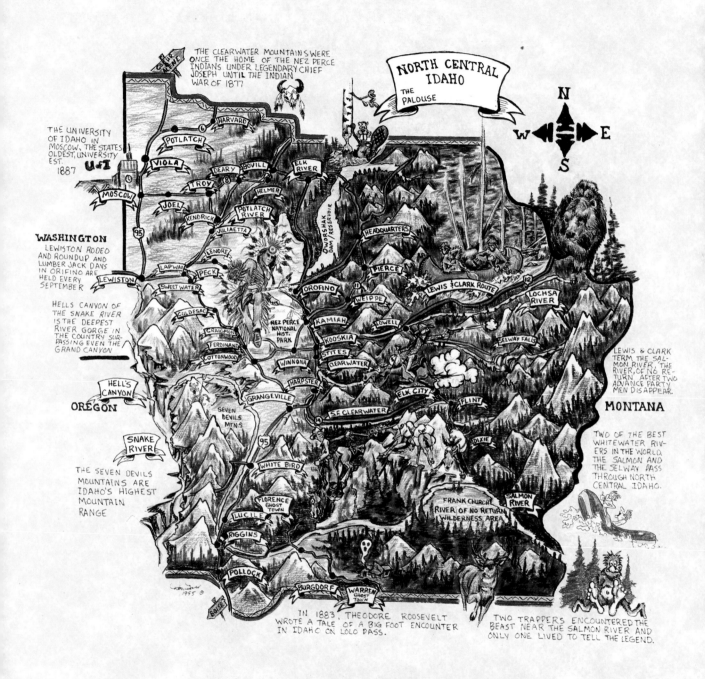

NORTH CENTRAL IDAHO
THE PALOUSE

THE CLEARWATER MOUNTAINS WERE ONCE THE HOME OF THE NEZ PERCE INDIANS UNDER LEGENDARY CHIEF JOSEPH UNTIL THE INDIAN WAR OF 1877

THE UNIVERSITY OF IDAHO IN MOSCOW, THE STATES OLDEST UNIVERSITY EST. 1887

WASHINGTON

LEWISTON RODEO AND ROUNDUP AND LUMBER JACK DAYS IN ORIFINO ARE HELD EVERY SEPTEMBER

HELLS CANYON OF THE SNAKE RIVER IS THE DEEPEST RIVER GORGE IN THE COUNTRY SURPASSING EVEN THE GRAND CANYON

OREGON

SNAKE RIVER

THE SEVEN DEVILS MOUNTAINS ARE IDAHO'S HIGHEST MOUNTAIN RANGE

LEWIS & CLARK TERM THE SALMON RIVER, THE RIVER, OF NO RETURN, AFTER TWO ADVANCE PARTY MEN DISAPPEAR.

MONTANA

TWO OF THE BEST WHITEWATER RIVERS IN THE WORLD, THE SALMON AND THE SELWAY PASS THROUGH NORTH CENTRAL IDAHO.

IN 1883, THEODORE ROOSEVELT WROTE A TALE OF A BIG FOOT ENCOUNTER IN IDAHO ON LOLO PASS.

TWO TRAPPERS ENCOUNTERED THE BEAST NEAR THE SALMON RIVER AND ONLY ONE LIVED TO TELL THE LEGEND.

Chapter III
NORTH CENTRAL IDAHO
Region 2

Wheat lands, timber lands, fish from sea. Beauty, brains, the wildness of nature. A wildness watched over by a civilized eye. North Central Idaho reveals a big bounty.

It cannot be described with one breath or with one set of adjectives. It changes so quickly by the mile and by the angle of sunlight. But one can choose any moment and try.

At sunset the Palouse rolls like billowing swells on a dark earth-sea, with darker timber-filled troughs and golden grain-tossed crests. Beyond the Palouse,

the wide forests flow like a blue-green ocean. On this sea's horizon the snowtopped Bitteroots surge up out of a great stormy wilderness, like whitecaps, breaking north.

That's just one perspective of North Central Idaho, a grand mixture of mini-regions, each one its own world.

The Palouse spreads north from the top of Lewiston Hill. It got its name, some have said, from early French trappers who thought it looked like a beautiful green lawn, or *pelouse*. Others have said that the name is Nez Perce Indian, pointing out that it sounds like "appaloosa," the beautiful spotted horse that the Nez Perce developed. Although the Palouse probably derives from an Indian word, any certainty is lost. Whatever its name's origin, the Palouse is green-gorgeous — as a lawn, as rich farmland and as a heaven for horses. ☞

COMING IN ON HIGHWAY 12

by Karen Swenson

It was late August, a windless silence of heat, as I wound my way up Lolo pass. I am a New York City person. Silence impresses me and I carried that silence with me all morning among the thrust and crest of rocks. I meet no one until, almost at the top of the pass, I came upon an ill-advised trucker maneuvering many wheels around a hairpin at the edge of a precipice. I pulled off the road and once he passed me stayed where I was listening to audible emptiness. There was no wind in the firs and the silence was huge as the sky. My cat, Miscegenation, so called because she was all the colors allowed to cats by God, came and sat in my sun filled lap. We watched light glint off mica in the roadside rock, a sharpness in the eye as stabbing as the occasional harsh

Idaho shares the Clark Fork river with Montana, and each year used to send wild mustangs from the Camas prarie across the border.

call of a jay which made her shift her ears to a new angle.

I took some pictures with a camera which was later melted into a puddle of black excrescent plastic by the sun in Yellowstone on the back window ledge of my car. But they never showed me quite what I saw the heights, the depths, the bigness, the silence, the aloneness, the un-human self-sufficient certainty of that landscape with one snowy crest peaking out among bare bouldered shoulders in the distance. All of which said quite plainly I was not necessary, that things would go on without me, although the unhuman inhabitants would be quite pleased to fold my bones into the stew they were making, had been making, intended to continue to make.

Along the Lochsa that morning there wasn't much doing except sunlight on water. I stopped, walked down to the edge. The water,

THE APPROACHING STORM.

👉 Eastward from the Palouse stretch the wide productive forests of fir, cedar, pine and larch. The nation' s largest stand of valuable white pine once grew here. One giant, felled in 1911 at an age of 425 years, stood 200 feet tall and seven feet in diameter. Although much diminished by harvest and disease, these forests still provide millions of board-feet of timber.

South of the Palouse begin the North Central Idaho canyonlands. All are deep. Two are deeper than the Grand Canyon. Indeed, the Snake River's Hells Canyon can seem too deep as it slices between two great mountain ranges — Oregon's Wallowas and Idaho's Seven Devils — rising on both sides to elevations of over 9,000 feet.

flecking the sun off its back in shards of gold, gave color and an aura of preciousness to pebbles on the bottom. The river filled silence with liquid chatter. Miscegenation watched from the hatchback sniffing the air like a wine connoisseur encountering a series of exceptional vintages. No one seemed to own anything but a flatbed Ford and everyone raised a hand just above the steering wheel in greeting despite my New York license plate. As the road twisted along beside the river keeping it company on one side, it was shrouded right to the edge with firs on the other. I remember occasional spidery bridges across the current. Again and again I stopped. What is it that is so attractive in the sparkle of a river? In backwater pools I watched the droplet shadows of water striders skid over the pebbled bottom.

Exactly where it happened I can't remember but after Lowell and Syringa. The little garrulous river was gone and there was a broad more dignified channel. Above it rose the hunched tawny shoulders of bluffs as though a thousand prides of lions were in their manes glowering from those heights. Why had no one told me about these? What were these awesome in their wild barrenness? Historical signs along the way retold Indian myths which seemed highly likely in this terrain.

Up switchbacks on a two-lane road I climbed these dry golden backs as though clambering over a somnolent anima. I could see the earthy foundation under the matted coat which looked like rock that had been shattered by the blow of a sledge hammer. What would be at the top? Mountains? Desert? The map said no to mountains but wasn't otherwise informative. I was not prepared for the great open vista at the top of long-bellied hills striated with furrows of stubble, ripened wheat and fallow. A magnificent monochrome landscape. Why hasn't this locale produced a school of abstract painters? Why did Georgia O'Keefe miss this? She would have known what to do with these subtle variations of browns and beiges.

As I approached Moscow I turned off the main road onto a narrow stretch of pavement that promised a town named Genesee. Beyond a salvage of pavement on either side the fabric of grain undulated away. Out of it suddenly rose a hawk, his small gray prey in his talons, and crossed my windshield perilously but thrillingly close: my blessing from this strange new country I was to live in. ◢

TRAVEL JOURNAL
by Bill London

Begin with hundreds of square miles of Idaho forest, all open for hiking and camping. Add a village in the middle of that backcountry, at the end of a state highway. A village barely big enough for a stop sign and certainly much too slow for a stop signal. Drop in an unpretentious family-run resort hotel where the night-life revolves around the fireplace and the hot tub. Now stir in a handful of unique attractions, like

The aptly named Clearwater River cradles green garden lands and much of the region's population. The famed Salmon River canyons channel the largest undammed river system in the contiguous U.S. These canyon rivers flow out of a wilderness that some have come to call "The Big Wild," or "America's Serengeti," because of its great size, environmental integrity, and abundant wildlife.

Only two roads penetrate through North Central Idaho's portion of this wilderness. The gravel Magruder Corridor road closes every winter. Paved Highway 12, which follows the Clearwater and Lochsa Rivers to Lolo Pass, has only been in existence since 1962.

Before the first few roads entered North Central Idaho, ragged ridgetops and roaring rivers allowed the biggest tree east of the Cascades and the tallest waterfall in Northern Idaho. The resulting prescription is just what any wise physician would order - a naturally-relaxing vacation, a comfortable destination, the town of Elk River Idaho, population 180.

After the last mill closed down there in 1980, yet another timber town faced what could charitably be called an uncertain future. But mostly due to the enterprising new owners of the town's only hotel, and the mini-infusion of visitor dollars they've created, Elk River's economy continues to exist.

"We've built our business on keeping people comfortable," explained Andre Molsee, one of the new owners of Huckleberry Heaven Lodge, Elk River's finest. "On vacation, when people are roughing it in Idaho, they just won't settle for a buggy old cabin without a good hot shower-and I don't blame them, I won't settle for that either."

For Elk River visitors the available choices extend far beyond the difficult dilema of choosing between huckleberry pie and huckleberry donuts for dessert. The town is surrounded by some extraordinary outdoor attractions.

Of all those sites the most awesome is the Big Tree. Only 10 miles north of Elk River, this giant western red cedar-more than 18 feet in diameter, taller than a 15-story building, and at least 3,000 years old, is the largest tree of any species in North America, east of the Cascades. Until 1979, the huge cedar was undiscovered in the vastness of Idaho's backcountry.

Swimmers will want to head for Elk River Pond, a delightful mountain lake a quarter mile from town. The Elk River Recreation District has placed three small campgrounds around the lake to encourage visitor use of the area, and offer the camping places for free. But as you might expect at that price, none of those sites provide RV utility hookups. If you are interested in sites with hookups, a total of nine such spaces are available within Elk River.

Twenty miles past the pond is a larger mountain lake, Dworshak Reservoir, created by the damming of the North Fork of the Clearwater River. At Dent, where the road from Elk River bridges the lake, the U.S. Army Corps of Engineers built a full-service-including hot showers and utility hookups-50-unit camping area and a boat launch ramp.

But Dworshak is worth visiting for more than the waterskiing opportunities. Its 53-mile length is an open highway into what had previously been some of Idaho's most inaccessible backcountry. Now that the reservoir has provided a water highway, more than 140 "mini-camps" have been built along the shoreline, with access by boat only. Set on isolated coves and pockets, these single-site camping areas offer only a pit toilet, table and grill-and of course, serenity.

If you tire of the water and are ready for a return to the big trees, there are more. Two protected groves of uncut forestland are located north of Elk River, at Morris Creek and at Elk Butte.

The Morris Creek Old Growth Cedar Grove is the only remaining stand of uncut western red cedar in the area. Within the 80-acre preserve it is all cedars, most five to eight feet in diameter, packed tightly together on a gentle, north-facing slope. Foot trails provide the only access into the area, from the gravel road a quarter mile away.

Elk Butte Mountain Hemlock Natural Area is 140 acres of, not too surprisingly, mountain hemlocks, a tree which only rarely grows in pure forest stands. The preserve contains the only grove of big hemlocks in the area. A smaller, high elevation species, these

only the most primitive travel. The geography is underlain by a fascinating geology. "Worlds in collision" summarizes part of the story.

The Seven Devils Mountains rise as gorgeous grotesques. He Devil, She Devil, the Tower of Babel and other rocky goblins haunt a high country of timber and lakes. Strange to look at, the Devils are stranger to ponder. One hundred million years ago, parts of the Devils formed North America's "west coast." Then the global dynamism of plate tectonics produced what geologists call "exotic terranes" and sent them crashing onshore. These terranes were remnants of lands once located in the tropical Pacific Ocean, thousands of miles to the southwest, in an area of palm trees and coral reefs.

hemlocks are three to four feet in diameter. As a bonus, don't forget to look beyond the trees and the forest to the view from the top. Most of the spine of the Bitterroot, Mountain Range, on the Montana border, is visible from the butte.

In addition to all those special and spectacular places, Elk River is the gateway to the miles of National Forest that surround it. Because there are so many miles of trails and acres of forest with so few human visitors, camping, fishing, hunting and hiking are allowed virtually everywhere-and game, from deer and elk to hawks and ducks, is not difficult to see. Elk River is remote and undiscovered enough that it is actually rare to meet other people at any of the forest preserves in the area.

For anyone who is interested in rustic, but comfortable destination, Elk River is a pleasant place to rough it, in style.

Horses have always been a part of working life in the "Palouse" territory, from Nez Perce tribes to mule-driven loggers.

TEDDY ROOSEVELT AND SASQUATCH ON LOLO PASS

"They were surprised to find that during their short absence something, apparently a bear, had visited camp, and had rummaged about among their things, scattering the contents of their packs, and in sheer wantonness destroying their lean-to. The footprints of the beast were quite plain, but at first they paid no particular heed to them, busying themselves with rebuilding the lean-to, laying out their beds and stores, and lighting the fire.

While Bauman was making supper ready, it being already dark, his companion began to examine the tracks more closely, and soon took a brand from the fire to follow them up, where the intruder had walked along a game trail after leaving the camp. When the brand flickered out, he returned and took another, repeating his inspection of the footprints very closely. Coming back to the fire, he stood by it a minute or two, peering out into the darkness, and suddenly remarked: "Bauman, that bear has been walking on two legs." Bauman laughed at this, but his partner insisted that he was right, and upon again examining the tracks with a torch, they

certainly did seem to be made by but two paws, or feet.

The men, thoroughly uneasy, gathered a great heap of dead logs, and kept up a roaring fire throughout the night, one or the other sitting on guard most of the time. About midnight the thing came down through the forest opposite, across the brook, and stayed there on the hillside for nearly an hour. They could hear the branches crackle, as it moved about, and several times it uttered a harsh grating, long-drawn moan, a peculiarly sinister sound. Yet it did not venture near the fire.

In the morning the two trappers, after discussing the strange events of the last thirty-six hours, decided that they would shoulder their

---

The Seven Devils are the what the Indians once called "the place of the big jumping off" — into the Hells Canyon, America's deepest gorge. The power of the Snake River has taken fifteen million years to carve this sensation.

The Devils, the Hells Canyon and much of western North Central Idaho are also in the province of the Columbia Basin Basalts vast flows of lava which flowed across the area when the Hells Canyon began forming. These basalts formed the wonderful rimrock and "book cliffs" that characterize much of the area.

The lava was stopped on the east by another rocky wonder, the Idaho Batholith (which means "deep

packs and leave the valley that afternoon. They were the more ready to do this because in spite of seeing a good deal of game sign they had caught very little fur. However, it was necessary first to go along the line of their traps and gather them, and this they started out to do. All the morning they kept together, picking up trap after trap, each one empty.

In the high, bright sunlight their fears seemed absurd to the two armed men, accustomed as they were, through long years of lonely wandering in the wilderness to face every kind of danger from man, brute, or element. There were still three beaver traps to collect from a little pond in a wide ravine near by. Bauman volunteered to gather these and bring them in, while his companion went ahead to camp and make ready the packs.

On reaching the pond Bauman found three beaver in the traps, one of which had been pulled loose and carried into a beaver house. He took several hours in securing and preparing the beaver, and when he started homewards he marked with some uneasiness how low the sun was getting. As he hurried towards camp under the tall trees, the silence and desolation of the forest weighed on him. His feet made no sound on the pine needles, and the slanting sun rays, striking through among the straight trunks, made a gray twilight in which objects at a distance glimmered indistinctly. There was nothing to break the ghostly stillness which, when there is no breeze, always broods over these sombre primeval forests.

At last he came to the edge of the little glade where the camp lay, and shouted as he approached it but got no answer. The camp fire had gone out, though the thin blue smoke was still curling upwards. Near it lay the packs, wrapped and arranged. At first Bauman could see nobody; nor did he receive an answer to his call. Stepping forward he again shouted, and as he did so his eye fell on the body of his friend, stretched beside the trunk of a great fallen spruce. Rushing towards it the horrified trapper found that the body was still warm, but that the neck was broken, while there were four great fang, marks in the throat.

The footprints of the unknown beast-creature, printed deep in the soft soil, told the whole story.

The unfortunate man, having finished his packing, had sat down on the spruce log with his face to the fire, and his back to the dense woods, to wait for his companion. While thus waiting, his monstrous assailant, which must have been lurking nearby in the woods, waiting for a chance to catch one of the adventurers unprepared, came silently up from behind, walking with long, noiseless steps, and seemingly still on two legs. Evidently unheard, it reached the man, and broke his neck by wrenching his head back with its forepaws, while it buried its teeth in his throat. It had not eaten the body, but apparently had romped and gambolled round it in uncouth, ferocious glee, occasionally rolling over and over it; and had then fled back into the soundless depths of the woods.

Bauman, utterly unnerved, and believing that the creature with which he had to deal was something either half human or half devil, some great goblin-beast, abandoned everything but his rifle and struck off at speed down the pass, not halting until he reached the beaver meadows where the hobbled ponies were still grazing. Mounting, he rode onwards through the night, until far beyond the reach of pursuit." ◆

From 'Hunting the Grisly',
Teddy Roosevelt 1909

---

rock"). The batholith is an enormous structure of beautiful granite, which formed under tremendous heat and pressures way down in the earth and rose to the surface, some seventy and more million years ago.

North Central Idaho's higher mountains were more recently scarred by glaciers. Many high country lakes sit in cirque basins carved by the great ice during an epoch that was also a time of great beasts. Idaho's Age of Mammals is nowhere better preserved than at Tolo Lake, near Grangeville. Here the remains of imperial mammoths, bison, and other ice age creatures have been uncovered, a treasure of scientific wealth. One mammoth tusk is seven feet long. The precursors of North Central Idaho's modern-day natives — the Nez Perce Indians — may have hunted these animals, 10,000 years ago. Investigations

The Western White Pine is the state tree of Idaho. And the virgin stands of this tree are gone.

The tree was named by the Scot, David Douglas, for whom the Douglas-Fir is named. Because of its light, even grain that doesn't warp or shrink much, white pine is in demand for the manufacture of door jambs and window sashes. But we didn't lose our White Pine forests just because of logging, we lost it because of fire, and I don't mean forest fires.

Before we had electricity, paper matches, and disposal lighters, everybody used wooden safety matches to light lamps, fires in the stoves, besides tobacco in pipes, cigars, and cigarettes. Americans were using over 100 million matches a day. Because matches made from Idaho's Western White Pine don't break when struck, is why the match business got started. And though they still make matches from the trees, the trees are from forests grown for that purpose. But we burned up the magnificent virgin growths of Western White Pines one match at a time. ❧

WESTERN WHITE PINE

THE CROWN JEWEL   *By Margaret Fuller*

If you were sitting on the porch of Sleeping Deer Lookout in central Idaho near sunset on a summer evening, you'd be on top of the world. Below, cliffs drop hundreds of feet to a basin of blue-green lakes. In every direction rows of beige and dark green ridges merge into blue haze. From here the Frank Church - River of No Return Wilderness stretches 20 miles south, 10 miles east, 40 miles west and 60 miles north.

Toward the orange, western sky, a slice of shadow marks the course of the Middle Fork of the Salmon River, the third deepest canyon in North America. The second deepest, the canyon of the main Salmon River, cuts across this wilderness several miles to the north. (The deepest is Hells Canyon on the Snake River.)

A Nez Perce encampment in Palouse territory.

continue.

The Nez Perce Indians have long been one with North Central Idaho. Historically, the Nez Perce's area of influence stretched south to Boise and into the Wallowa country of northeastern Oregon. Their lifestyle was based on the abundant salmon in the area's rivers and on local vegetation, such as the camas root, which then grew in profusion in areas around Moscow and Grangeville.

When Lewis and Clark encountered them in 1806 the Nez Perce had already mastered all aspects of horsemanship and become expert buffalo hunters. The Nez Perce never accepted the EuroAmerican concept of land "ownership," although many adapted to the farming introduced by religious missionaries in

Containing 2.3 million acres in six national forests, The Frank Church is the largest wilderness in the United States outside of Alaska. It has some of the most varied terrain, from gentle hills along the Salmon River at 2,000 feet to the granite summit of Mt. McGuire at 10,082 feet.

This wilderness is also one of our wildest. Judging by the hoof prints, more elk and deer use the trails than humans. You can reach lakes 30 miles from a trailhead, such as the lake where my son Stuart once caught a limit of trout in 45 minutes. One evening a moose came up to our tent and bellowed at us for occupying its dust bath, which was the only space not covered by beargrass. That same night I heard the howl of a wolf.

Rivers are the lifeline of Idaho, nowhere more evidenced than (Below) North Central Idaho, where the Clark Fork rushes and tumbles; the Clearwater hosts this cook's shack on a barge for loggers...complete with stove, tables, chairs (Opposite).

The Frank Church Wilderness is easlily reached for an area that is so distant from population centers. That is because the act which created it allows airplanes to land at the established air strips, and jet boats to travel on the main Salmon River. You can stay at one of the guest ranches, arriving by jet boat or plane. A pilot can leave food for you at one of the ranches or guard stations inexpensively.

Another reason access to this wilderness is unusually good is because nine road corridors reach into the wilderness on the east, west and south, offering car-camping and day hiking.

This wilderness also has more types of recreation than most. Whitewater kayakers and rafters come from all over the world to float the Middle Fork and main Salmon Rivers. Many Idaho outfitters offer guided trips on the rivers. The Middle Fork trips begin at Dagger Falls in thick forest where willows edge the river, which plunges down in rapids and falls pinched by dark walls of rock. As the river descends, sagebrush replaces forest and canyon walls become peaks faced by 1,500-foot cliffs. Catch-and-release fishing here allows trout to grow to two and three pounds. At night while you sit around a campfire (built in a fire pan to keep the sand clean) your outfitter fixes gourmet meals.

In the fall planes fly in to the airstrips, especially in Chamberlain Basin, ferrying in hunters from all over the country. Other hunters ride in to one of the dozens of large meadows with encouraging names like Moose jaw and Wapiti. Backpackers can take overnight or longer trips.

the mid-1800s. Their original "reservation" was reduced in size by the American government in 1863. In 1877, all Nez Perce were ordered to move onto the new smaller reservation.

What followed was tragedy: the epic Nez Perce travail and war, in which Nez Perce men, women and children were led by their leaders Joseph, Looking Glass, White Bird, and Yellow Wolf from the first battle at the foot the high hill now known as White Bird, up the Clearwater and Lochsa Rivers over Lolo Pass in Montana, up the Bitterroot River into the Yellowstone Country back into and across Montana and almost into Canada, before the tragedy ended in the snow. "Hear me, my chiefs," were Joseph's words. "From where the sun now stands I will fight no more forever."

You can bathe in one of the 24 backcountry hot springs, such as the little-known Showerbath Hot Springs on Warm Spring Creek, reached by trail from the Sleeping Deer Road near Mahoney Creek Campground. Here a narrow gorge choked with shrubs holds six separate hot springs within one-quarter mile. At the sixth, hot water showers off the canyon wall into a rock-lined pool.

With all these superlatives: largest, wildest, most historical, most varied recreation and most accessible for a remote location, this wilderness lives up to the stature of the man it is named after, former Idaho Senator Frank Church.

Church's words, spoken after passage of the 1980 bill that created the Wilderness, demonstrate his recognition of the high quality of this wilderness: "The winners are the people of Idaho who will have, to enjoy, the finest wilderness in the West, the crown jewel of the National Wilderness System."✍

IDAHO'S SEAPORT?

by Bill London

The Nez Perce called it "Tsceminicum." The confluence, the meeting place, where the Clearwater brought snowmelt from the Bitterroot Mountains to mingle with the water from the south, from the big river, the Snake.

Every spring the waters churned and growled there, flooding the low plains and scouring the treeless canyons, forcing the people living there to higher ground. Every autumn the water calmed and receded, but flashed and danced with the slicing fins and thrashing tails of the salmon returning to their spawning beds to breed and die. Then the people wade the rivers, sharing the bounty with bear and eagle.

A century ago a different people came to the confluence, determined to stay with the river whatever its mood, to use the flowing waters as a river highway, to haul themselves upstream to the gold strikes at Pierce and Orofino, to return downstream to the coast laden with yellow metal newly-plucked from the Idaho mountains.

They dreamed of a tamed river, safe for transport, and even a seaport at the upper end of a Columbia/Snake River Highway.

The discovery of gold in 1860 by E.D. Pierce at Orofino was Idaho's first gold strike of many. It brought in miners, merchants and desperadoes. It created the tent city of Lewiston, Idaho's first territorial capital. It pressured the Indians. It presaged what was to happen again and again, all around Idaho: great commotion, great discoveries, and dastardly deeds.

The murders of the Lloyd Magruder party, in 1863, is one of Idaho's best bad guy stories. They were axed to death in their sleep by bandits, deep in the wilderness, for their $30,000 in earnings from a supply trip to Montana. Their killers would have gotten away clean if it were not for Hill Beachy, owner of Lewiston's Luna Hotel.

If rivers and horses were the lifelines for people of the Palouse, then timber was their lifeblood for generations. Mother Nature's lightning strikes along the Clearwater were annual challenges.

and a thousand feet of elevation away. Then in summer, the steep canyon walls are baked, allowing the stubby grasses only a seasonal resting place before they, too, are browned like the rocks rising above the slack water.

But it was not until 1975 that the eighth dam on the Columbia and Snake closed the lock on the roaring, waters and brought the slack water to the confluence, to Lewiston. Now the river crashing and twisting through Hell's Canyon is calmed, held to pond-stillness on the uppermost lake of the stairstep system leading downstream to the Pacific.

Sunshine here at the confluence, the lowest spot in Idaho, slices often through the cloud cover so prevalent in the Panhandle. Some winters, no snow touches ground in the valley floor, but drifts downward to melt in transit and fall finally as rain. Spring arrives months earlier here than on the upland prairies a few road miles

Amazing, certainly, but also the fruition of a century of dreams and plans. Lewis and Clark probably didn't consider the confluence a potential seaport when they camped there in 1805. But when the big paddle wheeled steamboats pushed upriver to land at Lewiston, discharging supplies and passengers bound for the gold fields and eventually loading grain and fruit grown in the inland region for market downriver, the idea of a tamed river returned with every lost boat or damaged cargo.

The water here at the Port of Lewiston is not sea-salty, but fresh from the Idaho mountains. No tides lift and lower the tugboats and barges. Instead, the water level is constant and waveless, controlled by the eight dams downstream. But this is a seaport nevertheless.

Before Magruder had left Lewiston, Beachy had dreamed of his friend being murdered by some toughs he had seen loitering around Lewiston. Later, when he saw these same toughs come through town with boxes of gold, Beachy remembered his dream. Beachy pursued the criminals through Walla Walla and Portland to San Francisco, where he persuaded authorities to arrest them. Later, one confessed and the killers were hanged, back in Lewiston near the Luna Hotel.

Lewiston wasn't Idaho's capital for long. Richer diggins were discovered in the Boise Basin, and when Boise's population boomed and Lewiston's busted, the legislature decided to follow the political power. One day, Idaho's governor and chief scalawag Caleb Lyons left Lewiston to go "duck hunting," never to

LATAH COUNTY PARKS
by Keith C. Petersen

East Moscow is a county recreational site known as Robinson Lake Park, although there is no longer a lake here. It was donated to the county by one of the region's most colorful characters, Frank Bruce Robinson.

Frank Robinson moved to Moscow in the 1920's and took a job in a drugstore. In 1929 he placed an ad in a national psychology magazine under the headline, "I talked with God - yes I did - actually and literally," and inviting people to write him for further information.

Write they did, and Robinson's newly-founded non-Christian sect, Psychiana, shortly became the largest mail-order religion in the world, with thousands of students in over 60 countries.

Many in Moscow believed Robinson got rich from his religion, but actually he pumped most of his profits back into it. Even so, he did all right. What ever else Robinson might have been, he was also a philanthropist, putting some of his money to good work in his home town. His charitable contributions still inspire people of the area.

Among Robinson's charitable acts was the purchase and donation of property around a shallow lake east of town, since drained. His only stipulation was that the park be permanently opened to the public, and that it carry his name.

Robinson died in 1948, and Psychiana ceased operation in 1952. But Robinson Park is still popular with picnickers, a reminder of this innfluential man who, as much as anyone, helped shape Moscow's history.◈

THE BLUE BUCKET

More than half a century ago, a lone pioneer journeyed through Idaho on his way to Oregon and camped one night on Paradise Creek near Moscow. In filling his bucket with water from a creek, he scooped up gravel, and observed later that it was rich in gold. Being more interested in farming than in mining, he left the bucket and resumed his journey; but returned after a year, defeated in his agricultural efforts, to find the bucket and the rich placer deposits which he had left behind. He never found the Blue Bucket Mine, nor has anyone since, though many have searched for it.◈

return. Later, a detachment of federal troops arrived from Fort Lapwai for the Territorial records. Lewiston wasn't the only community scathed by Lyons. After plundering the Territory's Indian monies, he left Boise, never to return.

Another famous North Central Idaho citizen was a certain Mrs. Bemis of Warrens, known affectionately as China Polly. As a young girl Polly was sent from China to the U.S. and sold into virtual slavery as a prostitute. Later a Warrens hotelman married Polly and she became the beloved first lady of an entire region. Much later, China Polly became the subject of the book and movie, "A Thousand Pieces of Gold."

As with much of Idaho, cities in North Central Idaho are blessedly rare. And each city and town has its

The railroad brought people into Idaho, and timber out.

INDOORS IN MOSCOW *by Ron McFarland*

Moscow, Idaho, is occasionally described as a "typical New England town," except that it's located on the shores of a wheat desert known as the Palouse instead of an ocean known as the Atlantic. The Chamber of Commerce describes it as "The City with a Smile," and it is generally regarded as a "great place to raise kids."

In the wheat, pea, and lentil fields surrounding the town, you can find flocks of Hungarian partridge and fat pheasants. On Moscow Mountain, about five miles out of town, you can find deer, a few grouse, some luxury homes, and, if you go to the right place, weekend keggers held by the scions of college professors.

If I had to spend the afternoon indoors in Moscow without my word processor or a ball game on television, I wouldn't mind spending it at the Garden Lounge, as it was when I first visited the place almost twenty years ago or as it is now, and as I hope it will always be, except maybe worse. No one wants to see his favorite bar improve significantly over the years. I'd rather it got worse than better. I don't care to hang out at a place that's looking much better than I am.

Not that I don't have a soft spot for my home, with its huge deck that would look out on Paradise Ridge if I cut down the sprawling apple tree, which produces Red Delicious peppered with those challenging wormholes that mark the difference between supermarket and real apples. Elsie, my long-suffering wife, would like the house to look like her meticulous friend Janice Brandal's. I tell her she too should have married a Scandinavian. I represent the cluttered places of the world, the sloppy, self-indulgent landfills of the mind.

The Garden Lounge remains faintly unsavory, but not dangerous. Nick Bode, the part-owner and bartender who's usually on tap when I'm there, also seems a little unsavory, I've always thought, but I guess he isn't very dangerous either. That's just a guess. I think he has a bad streak of respectability in him, like most bartenders. Most English professors are would-be writers, and most writers, would-be or otherwise, also have a streak of unsavoriness. Somehow all of this gets together reasonably well at the Garden Lounge. I saw a police officer in there last week, but he didn't even arrest anyone. It's that kind of bar.

---

own uncommon character.

Potlatch is a marvel. It was the epitome of a "company town," owned and operated by the Potlatch Lumber Company for the primary business of logging and milling the ocean of Idaho White Pine. But the company had the business of benevolence in mind, too. Everything was provided here for its workers. Schools, churches, houses, even a company store so well stocked with reasonably priced goods that non-company people came from Idaho and Washington to shop in what must have been the area's first mall.

A story goes that Moscow was first called "Hogs Heaven" by the menfolk of the first EuroAmerican families to move to the area, because their pigs so loved rooting there for camas. The womenfolk pre-

TIMBER

by Barbara Coyner

Quarter to four. The alarm sounds and he reluctantly swings his lanky frame out into the chilly stillness of another work day. Groping for his clothes, he dresses quickly. A wool plaid shirt, black pants with frayed hemlines, suspenders and corked boots. In the kitchen, a small fire is coaxed in the woodburner, the coffee is brewed and a cooler is hastily packed with sausage, bread and cake. No time for breakfast today. It's load the chain saw and head for the woods.

So the logger makes his way out into the half-dark, half-light of morning where he becomes legion. The individual is swallowed up in a giant network of trucks, rail lines, mills, small companies, multi-national corporations, federal agencies and global politics. Logging is big business, accomplished one tree at a time, one logger at a time, with one mighty chain saw.

Nature's terrifying nitelight glows along the Clearwater.

ferred "Paradise Valley." Later, in typical Idaho fashion, somebody renamed it Moscow, after his other two hometowns, the Moscows in Ohio and Pennsylvania.

Moscow lies in the fine Palouse grain country, but it is most famous for its fine school, the University of Idaho, established in 1889. Another story goes that Moscow got the state university because Boise wanted the more profitable establishment, the territorial penitentiary. Perhaps they both wanted just to keep the student lawyers and the career prisoners separated. Besides law, the U of I's major schools include forestry, agriculture, wildlife management and engineering.

The University is a major employer and benefactor of North Central Idaho. Serious scholarship rubs off

In the dawn's earliest moments, a logging truck growls into a lower gear as it enters the still-sleeping town of Potlatch. The lone driver sips his thermos cup of coffee as his eyes fall on the empty expanse to his right. Funny how it looks like just another farm field in the darkness. Ah, but the logger knows better. A closer look shows sporadic hunks of concrete jutting upward like grave markers in a cemetery. Indeed, isn't it a cemetery of sorts, with the hopes and dreams of the company town buried now in the tangle of weeds? Weeds and concrete ... it's all that is left of what was once the largest white pine mill in the world. A mill that offered cradle-to-grave security to its town, jobs to its people.

"Support the Potlatch Loggers," reads the sign across from the empty mill site. Alluding to the local team, the bright billboard marks the location of Potlatch High School's football field, where his 16-year-old son plays ball in these last 20 years or so, he has quit the same school, married, fathered three children, seen a grand-child born, turned 40 .., and he's logged. Following his brother's lead, he gravitated toward the mill, the steady paycheck, then the more promising future with the chainsaw. Now he sees his own son's ease with the woods and a saw come smack up against a lack of enthusiasm for the classroom. He knows, too, that his daughter has married a logger. Will there be a decent future for them?

Yet he still logs. It's all he knows. And according to his wife of 20 years, it's what he likes. He enjoys being out, scouting for timber, working with his hands, being his own boss. A "gyppo," an independent logger-that's what he is. The truck and self-loader cast a silhouette against the awakening sky as they move out onto the open road headed for the North Fork country. It's good to be back at work after six weeks of spring break-up and no income. Up a washboard of a road, another independent waits for him in the clearing, his "Cat" ready to provide support services to the two-man logging operation. Together they have bid and bargained for this small sale and now they will fall, skid, load and haul timber for a paycheck. It's all part of the job when you're a gyppo.

Yet he remembers he was born a steward, not a logger. Some of the practices of sawing down life's giants and clear-cutting stands of timber stir controversy out there in the world beyond. But how else is he to feed his son? Born into a logging town, indeed, into a logging family, this is the only vocation he knows. What's more, it's a vocation he defends.

"Trees are a renewable resource," he reminds. "I see myself as a farmer of sorts. It's just that it takes my crop longer to mature."

Meanwhile, Idaho's midsection pulses to the tune of the chain saw. Gyppos, small companies, large corporate fleets, all press in on the scaling shacks. The cedar, fir, tamarack and pine all get translated into board feet before being deposited in a huge sea of saw logs. All identity lost, the logs are systematically pulled, lifted, sawed, shaped, dried and stacked, as humans carry on the monotonous tasks of making logs into lumber. Hour after hour, men and women grade and sort, debark and saw, jockeying fork lifts and tolerating the elements to produce chips, boards, plywood, particle board-hopefully profits.

Mix in that stockholder's zeal, a healthy dose of environmentalist's doubt, then add some advanced technology. Watch the timber industry bob and reel as it adjusts to mandates on clear cutting, water quality, market conditions and consumers' preferences. ◢

The Snake River's Hells Canyon is shared with Southwest Idaho – the gorge America's deepest.

in many ways. Even the countryside around Moscow is studded with the signs of higher education. Area towns, railway sidings, and sometimes just signs often announce scholarly names: Harvard, Princeton, Yale, Stanford, Vassar, Purdue, Cornell and Wellesley.

Lewiston is North Central Idaho's idea of a metropolis, population 31,000. It sits at the confluence of the Clearwater and Snake Rivers at Idaho's elevational low point, 800 feet above sea level. Lewiston serves as the sea port of the Northern Rockies, filling barges with grain from Idaho and Montana. It is also the setting-off point for guided hunting and fishing parties up the rivers, and it's the home of Lewis-Clark State College.

Up the Snake River from Lewiston there are no towns for a hundred miles. Up the Clearwater, Orofino is a major sportsman and logging center. It could boast the world's only combination motel and sawmill the Konkolville where guests fall asleep to the perfume of fresh cut cedar.

River towns Kamiah and Kooskia — a.k.a. "kam-ee-eye" and "koos-kee" — retain vestiges of their Nez Perce pronunciations. The Nez Perce did not name whole rivers. Lewis and Clark mistook their word "kooskooskee" ("confluence") for "clear water," and so it goes.

To the south of the Clearwater River up on the camas prairie, a rich grain country supports the towns of Winchester, Nezperce, Craigmont and Grangeville. The fields here are often cultivated right up to the

road pavement, so that driving this prairie is like a scene out of Currier and Ives.

South of the Camas Prairie lies Salmon River country, which is anything but recumbent. It is standing on end, rugged beyond belief, and absolutely gorgeous. Little Riggins is the big town hereabouts, where the Main Salmon and the Little Salmon join. When Riggins holds its rodeo, the first week in May, the parade shuts down Idaho's only north-south highway. Since its sawmill burned, Riggins has transformed itself into a mecca for outdoor recreationists the gateway to the River of No Return and the Hells Canyon-Seven Devils Wilderness.

Even smaller villages dot North Central Idaho's near backcountry, each with its own character and

Without detection, five Chinamen quietly gained entrance to the Fraser store in Pierce one summer's night in 1885, while their fellow counones were planning to blame the older ones, who didn't have much longer to live and might as well take the punishment and die on a rope as in bed.

Sear's ruse had not quite the desired effect, so the next day the court arranged a mock hanging, thinking it might be possible to frighten the guilty ones into confessing. A hangman's rope was hung from a tree near the well at the south end of Main Street (for years it was to be known as the confession tree).

The court, unable to determine guilt, released the two oldest men. The five remaining men were turned over to a deputy sheriff and loaded into a hayrack wagon and started on a long journey to another court for further trial.

Three miles out of Pierce at a place called Hangman's creek, the entourage was met by a band of masked vigilantes. Without any hesitation or further ado, the vigilantes slung a pole between two black pine trees, put up five ropes and hanged all five of the prisoners.

When news of the hanging reached Portland, the Chinese merchant community in that city sent agents upriver to Lewiston and into northern Idaho, both to safeguard the property of their people and to check the facts in the case. The agents found that the dead men had indeed been guilty and richly deserved their fate.⌒

story to tell: Elk City, Elk River, Headquarters and Pierce. Beyond them, all is wilderness and another world altogether.

A paraphrase of Omar Khayam's famous poem *The Rubaiyayt* could be applied to North Central Idaho's lovely combination of resources talents and beauties. "A loaf of bread, a jug of wine and you, my sweet. Ah! Wilderness and paradise, complete."

CALENDAR

Lionel Hampton Jazz Festival, Moscow, February: Some of the world's top jazz musicians gather for this famous Northwest festival Contact: Moscow Chamber of Commerce (208) 882-1800.

Salmon River Jet boat Races, Riggins, mid-April: World Class jet boat racing on the Salmon River. This is the first leg of the U.S. Championship jetboat Race. Competitors come from as far away as Canada, Mexico, and New Zealand. Contact: Salmon River Chamber of Commerce, (208) 628-3440.

Dogwood Festival, Lewiston, Late April: A city celebration that includes a rodeo, arts and crafts fair, garden tours, concerts and plays. Contact: Lewis-Clark Artist Series, Lewis-Clark State College, (208) 799-2243.

Riggins Rodeo, Riggins, early May: Wild West action with parade on Sunday morning starting off the final day of rodeo action. The steep canyon walls at Riggins provide a natural stadium. Contact: Salmon River Chamber of Commerce, (208) 628-3440.

Grangeville Border Days Rodeo, Grangeville, weekend before July 4: Three days of street fairs, parades and rodeo. Contact: Grangeville Chamber of Commerce, (208) 983-0460.

Clearwater Riverfest, Kamiah, 1st weekend in July: Arts and crafts exposition by local artists with a Bluegrass concert in the park. Contact: Kamiah Chamber of Commerce, (208) 935-2290.

Rendezvous in the Park, Moscow, July: Magical music and festival held in beautiful East City Park. National and international stars perform jazz, folk, blues, country and classical music under the canopy of the trees. Arts and crafts, children's activities, silent movies, and more. Contact: Moscow Chamber of Commerce, (208) 882-1800.

Hot August Nights, Lewiston, mid-August: A "blast from the past" with music, dancing and a classic and nostalgic car show and cruise. Contact: Port City Action Corporation, (208) 746-4845.

Chief Looking Glass Days, Kamiah, mid-August: A traditional Pow Wow by descendants of Chief Lookingglass of the Nez Perce Indian Tribe. Native American dancing and cultural ceremonies are exhibited by the Nez Perce people. Contact: Chief Lookingglass Days Committee, (208) 935-2525.

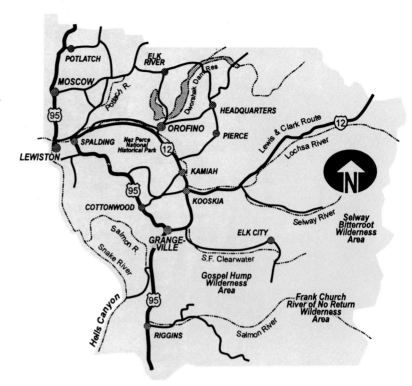

Lewiston Roundup, Lewiston, September: World-famous Rodeo events and a cowboy breakfast are featured. Contact: Lewiston Chamber of Commerce, (208) 743-3531.

Clearwater County Fair and Lumberjack Days, Orofino, September: An international event which attracts logging competitors from all over the world. The excitement includes a carnival and parade. Contact: Orofino Chamber of Commerce, (208) 476-4335.

TIPS: FOOD & SHELTER

The **Biscuitroot Park** in Moscow and **The Broiler** in the University Inn have been popular eateries for years.

The **Lodge at Riggins Hot Springs** is pricey and special -rates include all meals. A hot springs spa on the Salmon River.

The **Huckleberry Heaven Lodge** in Elk River is a treasure to stay both summer and winter. Reasonable prices with many amenities and renown huckleberry ice cream.

Nice atmosphere with a view and food to match can be found at the **Three Mile Inn** outside of Lewiston.

Southwest Idaho
Region 3

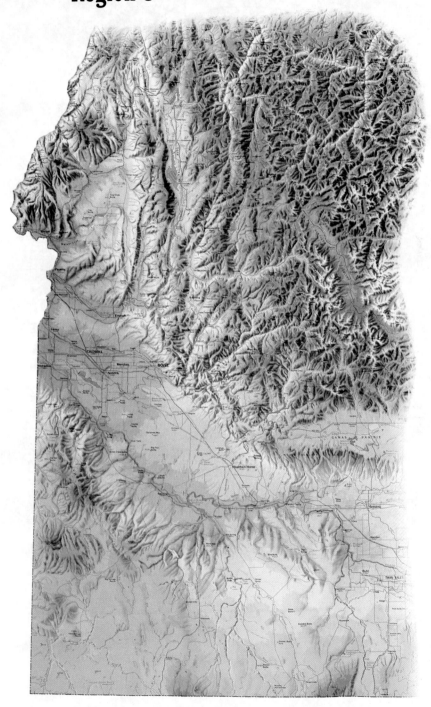

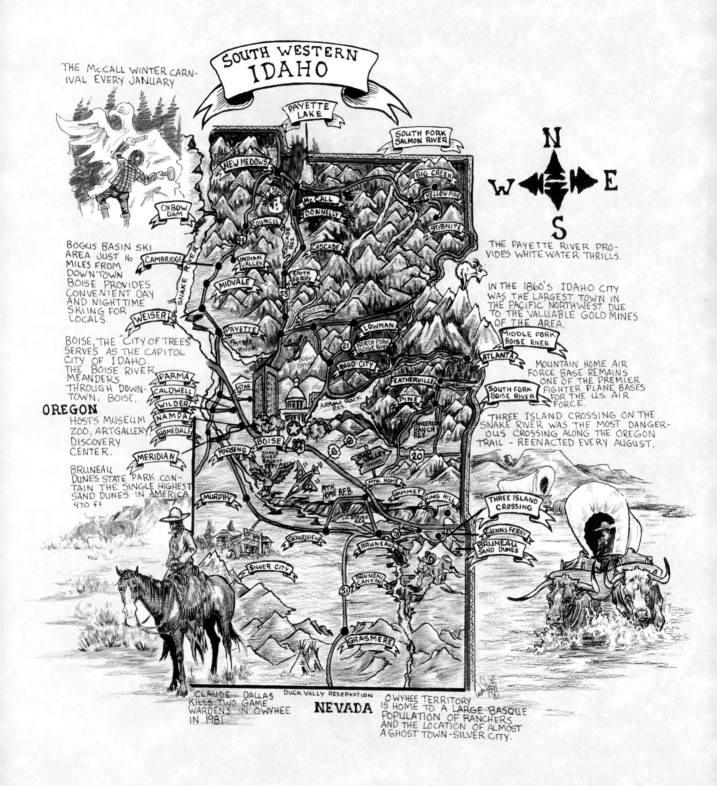

SOUTH WESTERN IDAHO

THE McCALL WINTER CARNIVAL EVERY JANUARY

BOGUS BASIN SKI AREA JUST 16 MILES FROM DOWNTOWN BOISE PROVIDES CONVENIENT DAY AND NIGHTTIME SKIING FOR LOCALS.

BOISE, THE "CITY OF TREES" SERVES AS THE CAPITOL CITY OF IDAHO. THE BOISE RIVER MEANDERS THROUGH DOWNTOWN, BOISE, HOSTS MUSEUM ZOO, ARTGALLERY, DISCOVERY CENTER.

OREGON

BRUNEAU DUNES STATE PARK CONTAIN THE SINGLE HIGHEST SAND DUNES IN AMERICA 470 ft

THE PAYETTE RIVER PROVIDES WHITE WATER THRILLS.

IN THE 1860's IDAHO CITY WAS THE LARGEST TOWN IN THE PACIFIC NORTHWEST DUE TO THE VALUABLE GOLD MINES OF THE AREA.

MOUNTAIN HOME AIR FORCE BASE REMAINS ONE OF THE PREMIER FIGHTER PLANE BASES FOR THE U.S. AIR FORCE.

THREE ISLAND CROSSING ON THE SNAKE RIVER WAS THE MOST DANGEROUS CROSSING ALONG THE OREGON TRAIL - REENACTED EVERY AUGUST.

CLAUDE DALLAS KILLS TWO GAME WARDENS IN OWYHEE IN 1981

DUCK VALLY RESERVATION

NEVADA

OWYHEE TERRITORY IS HOME TO A LARGE BASQUE POPULATION OF RANCHERS AND THE LOCATION OF ALMOST A GHOST TOWN - SILVER CITY.

PAYETTE LAKE
SOUTH FORK SALMON RIVER
N W E S
NEW MEADOWS
BIG CREEK
YELLOW PINE
McCALL
DONNELLY
COUNCIL
CASCADE
STIBNITE
OXBOW DAM
CAMBRIDGE
INDIAN VALLEY
MIDVALE
SMITH FERRY
WEISER
GARDEN VALLEY
PAYETTE
PAYETTE RIVER
LOWMAN
NORTH FORK BOISE RIVER
MIDDLE FORK BOISE RIVER
BOGUS BASIN
IDAHO CITY
ATLANTA
PARMA
CALDWELL
WILDER
NAMPA
HOMEDALE
STAR
ARROW ROCK RES.
FEATHERVILLE
PINE
SOUTH FORK BOISE RIVER
MERIDIAN
BOISE
ANDERSON RANCH RES.
MARSING
SNAKE RIVER BIRDS OF PREY AREA
SUN VALLEY
MURPHY
MTN. HOME A.F.B.
MTN. HOME
HAMMET
KING HILL
THREE ISLAND CROSSING
C.J. STRIKE RES.
GRANDVIEW
BRUNEAU
GLENNS FERRY
BRUNEAU SAND DUNES
SILVER CITY
BRUNEAU CANYON
GRASMERE
SNAKE RIVER

Chapter IV
SOUTHWEST IDAHO
Region 3

And yet how beautiful it is! For the first time I understood Oliver's enthusiasm. We went softly on that sandy trail among the sage, and that dry magical wind from the west blew across us, until at last we came out on a long bench above a river valley, with mountains close behind patched with snow and forest. To our right, the stream broke out of a canyon cut through the sagebrush foothills. To the left, across a bridge, was Boise City climbing up its stepped benches. Below town the crooked line of cottonwoods marking Boise Creek groped across the plain until in the distance trees and river sank below the benches and the plains healed over. From a mile or two away, unless one is on a high place, neither the Boise nor the Snake can be seen at all, sunken in their canyons." ⟋

WALLACE STEGNER – from Angle of Repose

Southwestern Idaho's feel was never captured more adroitly than Mary Hallock Foote's paintings a hundred years ago.

Southwest Idaho may seem a country of contrasts, but it is really a land of marvelous blends. Forest to desert. Wetland to dune. Valley to canyon to mountain. Urban amenities to rural comforts to primitive wilderness ordeals. Southwest Idaho provides an excellent example of the New-And-In-Many-Ways-Yes-It's-Better-West, where the cutting edge of high technology meets the healing touch of nature.

Mountain bikers leaving Bonneville Point follow 150-year-old wagon ruts of the Oregon Trail down through the pale green sage atop purple cliffs. Within minutes they are pedaling past the modern industrial campus of Micron Technology and on into bustling Boise. Farmers, fighter jet pilots and office workers keep the racks on their rigs always ready for their rec gear: kayaks, skis, bikes, fishing poles and compound

THE HIGHWAY HOME

By: Rick Ardinger

October. The deer herds aren't down on the road yet. In a month, when snow cements the higher elevations, Highway 21 will twist along More's Creek with occasional carcasses, abandoned radiator-crushed pickups, and magpies swooping and diving at the roadkills.

I drive the highway to Boise everyday, nearly a twenty-mile ride each way. Veterans of the road know each other's cars and wave, steam rising from coffee cups in the morning, eyes gleaming with release in the afternoon.

I like the road, the ride, the distance from Boise perhaps for all the same reasons you hear from people who live outside cities. I use the time on the road to prepare for and unwind from the day. I've also time for road-fueled illusions. Each way, the drive holds its promise, and I find it somewhere along the way.

I've grown to know the road where slides most often occur, where rocks tend to tumble after rain, where to back off the gas for black ice, where the school bus pulls off to let cars pass, where troopers set speed traps in the sage. Each morning over coffee, I envision the road between me and the kitchen table, how I'll weave and climb and descend, or coast toward the river till it's time to go.

I drive a Volkswagen, an old one and cranky. I turn the key and let it warm, listen to the rocker arms, prime it when it idles rough. Then the house retreats in the rearview mirror to yellowing aspens and a pasture of sage and cheat grass again. Why leave? Why work? The gravel shifts under my tires till I make pavement. Something to think about on the road.

Crossing the high bridge over More's Creek, I recall that a while back someone jumped off the bridge and lived. On the bridge, the tires whir with new sound, and I think of jumping myself - not suicide, but Johnny Weissmuller-style to save a friend, or just to dive, a ragged loincloth my shield, a yodeling call to the elephants as I fall.

From Hilltop, the Owyhees crawl off in the distance. I believe in everything: every sign and symbol, the I Ching, St. Francis in the garden, my horoscope, Lou Boyd. A morning moon over the road leaves me blushing for a truth I can't articulate. There's something prescient about roads in autumn, when aspens yellow, cornstalks stiffen, and we're running out of good weather to drive.

Highway 21 runs all the way from Boise to Stanley, plenty of sidewinding curves between Idaho City and Lowman. During the winter, vulnerable to snowslides, patchy ice, top-heavy motor homes, barreling logging trucks, drunks, and deer, the road's earned a reputation as beautiful but dangerous. Autumn makes you wonder why you haven't traveled it more often.

There are days in October when I need more than just a commute. I need more distance under my wheels, the broken yellow line shooting like tracer bullets. I'm not alone with this impulse. I share it with friends who show up unexpectedly after a ride from Pocatello through the Arco desert, through Craters of the Moon or over Galena Summit to Stanley and the loneliness of Highway 21. They wander it like refugees for beer, a meal and a bed. Then hit it early again in the morning, the road burning out whatever fever's in the blood to move, to level vision with nothing more than sage and mountains.

---

bows. Their lifestyle is as wide open as Southwest Idaho skies which are shared by soaring falcons.

From top to bottom Southwest Idaho begins at 11,000 feet high in the Sawtooth Mountains. It drops past granite and snow into the thickly wooded wilderness, through the wildly historic gold rush country past picturesque towns like Idaho City and Atlanta. It then falls into canyons over sheer rimrock walls and spills out into wide and fertile agricultural valleys, which are quickly filling with houses. It includes an arc of the great Snake River, two other main rivers (the Payette and Weiser), the lonesome massif of the Owyhee Mountains, and — wonder of wonders — a big city in Idaho, the sudden metropolis of Boise. At its bottom Southwest Idaho seems bottomless as it drops into the Hells Canyon.

In spring the urge wells up again. But it's not the same as in autumn. A "last call" urge tests the tautness of an impulse that most shrug off but some embrace. I expect visitors any day.

Meanwhile, a daily forty-mile ride attends my need. And when days wring me out till I'm on the edge, I take the road home like a fugitive, climb past Lucky Peak, over High Valley Summit, and descend. Each time, it seems, a change occurs: a release like an unclenching fist, after a mountain's wedged between me and town, and I'm among the coyotes again. The moment is as true as anything Jack Kerouac might have cried "Yes!" about before passing the jug around.

"Entering Boise County," the road weaves and climbs again, then flattens out far enough to see the dirt turnoff to home. I lift my foot off the gas and coast to make the turn. Daisies bob and weave along both sides of the drive. An escort of laughing, barking dogs runs alongside. Shirts, sheets, and dresses billow from the clothesline. The mountain's there like yesterday.✍

Despite Payette Lake's short drive north from bustling Boise, it offers summer and winter recreation that has surprisingly remained uncrowded.

Geologically and simplistically, Southwest Idaho can be divided into rock and soil. A lot of the rock comes from the great Idaho batholith, the biggest chunk of granite in North America. It provides the bedrock and big scenery nearly everywhere north and east of Boise, and perhaps for the Owyhee Mountains too. This batholith "floated up" from deep in the earth's crust 80 million years ago. The rest of the rock comes from millions of years of volcanic activity, layer after layer of rhyolites and basalts. These created many of Southwest Idaho's buttes and rimrocks and formed dams which impounded enormous lakes. From 8 million to 2.5 million years ago much of the Boise, Weiser, Payette and Snake valleys was filled by the ancient Lake Idaho, which in turn filled with mud and sand. This is the source of much of the good valley

BASQUE COUNTRY

by Scott Preston

The serene hills of Nevada and Idaho are a far cry from the Basque homeland in northcentral Spain, a region of verdant mountains washed by ocean air. Though Ernest Hemingway once compared the dry, sagebrush-covered hills of Idaho to those of Spain, he was talking about southern Spain. The desert confluence of Idaho, northern Nevada, and eastern Oregon is more akin to a trip to the moon than the land of the Basques. And yet they have made it their home, preserving Old World traditions more intensely than they would in Europe.

Hells Canyon. Wonder where the name came from – the Snake is somewhere down below...far, far down below.

The sidewalk rolls up early in downtown Boise on a Sunday night. Here, in the heat of Idaho's Basque country, most of the restaurants and shops close in the afternoon if they open at all and traffic is sparse all day.

Everywhere, that is, except the corner of Grove and Sixth, a few blocks southwest of the Capitol building. Sunday night is always a busy time at the Boise Basque Center, the oldest such social club in North America, and the center of Idaho's Basque population.

At 4 p.m. a few patrons sit at the center's small bar, sipping beer and glancing at the NBA All-Star game on the TV set mounted overhead. Across the room, glass cases hold trophies and souvenirs, including a letter from Ronald Reagan congratulating the Oinkari Dancers on their 1985 European tour, and accordionist and troupe accompanist Jimmy Jasauro's certificace from the National Endowment for the Arts, recognizing his contributions, as a "Master Folk Artist," to the preservation of his heritage and the United States' cultural diversity.

The Oinkari Dancers were formed in 1964, after a group of Idaho Basques toured the old country and were immediately attracted to traditional festival dancing. Although no other group quite like the Oinkaris exists in the United States, their example has inspired the creation of many small social dance groups in Basque communities throughout the West.

The Oinkari Dancers have become central part of American Basque culture, performing at festivals and gatherings far from home. Participation in the group is a virtual rite-of-passage for some young Boise Basques-one can join at age 14.

No one knows where the Basques originated. They are the true mystery people of Europe, their language completely unrelated to the Indo-European language groups found else

topsoil and the fine Boise sandstone at Table Rock.

Southwest Idaho can also be seen as one big geologic hotspot. Here, the earth's hot mantle is close underground. An airplane flight over the backcountry on a cold winter's day reveals dozens of steam plumes from geothermal springs. Many buildings in Boise — including the capitol mall — are heated with natural hot water. Hot water has done more than to heat homes. In the ore bearing seams of the Boise Basin and the Owyhees, it helped to concentrate the gold.

Early humans in Southwest Idaho no doubt enjoyed the hot springs when they arrived here during the Ice Age, perhaps 14,000 years ago. Much later, Indians from all over the Northwest gathered near the

where on the continent. The Basques call this language Euzkera, and it is central to their identity. The Basque country, Euzkadir, has been inhabited by the Basques for more than 2,000 years, making them solid candidates for distinction as the oldest European culture to continuously occupy a specific geographical area: seven provinces, four in Spain, three in France, split by the Pyrenees Mountains and bounded by the Atlantic Ocean. Bilbao, one of the major deepwater ports of Europe, is one of the largest Basque cities, with a population of approximately 1 million (not all Basque).

Bilbao is a testament to Basques' close association with the water. A maritime people renowned for their seamanship, Basques played a major role in the discovery of the New World. They sailed with Magellan, and were a crucial component of the first voyage of Columbus, the flagship Santa Maria being Basque-owned and, like the Nina, largely crewed by Basques.

Despite enclaves of Basque people throughout North America and South America, their arrival in Idaho and the high desert country of the surrounding Great Basin was something of an accident. The mythic promises of the California gold rush brought fortune seekers of many nationalities to the West, Basques among them, but reality proved harsh.

Desperate to obtain work, a number of Basques found themselves in northern Nevada, where they were given employment by local sheep ranchers. Their strong cultural propensity for honesty and hard work made them immediate successes in that business, and sheep herding became the primary employment for the first immigrants, though they were anxious to move on to other ventures at the earliest opportunity. These days, Basques can be found in all professions.

OLDEST MAN: BOISE

As long as I've been in Idaho I don't understand how come they name things like they do. How can you have Bogus Basin on top of a mountain as a ski area and Lucky Peak as a reservoir down in a canyon? And they keep moving places around. Like Boise, there have been three different Fort Boise's near what is now Parma, before they built the city of Boise around the U.S. Army's Fort Boise at it's present location.

The first Fort Boise was started by John Reid of John Jacob Astor's Pacific Fur Company in 1813. He was killed by Indians and the fort burned to the ground in 1814. Donald McKenzie who had worked for John Jacob Astor's Pacific Company built another Fort Boise for the Northwest Company of Canada at the same place in 1819, but he was run out by the Indians also. In 1832 Thomas McKay of the Hudson Bay Company built another fort north of the earlier sites, but it got washed away in a flood in 1853. So they built another one in 1854 and it got washed away in the 1862 flood. In 1863 Major Pickney Lugenbeel built the U.S. Fort Boise, to house the soldiers that were sent west to protect the emigrants on the Oregon Trail and the town of Boise grew up around the fort at it's present location.

Boise sure was persistent.

---

confluences of the rivers to fish for salmon and to trade at an annual fair. Paiutes may have brought obsidian arrowheads from central Oregon. Nez Perces and Cayuses may have brought shells from the coast. Shoshones may have traded buffalo skins from the upper Snake River Plains.

Some researchers have said that one name for this gathering — and the whole area — meant "peace." But the Shoshones and Nez Perce were often at war. And when the first EuroAmericans passed this way in 1811, a period began of alternating peace and war between Indians and whites and Indians.

The Astorians were mainly French Canadian voyageurs scouting beaver country for the New York financier John Jacob Astor. More accustomed to the central Canadian flat waters than Idaho whitewater

from: BREAKFAST IN IDAHO CITY

By: Rick Ardinger

I sit at the counter of Calamity Jayne's on a March Sunday morning in Idaho City waiting for my order of "Sobbing Potatoes" to sizzle and brown to the cook's approval. It's a house specialty, a scramble of sliced potatoes, shredded onions, and enough cheese to clog an artery. I swallow black coffee down like fuel and read the latest *Idaho World*: police citations for inattentive driving, discharging firearms within city limits, two divorces, a letter to the editor we've read a hundred times.

One of many popular whitewater rafting rivers, the South Fork of the Payette flows down toward Boise from Payette Lake.

Breakfast looks as if I'd cooked it. No Perkins frills here, no cloth napkins, no parsley, no twisted orange peel. I swallow more coffee and dig in. Delicious.

My wife Rosemary attends Mass at St. Joe on the hill, one of the oldest Catholic churches in Idaho. Each week a priest comes up from Boise for a dozen parishioners. I imagine them singing, the lapsed and the faithful exchanging signs of peace on the edge of this great wilderness

In CJ's the waitress keeps our cups filled without a word. We're all comfortably anonymous, lost in our newspapers, omelettes, and silence. Outside a wash of grays you'd try to rub out of the bottom of a glass. But the color envelopes us like a quiet good mood we all know and don't acknowledge. The stove melts ice from the windows. Too cold, too lazy and comfortable to get up for one of the Park & Skis north of town. It's a day to plan no further than breakfast, the next bite, the next classified ad.

they had left their horses far upstream and embarked in canoes upon the Snake River, only to have their plans dashed to pieces by what they called "the mad accursed river." Indians showed them a trail to the Boise Valley and they exulted, "Les Bois !"— Trees ! — when they stumbled upon the wooded valley. They found more help from Indians at a large encampment near Boise's hotsprings, and then headed on west into Oregon. Three years later, three of the party were killed by Indians while trapping in Southwest Idaho.

In the years to follow all of southern Idaho was a commercial battleground between U.S. and British fur interests. The Hudson's Bay Company wanted to wipe out the beaver in the Snake River country in order to forestall the northwestern advance of the Americans. The "honorable company" established Fort Boise,

After Mass, Rosemary joins me at the counter for poached eggs. The world's more right than an hour ago. She believes this. I do too, caffeine coursing through my veins. We share a glass of milk, decide for no particular reason to visit the Pioneer Cemetery before taking the road home. I gather up the paper, tip the good waitress, search my pocket for the car keys.

Idaho City looks worn out from the night before, clapboard buildings leaning into each other, wood smoke in the air like always, stray dog crossing the street. Without the cars strewn randomly about, the town wouldn't look much different than it did a hundred years ago. Spring will become this place if it ever comes. Meanwhile, ankle-deep slush, roof-sagging snow dripping in the sun, and folks walking in shirtsleeves prematurely proclaim the promise of a new season. ᵔ

Most regions of Idaho are dotted with gorgeous but little known lakes. This gem of the Southwestern region is Warm Lake.

west of present day Parma in 1834, only to abandon it in 1855 because of the Indian threat.

The Oregon Trail land rush began around 1843, but even then Southwest Idaho was seen by white Americans as on the road through nowhere. A U.S. Army Fort Boise was established in 1863. When gold was discovered in Boise Basin by George Grimes in 1862, the city of Boise had its future secured. Becoming Idaho's capital helped a lot too. Situated at the head of a fertile farming valley halfway between the great mining areas of the Basin and the Owyhees and on the main road from old to new, Boise has generally prospered.

Southwest Idaho still offers its residents a blend of history and modernity and nature. This blend draws

FROZEN FANTASIES IN McCALL

By: Frances W. Ford

Snow sculptures, fantasies in ice and snow, draw thousands of visitors to McCall, Idaho each February for Winter Carnival. Although there are many other activities connected with the Carnival, the unique frozen figures are what people come to see.

The variety is dazzling. Some sculptures, replicas of famous monuments, amaze the viewer with their sheer bulk and size. Others, depicting whole scenes such as Santa's workshop or the Knights of the Round Table, delight the visitor with their detail and scope. And some, recreations of favorite childhood characters such as Winnie the Pooh or Mickey Mouse, are friendly guides along the way.

There are no ropes or guards to separate the viewer from the work. Some of the sculptures, with built-in slides, caves or miniature golf courses, invite the viewer to climb aboard, to explore, to play. Children and adults alike are reminded of their own experiences building backyard snow families, and few can resist the urge to touch or pat or even hug a particularly appealing figure.

And sooner or later the viewer exclaims, "Wow? How do they do that?" Then, perhaps shivering in the cold, the more practical among us ask "Why? What drives them to do it?"

The answers are as varied as the sculptors one can find to question. Some do it professionally, for money. A few others do it out of a sense of obligation, for family or business. But most do it for love.

The first Carnival was pronounced a success. There were 28 sculptures, and the McCall-Donnelly High School Junior Class took first prize with a giant reproduction of Sharlie, McCall's resident lake monster. "It was a stunning sculpture, sprayed with green paint," Scoles remembers. "Of course, we now know that paint melts the sculptures and its mainly for that reason that all our sculptures now are white. It's not from any idea of purity or attempts to make them resemble marble."

For three years in a row, rain and January thaws reduced the sculptures to slush, so the

Hot and cold bath and shower, Idaho style.

newcomers in increasing numbers as the whole region grows up into a metropolis and its suburbs.

The history is best experienced in three separate corners of the region. Silver City, in the rugged Owyhees, has been called the "Queen of America's Ghost Towns." Idaho City, just upstream from Boise, is a livelier — and much more livable — old dame. Near Gooding, the annual re-enactment of the Three Island Crossing of the Snake River brings the Oregon Trail experience back to life.

Even in boomtown Boise, history keeps several addresses. The Territorial Penitentiary, the Morrison-Knudsen Depot, the mining barons' mansions on Warm Springs Avenue. In Caldwell, Nampa, Payette, Weiser and elsewhere, great old homes and buildings remember the past.

date for the event was changed to the first week in February. At the same time, local sculptors came up with the idea of building with slush, instead of snow, and a whole new concept was born. The Carnival gained a second wind.

Bob Scoles continues to be enthusiastic about and involved with the snow sculptures of Winter Carnival. "Anybody," he says, "can do it. It's fun, and the camaraderie is special."

Scoles marvels that a town the size of McCall can come up with something so special, and credit~ the involvement of many locals. "Shopkeepers, ministers, Forest Ser-vice workers, teachers, barbers - everyone is on the same level. It's gone beyond economic reasons; we retain the Carnival because we've got something special to belong to."

Early dog sleds and skiers in Long Valley.

DIAMONDFIELD JACK

He got his nickname from his belief that there was a diamond mine near Silver city in Owyhee County. Diamondfield Jack became a household name in Idaho for reasons that had nothing to do with mining, though.

Sheep are very efficient grazers. They're able to crop off grass right down to ground level. That doesn't leave a thing for cattle to eat, and that's why there were range wars in the West. In Idaho, this basic conflict resulted in the deaths of two sheepmen in Cassia County in 1896.

Diamondfield Jack was a gunman hired by cattlemen to intimidate sheepmen. He'd threatened all of them at one time or another, so it was natural to assume he was involved in the murders. The man was arrested, prosecuted, convicted, and sentenced to hang. But hanging Diamondfield Jack proved difficult. Frantic men on horseback twice galloped into Albion carrying postponements, saving him from the gallows at the last minute. The third time Jack was scheduled to hang, two cattlemen came forward and confessed to the murders. They were eventually acquitted on self defense.

Even with a confession, tests that proved the murder weapon wasn't his gun, and an alibi that placed him in Nevada at the time of the murders, many were still convinced that Diamondfield Jack pulled the trigger. There was enough opposition to keep him in jail for six years. But eventually Diamondfield Jack was released.

The man who was saved from the gallows three times moved to Nevada, where his luck finally ran out. Diamondfield Jack, who lived at least part of his life by the gun, did not die that way. He was run over by a taxi cab in Las Vegas in 1949.

Today, Southwest Idaho is mainly Anglo, with a vibrant Hispanic community, and a growing Asian presence drawn mainly by the booming high tech industry. Shoshones and Bannocks live on the Duck Valley Reservation, in the remote Owyhee Highlands. Shoshones dominated Southwest Idaho at the time of the coming of the Whites. In 1819 Donald Mackenzie reported 800 lodges at the site of present-day Boise. The city of Nampa derives its name from Nampuh ("Big foot"), an enormous Shoshone war chief.

The last of what Whites called "the Indian troubles" ended in Idaho in 1879 with the conclusion of the Sheepeater War. The mountain-dwelling Sheepeaters were pursued by the U.S. Army through the most rugged country imaginable: the Salmon River Mountains. Today this area is still unroaded as part of the

OWYHEE BONES

by Rodger Rapp

Owyhee County, 7,641 square miles of southwest Idaho, is a great place to get away from it all. My friend, Sonja, and I spend our weekends there escaping the pressures of workaday servitude by plunging headfirst into deep time. We can follow the arc of time's arrow for miles, seeing the land the way it once was, without ever seeing anyone else.

Civilization, what little there is, has been spread mighty thin here. Only 8,272 permanent residents were found and counted during the last government census. Less than sixteen percent of the county is privately owned. The rest, more than 4.1 million acres of semi-arid desert and scrub forest, is husbanded by state and federal agencies.

A long, Snake River slice of the federal government's 3.8 million acre Owyhee County public trust is included in the Snake River Birds of Prey Area. In the Owyhee badlands to the south, where we usually go, the Bureau of land Management systematically administers an East-meets-West land-use compromise: range-fed cattle are created separate but equal.

The steamer IMNAHA provided transport along the Snake.

Controlled grazing, according to some range-management "desert ecologists," actually stimulates the growth of additional plant cover. Grazing animals break up the soil as they move and trim back taller plants that monopolize the available sunlight and water.

Critics who grouse about the federal four-legged welfare system disagree; they call it hamburger hell. It's fairly quiet on the Western Front, whatever the case may be. Government grub-staked cattle tend to avoid human contact as much as possible.

The people who live and work in Owyhee County are surprisingly friendly. Getting to know the general lay of the land, however, is no easy task for a rank outsider. Few of its regularly maintained two-lane roads are paved; only two or three of these attenuated "medium-duty" arterials actually lead to the nearest version of Rome. Self educated backroad scholars must study at the school of hard knocks.

Topographic maps of the Owyhee's cow-path hinterlands, most of them drawn up by the U.S. Geological Survey in the 1950s and photo-revised in the 1970s, carry a fine-print disclaimer: "Revisions shown in purple compiled from aerial photographs. . . . This information not field checked." Newer roads and jeep trails-and they are legion-aren't shown at all.

Eventually, although we don't always know exactly where, we pull off to the side of a dusty "access" road, open the doors, lace up our thirsty boots, and get out. ✍

River of No Return - Frank Church Wilderness, the largest in the contiguous U.S. The wilderness is now home only to animals and a playground for recreationists. But Indian petroglyphs are frequently found here, as they are all over Southwest Idaho.

Three other ethnic groups are especially important to Southwest Idaho. Chinese came to the area to mine for gold after the completion of the transcontinental railroad. There were sizable Chinese communities in Boise and other towns. Near Warrens, north of McCall, Chinese farmers created the only system of Chinese-style terrace agriculture found in the New World. Japanese-Americans have contributed more recently to Southwest Idaho's welfare. After the indignities af the World War II internment camps, Japanese-

SILVER CITY
by Bessie M. Baker

Twenty-five years ago there were quite a number of ghost towns in our thriving west, but today there are few. Somehow they are disappearing, and the stories of their grandeur are becoming hazy and lost in legend. A very few achieve glamour as typical examples of the roaring west of gold-rush days, and are given tremendous impact through movies, radio and television.

Idaho has a ghost town which has all the glamour of any movie western. The old buildings still stand although weatherbeaten and deserted. The bank and court house, which were stone structures, have fallen down, and the few remaining walls, the bank vault, and the prison cells, are mute evidence that once this community was a thriving, brawling place.

Silver City is not for squeamish people; Silver City is for hardy people-people who can stand the excitement of riding 30 miles over narrow, brush-lined mountain roads that wind in hairpin curves up, and up, and up. The view from the upper reaches of the Owyhees is magnificent, and only those hardy adventuresome souls who are brave enough to make the trip will ever know the thrill of imagining how Silver City came to be. One standing at the top of the grade can almost see the freight wagons 50 years ago as they inched slowly up the winding road, their 10- to 12-horse teams straining at their collars, tons of supplies to the city of thousands. And what a city it was! It had a newspaper; a Catholic church; a barber shop which advertised baths in an actual bathtub as a specialty; barrooms with huge mirrors and polished interiors: six general stores; two hardware stores; a tin shop; two meat markets; two hotels; four restaurants; a brewery and bottling plant; a jeweler; photographer's gallery; a tailor shop; three barber shops; four lawyers; two doctors; and eight saloons.

The visitor today, as he walks the deserted streets can close his eyes and hear the raucous laughter and drunken cursing, the pistol shots ringing out in the sharp, clear night, and the tinny piano music of the dance halls. He can smell the cheap perfume and hear the rustle of silk skirts as prostitutes open doors. He can feel the sharp knife-edge of fear as he watches recruited thugs from two mining companies in desperate warfare before the old War Eagle Hotel.

Silver City has its boot hill, too. The cemetery has been restored by two fraternal organizations, the Masonic order, and the Odd Fellows lodge. New fencing around the cemetery, and a thorough cleaning away of the weeds and trash, which accumulated have improved the appearance of the cemetery.

Six thousand feet up, Silver City stands, a ghost town wrapped in Western legend romantic and raw, surviving winters of terrific, freezing winds which heap drifts of snow over the entire area, deep enough to bury the town. ᔭ

The Silver City Stage Stop conjures images: Mining boomtown. Outlaws. Ghost town. The infamous Owyhee desert. Claude Dallas. Running the little known Owyhee River.

Americans stayed on, and have contributed greatly, notably in the areas of agriculture, government and education.

Basques comprise the ethnic group for which Southwest Idaho is best known. Boise is the center of the largest Basque community outside Europe. Basques have been here since the mining days and they continue their contributions. While some say most Americans feel part Irish, anyone who grows up in Southwest Idaho probably feels a little bit Basque.

Most Southwest Idahoans also feel a part of the technological revolution. The Boise Valley has become a center for high tech manufacturing. Micron, Hewlett-Packard and Zilog are major employers and important

THREE ISLAND CROSSING

Jump Creek Falls near Homedale.

Emigrants on the Oregon Trail faced a tough decision when they reached what is now Glenns Ferry, Idaho. The story of Three Island Crossing is coming up next.

Three Island Crossing was a well-known, often dreaded, landmark on the Oregon Trail. When emigrants, on foot, in wagons, and on horseback, reached the Snake River across from the modern day town of Glenns Ferry, they had a choice to make. They could continue on a branch of the Oregon Trail through the desert south of the Snake, or they could cross the treacherous river for the greener grass and shorter route on the other side. Most chose to cross the river, using two of the three islands. Not everyone made it with their possessions. Wagons and carts were frequently swamped or overturned. Many horses, mules, and oxen lost their lives to the current.

Crossing the river could be a terror for settlers. Staying on the south side was not a certain joy, either. As one emigrant said, in his 1843 diary, "This is, perhaps, the most rugged, desert and dreary country, between the western borders of the United States and the shores of the Pacific. It is nothing else than a wild, rocky barren wilderness, of wrecked and ruined Nature, a vast field of volcanic desolations."

In 1869, Gus P. Glenn put an end to the agonizing, by starting a ferry service near the infamous crossing. Glenn's Ferry is named for that early Idahoan's business.

Today, the story of the Oregon Trail is told at Three Island Crossing State Park, just off the interstate at Glenns Ferry.

community boosters. Mt. Home Air Force Base is one of two "composite wings" in the country. Its high-tech aircraft and weaponry provide the nation with its front-line defense.

Boise State University provides Idaho with its only urban university. At 15,000 students and growing, BSU scurries to meet a booming community's educational and cultural demands and to provide the rallying siren call of college sports. Two fine valley colleges — Albertson's College of Idaho in Caldwell and Northwest Nazarene College in Nampa — are Northwest leaders in both academics and sports. Weiser tempos the area's musical spirits with its annual National Old Time Fiddlers Festival. Summer afternoons jump with jazz at Sunnyslope, above the Snake River near Marsing. And two of the nation's best rodeos are held in

SANDS OF TIME
by Mario P. Delisio

Bruneau Dunes. A great many Idahoans have heard of them and many have visited the area, perhaps even scrambled up and happily slid or tumbled down the steep-sided dune slopes, the largest of which towers some 470 feet high. Many, likewise, have enjoyed viewing or swimming or fishing the lakes next to the large dunes.

Few people, however, either understand the natural history or realize the number of features entailed within this 4,800 acre park within the Idaho State Parks & Recreation system.

Located near the town of Bruneau and close to the Snake River, Bruneau Dunes is easily reached from I-84. Traveling east, take Mountain Home exit 90 into town, go 18 miles southwest on State Highway 51, then east on State Highway 78 for two miles. Traveling west on I-84, take Hammett exit 112, then State Highway 78 for 15 miles.

Visitors can climb dunes, camp, fish for bluegill or bass, take nature hikes and photograph the myriad aspects of the area. The Park also features equestrian trails. Off-road vehicles, however are not allowed off the roads leading to the dunes.

What of the natural history of Bruneau Dunes? What is there to attract, to intrigue, to remember at this spectacular landscape of world-class significance? Let us explore!

Bruneau Dunes lies in Eagle Cove, a semi-circular basin cut by the ancient Snake River. Eagle Cove is a massive sand trap, the results of which are the various dunal structures. Wind-blown sediments from the surrounding landscapes, traveling in the direction of the cove, are deposited or carried further away. The heavier,

sand-size particles fall into the basin while the lighter, silt, clay and dust particles continue to float in the air. Wind, and, to a degree, water, have formed, piled and sculpted the present landforms and water features over the past thousands of years.

A major event within the cove occurred about 15,000 years ago. At that time a catastrophic flood called the Lake Bonneville Flood swept down the Snake River from eastern Idaho. Upon meeting Eagle Cove it swamped the basin to an unknown depth, eroding landforms and depositing sediment. with

a volume of water exceeding 200 times the present Snake River for a period of perhaps a month and a half, the flood probably destroyed any existing dunal structures. The present features at Bruneau Dunes, therefore, are believed to post-date the Lake Bonneville Flood.

The flood was caused by the partial collapse of the north shore of ancient Lake Bonneville. This lake, created during the last glacial age, occupied the present Great Salt Lake Basin stretching from a corner of

Nampa and Caldwell.

While the high tech companies inflate the economy's sails, agriculture and forest products are still the area's mainstay. Millions of board feet of timber are annually harvested from the Boise and Payette national forests. Cowboys ride herd on cattle on the great Owyhee range. And farms from Weiser, Payette and Parma, through Fruitland, Middleton and Emmett, to Meridian and Eagle produce nationally significant harvests of row crops. Even highly urbanized Ada County still has one-quarter million acres of farmland.

North of its farm belt and the population centers, Southwest Idaho presents a recreationist's dream of mountains, canyons, forest and wilderness. Forty minutes from the Boise Valley, the north and south forks

southeastern Idaho south to Provo, east from the Wasatch Mountain front flanking Salt Lake City-Ogden-Logan and west to the Nevada border. It was approximately the size of Lake Michigan, about 20,000 square miles in extent. Present Salt Lake City would have been hundreds of feet underwater as evidenced by the high staircase terraces cut into the north-south trending Wasatch Mountains. The massive erosional-depositional forces of the wall of water account for much of the present appearance of the Snake River Canyon extending some 250 miles from Pocatello through southern Idaho and into Hells Canyon.

Basque sheepherders still tend their flock after a hundred years. If people live here long enough, they convince themselves that they are part-Basque. The ghosts of these Long Valley sheep were driven up to prime Long Valley summer grazing land a hundred years ago.

Bruneau Dunes consists of essentially four areas: the large dune complex (often called the Big Dune), the North Dune Field, the "Little Sahara," and the south rim of Eagle Cove overlooking all of the other areas. Certainly the most dominant area is the large dune complex. Appearing as a single massive dune to the casual observer, the complex is composed of two large dunes that merge. Interestingly, the merging sections or arms of each dune curl around each other to form a crater. Each dune has a peak, with the higher one reaching 470 feet. Associated with the large dune complex is a massive sand ramp leading from near its ridge in a westerly direction. The sand ramp is delineated by a number of wave forms including a very distinctive depression or dimple about half way on the ramp.

Immediately to the north of the large dune complex is the North Dune Field. This consists of numbers of small to medium-sized dunes, some stabilized by vegetation while others are still active as evidenced by the lack of vegetation. The most accessible of these are the favorite playgrounds of dune climbers, besides the large dune complex. Most fascinating of all the areas, perhaps, is the seldom visited "Little Sahara." Reached either by horse or on foot, the "Little Sahara" entails a tremendous variety of dune structures, erosional features, oases, marshes, playas, wadis, wildlife, plants

of the Payette River offer the best whitewater adventures close to a big city. Farther north, the south and middle forks of the Salmon River, and the Hells Canyon of the Snake add a big wilderness impact to the experience. The Bogus Basin Ski Area can be seen from Boise to Parma. Bogus offers five chairlifts and night skiing within minutes of the city. Brundage Mountain, near McCall, is famous for its powder and its snowcat access to backcountry.

McCall sits at 5000 feet high on a blue-black lake surrounded by mountains and forest. Long a favorite summering grounds for Southwest Idaho families, it is quickly becoming a national summer and winter mecca. Other communities in the area's northwest corner — Cascade, New Meadows; Council and

and an array of other desert forms. Throughout, the tracks of mammals, reptiles, insects and birds bear evidence of the animal-life that thrives here.

The fourth area is the bluff (hammada) overlooking the Eagle Cove basin. The bluff consists of ancient lake-riverine sediments covered to a great extent by wave after wave of sand dunes, like a running sea. In most places the sand is only a few feet deep. While most of the sand field is stabilized by vegetation, the southwestern section of it is active. It is this active area devoid of plant cover that is presently contributing a major amount of sand to Eagle Cove. Why this area is destabilized is not clear. The area can be easily observed from anywhere in Eagle Cove as a sheet of sand overflowing the bluff to the southwest. In addition, some of the entire bluff area where the sand has blown away is covered by pebbles and cobbles.

Although many people believe deserts to be barren areas, in reality they often include numerous varieties of wildlife and plants. Since most animals are relatively inactive during the heat of the day, the best times to observe them are during the early morning and late afternoon. Some animals are nocturnal. The wail and barking of the coyote during these times is evidence of this as are the multitude of tracks which are apparent each morning on the various sand features.

Altogether, Bruneau Dunes offers a complex of scenery aad activities that captures the imagination of adventurous visitors. For those who view desert landscapes as reservoirs of introspective contemplation, Bruneau Dunes is that, too. Excitement, solace, magnificence of scenery ... all these are entailed at Bruneau Dunes.⋞

The "City of Trees" -named Le Bois by the French. Must have more park space and tree shade per capita than anythwere. Winter finds some of the buildings evident in the background heated by underground thermal springs, and skiers flocking to a resort a short 16 miles north.

CONQUERING THE BRUNEAU RIVER CANYON

Even in 1950, parts of Idaho's formidable back-country were unexplored. That summer, three Twin Falls men became the first to navigate the Bruneau River Canyon.

Upon their return, "They were weary and unshaven and their eyes were dull from their experiences," reported the Twin Falls Times - News on Aug. 1. "But through their weariness was shining a bright gleam - the gleam of having done what never had been done before."

Idaho is the nation's whitewater capital. Thousands come every year to float world-class waters: the Middle Fork of the Salmon, the Main Salmon, the Payette, Selway, Owyhee and Lochsa.

By 1950, all those streams had been explored - all but the Bruneau, isolated by a 2,000-foot canyon and an unpopulated desert.⋞

Cambridge — balance their lifestyles on ranching, timber and recreation. To the east, forests hide the quaint and remote villages of Yellowpine and Big Creek.

And that's just to the north. The World's Center for Birds of Prey and the half-million acre Snake River Birds of Prey area begin on Boise's south doorstep. The area is home to the continent's largest concentration of nesting raptors. South of the river begin the Owyhees, Idaho's big empty quarter. Toward the southeast, the Bruneau Sand Dunes contain the highest dune in North America.

Southwest Idaho blends the best with the best. No wonder everyone seems to be moving here, now.⋞

Calendar

McCall winter Carnival, McCall: One of Idaho's best annual winter events. Festivities include world-class ice sculptures, an international sculpture contest, snowmobile races, parades, fireworks, and many other family activities. Contact: McCall Chamber of Commerce, (208) 634-7631.

Idaho Shakespeare Frstival, Boise, June - August: Experience Idaho's renowned Shakespeare theatre under the stars. Contact: (208) 336-9221.

Cherry Festival, Emmett, June: A community celebration of the annual cherry harvest and an oppor-tunity to enjoy Idaho hospitality at its best. The fun includes hot air balloon races, pie eating contests, delicious foods, and events for the entire family. Contact: Emmett Chamber of Commerce, (208) 365-3485.

National Old-Time Fiddlers Contest, Weiser, June: The most prestigious fiddlers' contest in the country. The nation's best country fiddlers play throughout the city during the competition and informal jam sessions. Contact: Weiser Chamber of Commerce, (208) 549-0450.

Boise River Festival, Boise, June: A night-time parade with a brightly lit show and enter-tainment floats will high-light this celebration. Spectators will be able to view the parade along the banks of the Boise River. Other major events include a hot air balloon festival, air show, enter-tainment, parades, athletic competitions, and the grand finale. Contact: Boise Convention and Visitors Bureau, (208) 344-7777 or (208) 383-7318.

Snake River Stampede, Nampa July: One of the top 25 rodeos in the country. Nightly entertainment includes some of America's foremost Country and Western stars, as well as first-class rodeo events. Contact: Nampa Chamber of Commerce, (208) 466-8497.

Payette County fair and Rodeo, Payette, August.: ICA Rodeo. Food booths, agriculture and livestock exhibits. Contact: Payette Chamber of Commerce: (208) 642-2362.

Three Island Crossing, Glenns Ferry, second weekend in August: Contact Glenns Ferry Chamber of Commerce, (208) 366-2002.

Caldwell Night Rodeo, Caldwell, August: "The rodeo where the cowboy is the star!" Rodeo thrills last five nights and fetures top professional cowboys. Contact: Caldwell Chamber of Commerce (208) 459-7493.

Western Idaho Fair, Boise, August: Exciting carnival rides and games, agricultural exhibits, dozens of food booths, and big name entertainment. Contact: (208) 376-3247.

Art In the Park, Boise, September: Considered one of Idaho's largest and most elaborate art shows, artists from all over the country bring original works of art to display and sell at this three-day outdoor event. Music, food booths and childrens activities. For more information, contact the Boise Art Museum, (208) 345-8330.

Air Force Appreciation Day, Mountain Home, first Saturday·after Labor Day: Festivities start with an airplane "Fly-by" and a parade that ends at Carl Miller Park. At the park, there is a free barbecue and lots of booths and entertainment. Contact: Mountain Home Chamber Commerce, (208) 587-4334.

Arts for Christmas Fair, Boise, First weekend in November through second weekend in November: The talents of over 340 artisans are on display and for sale to benefit Boisa Art Museum. Contact: Boise Art Museum, (208) 345-8330.

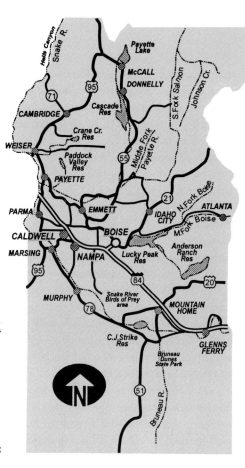

TIPS: FOOD & SHELTER

Shelter in Boise. The **Idanha Hotel** downtown is a piece of history, **Owyee Plaza** is top of the line, both offer great off season specials. **Shilo Inn-Riverside** is moderately-priced, friendly staff, but ask for a riverside room.

The Shore Lodge in McCall on Lake Payette one of the West's best kept secrets for both food and shelter. Brunch on the deck a summer and fall experience.

The Renaissance in Boise for excellent Northern Italian and seafood.

Best steak and prime rib, meeting place for ranchers, cowhands, and local bankers is the **Stagecoach** in Boise, operated by the same family for over 30 years. **Lock Stock & Barrel** also excels in beef and grilled fish.

Bar Guernica adjoining the Basque cultural center, offering Basque mini-meals (tapas) and burgers, similar fare to the Bar Boise in Guernica, Spain. Historic **Penguilly's Bar** is a local hangout for politicians & business professionals.

The Pacific Rim in Boise's lively Hyde Park area provides creative food at moderate prices.

Shige's Shushi downtown Boise can compete with **any** West coast sushi in quality and creativity.

The best hamburgers in Boise are at **The Dutch Oven,** and the **Crescent Bar** (no lawyers allowed).

For Breakfast without frills locals head to the **T&A Cafe** downtown, **Mrs. Bs** in the Burns Bros truck stop, and **Manley's** on Federal Way.

Short drives from Boise are the legendary **Sandbar River House** on the Snake River in Marsing, and **The Blue Canoe** south of Walter's Ferry.

South Central Idaho
Region 4

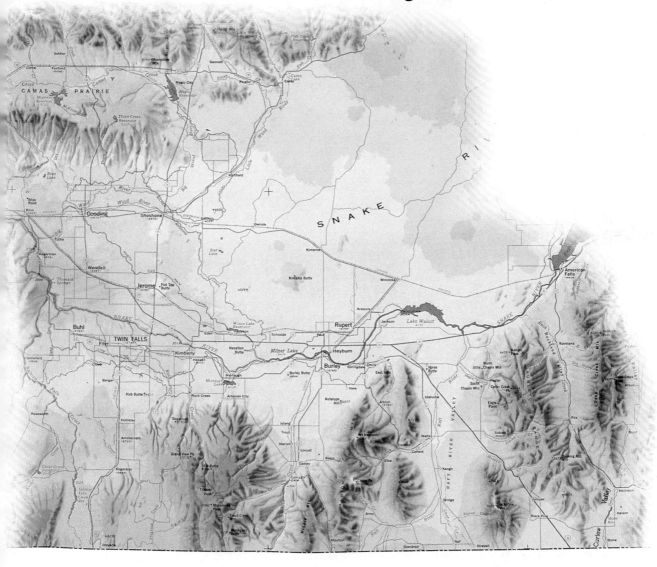

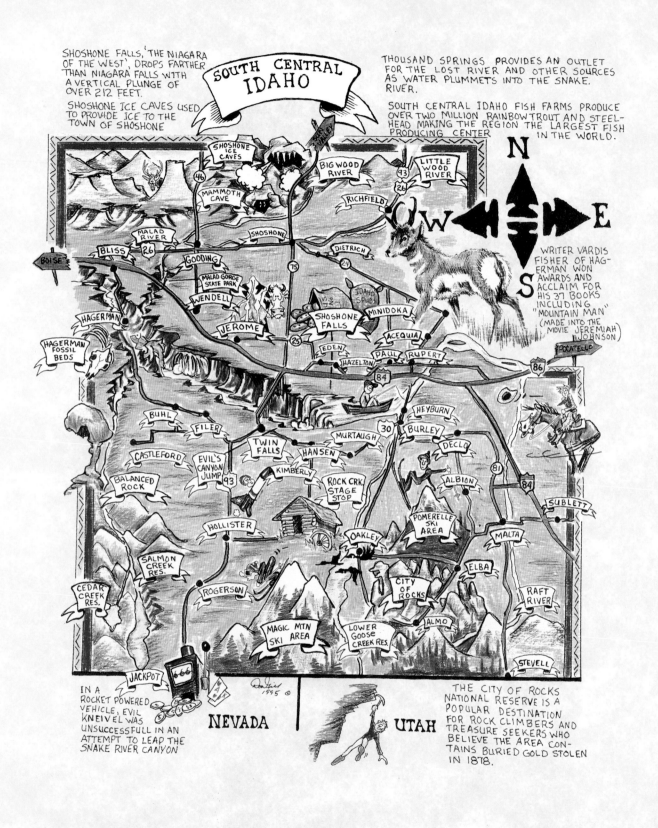

SHOSHONE FALLS, 'THE NIAGARA OF THE WEST', DROPS FARTHER THAN NIAGARA FALLS WITH A VERTICAL PLUNGE OF OVER 212 FEET.

SHOSHONE ICE CAVES USED TO PROVIDE ICE TO THE TOWN OF SHOSHONE

THOUSAND SPRINGS PROVIDES AN OUTLET FOR THE LOST RIVER AND OTHER SOURCES AS WATER PLUMMETS INTO THE SNAKE RIVER.

SOUTH CENTRAL IDAHO FISH FARMS PRODUCE OVER TWO MILLION RAINBOW TROUT AND STEELHEAD MAKING THE REGION THE LARGEST FISH PRODUCING CENTER IN THE WORLD.

SOUTH CENTRAL IDAHO

WRITER VARDIS FISHER OF HAGERMAN WON AWARDS AND ACCLAIM FOR HIS 37 BOOKS INCLUDING "MOUNTAIN MAN" (MADE INTO THE MOVIE JEREMIAH JOHNSON)

SHOSHONE ICE CAVES
MAMMOTH CAVE
BIG WOOD RIVER
LITTLE WOOD RIVER
RICHFIELD
SUN VALLEY
MALAD RIVER
BLISS
SHOSHONE
DIETRICH
GOODING
MALAD GORGE STATE PARK
WENDELL
IDAHO SPUDS
JEROME
SHOSHONE FALLS
MINIDOKA
HAGERMAN
ACEQUIA
HAGERMAN FOSSIL BEDS
EDEN
PAUL RUPERT
HAZELTON
POCATELLO
BUHL
FILER
HEYBURN
MURTAUGH
BURLEY
TWIN FALLS
HANSEN
DECLO
CASTLEFORD
EVIL'S CANYON JUMP
KIMBERLY
ROCK CRK STAGE STOP
ALBION
BALANCED ROCK
POMERELLE SKI AREA
SUBLETT
HOLLISTER
OAKLEY
MALTA
SALMON CREEK RES.
ELBA
CEDAR CREEK RES.
ROGERSON
CITY OF ROCKS
RAFT RIVER
ALMO
MAGIC MTN SKI AREA
LOWER GOOSE CREEK RES.
STEVELL
JACKPOT
BOISE

DaHill 1955 ©

IN A ROCKET POWERED VEHICLE, EVIL KNIEVEL WAS UNSUCCESSFULL IN AN ATTEMPT TO LEAP THE SNAKE RIVER CANYON

NEVADA   UTAH

THE CITY OF ROCKS NATIONAL RESERVE IS A POPULAR DESTINATION FOR ROCK CLIMBERS AND TREASURE SEEKERS WHO BELIEVE THE AREA CONTAINS BURIED GOLD STOLEN IN 1878.

Chapter V
SOUTH CENTRAL IDAHO
Region 4

PAUL BUNYAN WAS HERE TOO

And of course all old-timers in Idaho remember the night when Paul Bunyan drank nine kegs of rum in Idaho Falls and started for Seattle with his blue ox. It was a black wet night full of rain, and Paul wandered stupendously in a great drunken stupor, with his crooked trail behind him filling with water. The trail since that time has been known in all geographies as Snake River. ∽

Shoshone Falls of the Snake, higher than Niagara.

South Central Idaho is one big handsome country. Strong and productive, reticent and surprising, its lines show a character earned by hard work, done squinting under a sky billowing high with thunderheads.

These are the deep lines of wagon ruts, the green corduroys of irrigation, the listing and lonely lines of the old snow fences leading up to abandoned stone homes. Even the old timers' wry comments — halfjokes, half laments — characterize this great country. When they say, "And then it got interestin" they may mean beating a storm, navigating a box canyon, or battling a wildfire.

South Central Idaho is made handsomer by the light greens of spring grass, the pale purples of summer sages and sedges, and the wide winter whites as wise as the world. This sky here is always deepest azure.

SPRINGS ETERNAL

by Laurie Sammis

Thousand Springs. The name alone suggests wonder, excess, abundance. Pools of crystal blue water bubbling from below. Cool white streams gushing from a hidden source within the earth.

Even its location, in the center of the Magic Valley, implies mystery and myth. It is here, where the Snake River winds its way south of Hagerman, that Idaho reveals the solution to one of its most unique puzzles. The Big Lost River runs out of the mountains high in central Idaho, promptly disappears into the porous rock of the Snake River Aquifer at Craters of the Moon

Hidden below eyesight from most of South Central Idaho, the Snake winds and flows across the width of the entire state.

Monument, and finally rushes forth into daylight over 200 miles to the southwest. This is Thousand Springs: A series of instant waterfalls and spring creeks that tumble nearly 400 feet from the canyon rim to the river below.

At one time, the springs that gushed from the dark canyon walls were numerous enough to merit their name. Today, only three of the original 18 named and seven unnamed large springs remain undeveloped; most have been put to use for hydropower and fish production at nearby hatcheries.

Minnie Miller Springs, perhaps the most spectacular falls in the area, represents the last vestige of an ancient phenomenon. With over 450 cubic feet of water per second cascading into the Snake River, the springs are part of a 425-acre farm that contains more than three miles of river and stream frontage.

Thousand Springs Farm provides sanctuary for numerous forms of wildlife. Waterfowl flock to the 50-degree water, which flows at a rate of 1500 cubic feet per second through the springs and estuaries on the property. Within the crags and outcroppings of the canyon walls live golden eagles, various owls, and colonies of black crowned night herons, as well as other perching birds. One of the springs provides habitat for the largest known population of the rare and endangered Shoshone sculpin, a fish found nowhere else in the world. Yet it is the scenic beauty of the farm (contained on an approximately 65-acre island), and the springs themselves that make this a breathtaking spot worth cherishing and preserving.

Fortunately, that is exactly what is happening through the Nature Conservancy, a national environmental group that is in the "business of conservation." The Conservancy is a private, non-profit real estate conservation organization, international in scope. The major

Or else it is soon to be deepest azure. After the storm. After the snow. After the prairie fire. The weather can seem fickle in South Central Idaho. But here fickle means changing yet ultimately charming. One thousand springs gentle the ruggedness of vertical canyon walls.

South Central Idaho contains legendary wonders. Ice caves, devil's cauldrons, rock cities (not one, but two rock cities), gushing springs in great profusion, thundering waterfalls to out-Niagara Niagara, a world famous canyon, and a dry country's challenge made a garden through irrigation. Since the first wagon trains rolled through here over a century ago, South Central Idaho has been something to write home about. And before the first wagons, the Indian wrote for all the ages. Their petroglyphs make mystery novels

objective of its offices and affiliates (in 50 states and 11 Latin American countries) is to identify, protect, and manage or maintain over time, unique natural areas in the United States and abroad.

The Nature Conservancy works quietly to acquire the nation's best remaining natural and scenic wonders. Its goal is clearly defined, and because it is a private organization, executives are able to act quickly and concisely without a lot of bureaucratic red tape.

The Conservancy doesn't try to preserve the whole landscape, but instead concentrates on selecting jeopardized areas of the highest conservation value and concern.

In a sense, the Conservancy is an undeveloper. The organization has an extremely non-controversial attitude. They rarely expend funds on lobbying, and prefer to simply work within the free market system to purchase property from landowners.

A good example is a beautiful tract of land like Thousand Springs, where there existed a species habitat and an incredible amount of water, within a fast-growing area. A tremendous economic benefit could have been derived from dividing Thousand Springs into home sites or commercial fish farms. There were a number of developers who would have paid twice what the Nature Conservancy paid to be able to develop Thousand Springs.

Thousand Springs truly is a magical place. Walking around the property under the shade of tall oaks, picnicking within sight of the grave marker of Idalia Edgemoor the head cow of Minnie Miller's herd), or canoeing down one of the channels past the springs to the falls, brings one thought to mind: This is how life should be. It's not a big area, but there's something very special about it. It's the kind of place on which the Nature Conservancy likes to focus its efforts.❧

seem matter-of-fact.

The Snake River Plain is among the world's largest and most interesting volcanic areas. While on a relief map of Idaho, it looks like, well, like a plain — cut by deep gorges certainly, but almost everywhere flat — it attests to a time of remarkable pyrotechnics. And it will hit you when you least expect it with a vertical face — or precipitous plunge.

Most of the exposed bedrock is basaltic lava flows, capping great volumes of rhyolite. This rhyolite exploded from a long line of volcanoes, which began erupting 13 million years ago. These volcanoes erupted in a directional sequence from southwest to northeast, as the tectonic plate of North America drifted over

RAISED IN IDAHO

by David Clark

Trout are to Idaho as, well, potatoes are to Idaho. With over 75% of all trout consumed in the United States being produced in Idaho, people everywhere readily picture a trout dinner as originating in the cold, rushing streams of the high country of this state. But of the over 130 commercial trout hatcheries in Idaho, few are located in the mountains. Most of the 40 to 50 million pounds of trout (at a value of $70,000,000) destined to become meals each year, are raised in the sagebrush desert along the Snake River between Twin Falls and Bliss.

Although trout farming began in the United States in the 1860's, it wasn't until 1928, when the Snake River Trout Company was established in the Magic Valley, that the first successful commercial hatchery was built in Idaho. The farming operation, and the others that followed, were attracted by the spring water gushing out of the sides of the Snake River Canyon, in so many places that the area became known as "Thousand Springs."

The water that feeds these springs originates in the mountains of central Idaho and move southward until it reaches the Snake River Plain, a huge landscape created by millions of years of volcanic activity. Here, the rock is so full of cracks and holes, the water can no longer flow on the surface and is rapidly absorbed by the lava sponge. Once under the surface, this water

Irrigation of southern Idaho turned desolation into one of the most productive and fruited plains in the country.

continues to seep southward at a rate of five to ten feet each day. After moving more than 100 miles, the underground journey ends as the water suddenly exits through the walls of the Snake River Canyon at a steady rate of over 2,200,000 gallons per minute. The many miles of travel through this natural rock filter leaves the water crystal clear, at a constant temperature of 58 degrees-ideal for growing rainbow trout.

The trout industry has a saying, "If you don't have an egg, you don't have anything." To obtain eggs, special fish are raised exclusively for breeding purposes. These brooders are superior fish, bred to produce offspring that are fast weight gainers, have good body confirmation and appearance, and yield tasty, nicely textured flesh.

New developments seem to be occurring in the trout industry almost daily. One of the most interesting is its recent involvement in the raising of sturgeon (the fish that looks like a cross between a shark and a dinosaur), in cooperation with the College of Southern Idaho and the Idaho Department of Fish and Game. in this program, a wild sturgeon is caught to obtain a supply of eggs.

---

a "hot Spot" — a circular area of extremely thin crust.

That would be enough to interest earth scientists all by itself, but the progression of the volcanoes forms such a regular pattern — and the hotspot itself seems to be so circular, that some geologists have proposed that the initial perforation may have been created by a massive meteorite slamming into the earth in southeastern Oregon, some 17 million years ago.

The meteorite' s crater became an enormous lake of lava which overflowed and spilled to the north to form the extensive Columbia basalt flows that cover much of Oregon and Washington, and west-central Idaho. Then when tectonic drift floated the unpunctured North American continental crust over the impact

The eggs are then transferred to the hatcheries of the College of Southern Idaho, where they are fertilized, incubated and hatched. Some of the fry are then provided to the trout farms, where the sturgeon are reared until their first birthday, when 60% of the 12- to 20-inch fish are released back into the Snake River. To date, approximately 3,000 sturgeon have been returned to the river.

In return for rearing these fish, the commercial farms are allowed to keep some sturgeon for research purposes. If it transpires that these fish can be raised effectively in an artificial stream, then the excellent meat and caviar of the sturgeon may someday be produced for the market.

See the nice ladies? See the warden's wife? See Lyda, aka "Lady Bluebeard"?

LYDA SOUTHARD'S FAMOUS APPLE PIE

(Folksong sung to the tune of "Annie Laurie") - Rosalie Sorrels

Oh, Twin Falls' farms are bonnie
In the middle of July,
And 'twas there that Lyda Southard
Baked her famous apple pie.
Her famous apple pie . . .
Which ne'er forgot will be . .
And for Lyda's deep dish apple pie
I'd lay me down and die.

She sprinkled it with cinnamon,
A dash of nutmeg too,
And sugared it with arsenic,
A tasty devil's brew.
That famous apple pie . . .
Which ne'er forgot will be . . .
And for Lyda Southard's apple pie ,
Men lay them down to die.

Four times she picked her apples
And put them in a pie.
'Twas just dessert, she murmured
I never thought they'd die,
I never thought they'd die ,
I never thought they'd die,
She was just a country housekeeper
Who never thought they'd die.

Oh Lyda's got her just deserts,
She's in the jailhouse strong,
Her piecrust it was short and sweet,
Her sentence it is long.
Her sentence it is long . .
Her sentence it is long . . .
Oh, Lyda's in the jailhouse now,
Her sentence it is long.

site (at the rate of an inch-and-a-half a year) the geology changed from the less dramatic basaltic lava flows to the boom-boom-boom rhyolite explosive volcanoes that punched their way across South Central Idaho.

Later, the earth's crust stretched and ruptured in the area of the Great Rift, northeast of Twin Falls. This released more basaltic lava, which now covers much of the area. The cinder cones of South Central Idaho are the result of water seeping into the lava and then exploding as steam.

More of the work of water and lava now exists as the thousand springs. Water that percolates into the earth to the northeast — for example, the Big Lost River — springs out of the canyon cliffs and cascades into the Snake River. Some of the springs have been harnessed to provide the freshest, best temperature water

MINIDOKA'S DESERT EMPIRE

The first white people to traverse Minidoka County were the hardy pioneers who followed the crooked path of the Snake River through southern Idaho.

It was not until 1883 that what is now Minidoka County had a permanent settler. The Henry Schodde family arrived there in covered wagons and filed for a homestead on the windswept desert. For many years, this family lived an isolated life but they managed to build a cattle empire on a strip of land along the Snake River . . . in spite of the Indians and white outlaws who stole the cattle, horses and even frightened the children.

To the American farmer at the turn of the century, this area held little promise because he had to depend on nature to water his crops unless he had a strip along the river. This hot, dry, wind-blown wasteland seemed worthless. And quite fitting, the Shoshoni word-.Minidoka-

Crossed in the 1800s, bridged in the 1900s, this canyon of the Snake is not far from daredevil Evil Kneviel's attempted jump across. Attempted.

meaning "broad expanse," was applied to it.

About two miles above the Storey Ferry there was a drop in the Snake River which was called Minidoka Falls. This point presented an ideal place for the construction of a dam across the Snake River, which could be the starting point of a canal to irrigate land below it on the north .side of the river. The federal government in 1904 authorized the Minidoka Reclamation Project to be constructed at that point and work was shortly after commenced.

Although the first water was delivered in 1907, there were hectic years that followed. Spasmodic water delivery not only caused crop failure but discouragement for those who courageously looked toward a secure future from farming in Minidoka. However, with the building of the American Falls Dam, this agricultural future changed from dream to reality.

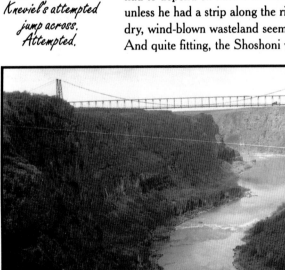

GOODING COUNTY

Those early-day pioneers would not believe their eyes if they had been privileged to see the country as it is today. Mile stretching upon mile of attractive farms, thoroughbred cattle in the fields, farm houses that would outshine the more palacial mansion of a century ago, and barns that would have made many a pioneer woman jealous of the lowly cow.

for South Central Idaho's famous fish farms, which lead the nation in the production of trout.

In the wondrous Hagerman Valley, there is more than just thousands of springs. There are beautiful farms and also the aquatic habitat for a living fossil, the gigantic Snake River sturgeon. Dead fossils reside here, too. At the Hagerman Fossil Beds, paleontologists have unearthed hundreds of skeletons of ancient, zebra-like horses, the oldest yet found on this continent.

More South Central Idaho geology lives as evidence of the great Bonneville Flood, around 15 thousand years ago which occurred when the gigantic precursor to the Great Salt Lake burst its banks and sent water in Amazonian amounts, splashing and crashing toward the sea. Shoshone Falls, 52-feet taller than Niagara

As the warm days of spring arrive in Gooding, the farmer mounts his tractor and turns acres of fertile soil each day. No longer does he follow along behind an ox hitched to a wooden plow. Here a field is showing feathery green from newly sprouted wheat breaking through the rich brown earth. There a field is all harrowed, awaiting the last frosts for planting of beans, potatoes or corn. Beyond is the velvet of growing alfalfa. Cattle are being moved into Mount Bennett Hills, where they will graze during the season ahead.

A few months later the landscape will change. The wheat will be tall . . . yellow . . . then turn a golden brown as the mechanized reapers move in for the harvest . . . 40 to 90 bushels per acre. The spring's fallow spots will be blossoming beans, that will yield up to 65 bushels per acre, potatoes that will produce from 200 to 600 sacks; waving corn that will run from 55 to 130 bushels. The alfalfa will produce two, three and four cuttings of hay. Herds of stock with their increase of calves will be worked down from the higher levels, to be readied for market.

The constant assurance of water, through irrigation, guarantees the farmer in Gooding County a good return from the soil.

In the heart of a large agricultural and grazing area, Gooding is located at the junction of three state highways, on the main line of the Union Pacific Railroad. Wendell is known as the turkey center of southern Idaho, while Bliss boasts one of the largest Rod and Gun clubs in the state.

What a revelation it would be if those pioneers could see the smooth paved highways where once wagon ruts and clouds of dust dogged the weary traveler . . . could see the huge steel bridges spanning the mighty river . . . could see the sage-encrusted desert covered with bounteous crops . . .could see plodding oxen

A vintage Buick navigates a snowy path down the canyon to the Snake River.

replaced by the mechanized farm machine . . . could see the harnessing of water to bring convenience to the homes, farms and industries.

As spokesmen over the country know, the Gooding Country affords some of the finest game-bird hunting in the west for pheasant, partridge, quail, sagehen and mourning doves. The Snake River, one of the greatest flyways of migratory waterfowl, is excellent hunting for duck and geese. Its rivers and streams are fine fishing haunts with rainbow, native and brook trout, as well as sturgeon.

Here are many notable scenic attractions including Thousand Springs, Clear Lakes, Dead Horse Cave, Lye Lake and the Gooding City of Rocks.⁓

and Twin Falls (now one orphaned twin because of diversion for power) were both created when swirling whirlpools dug deep holes along the path of the Bonneville Flood.Upriver from the Falls the Murtaugh stretch of the Snake River provides whitewater enthusiasts with the rides of their lives in spring and early summer after a big snow year.

The Malad River Gorge, which motorists fly over on the I-84 bridge, presents another magnificent sight. Here, in a narrow 250-foot deep canyon, a 60-foot waterfall vaults into a scoured hole called the Devil's Washbowl. Devil's Washbowl is one of at least 16 Idaho places named after the devil, in tribute to their fearsome ruggedness. Between Twin Falls and Jerome the Devil's Scuttle Hole was the name given by the

GOODING CITY OF ROCKS

Eleven thousand acres of rock is a bit too much for a fence, or a house, but it is ideal for a city of rocks. Little known, but inspiring in its majestic beauty is the Gooding City of Rocks (Not Cassia County's City of Rocks). Hidden among the seemingly endless waste of badlands of southern Idaho, and pierced by only a twisting thread of road, this spot of rugged beauty is well worth the time necessary for a visit to it.

HEALING OF THE HILLS
by Della Adams Leitner

Sometimes when I am hurt, despondent,
    lone,
I steal out to the hills and there I
    feel
Companionship with them; they seem
    to know
The inmost thoughts from others I
    conceal.
There is an understanding in their
    depths;
The shadowy vales are kind,
    protecting me
From curious gaze - I sense a
    fellowship
That lends me strength to overcome,
    be free.

The exploring visitor drives north from Gooding and heads into the mountains toward Fairfield, on state highway 46. Several miles out a "ranger station" road leads to the west, down into a small canyon which twists its way into sage-encrusted badlands. Continuing on for about eight miles, the visitor drops down a steep incline into a deep wash; here is the Gooding City of Rocks.

Stretching endlessly, in all directions, nature has carved great towers of tough, everlasting rock into 11,000 acres of fantastic shapes. Every turn in the road presents an entirely different and changing scene. The play of light and shadow on the rock (which sometimes spires to 100 feet in the air) creates grotesque shapes that only the imagination can limit.

Upon entering the City of Rocks, one is struck with its utter desolation. The answer to the query, "What a place for a badman's hide-away!" is partly revealed by the story of two early-day robbers who were reported to have held up a stage coach carrying $50,000 in gold, and then made their attempted get-away through this natural haven. Both were killed without revealing the hiding place of the gold. Many searching parties have scoured likely spots here, but no one has yet discovered their cache.

Returning to the highway, the open road beckons one on to view Camas Prairie, which in late spring spreads its carpet of blue camas in all directions. Further on is Fairfield, one of the lesser known and perhaps most beautiful entrances to Idaho's hinterlands and wilderness areas . . . ideal for vacation, fishing and big game hunting.

Astorian Expedition in 1811 to a particularly bad hole in a 35-mile stretch of rapids that wreaked havoc with their canoes.

Speaking of devils, in 1974 near Twin Falls, self-made-famous dare-devil Evel Knevel promised to jump the Snake canyon in a rocket powered motorcycle. Knevel drew national attention. Tourists thronged in. A few locals saw dollar signs, but many feared an invasion by motorcycle toughs riding in to watch their kamikaze comrade. But when the big day came and Knevel launched himself semi-skyward off the north rim, his parachute deployed "by accident" and he crashed on the rocks below. Not to worry. Knevel had been hurt worse jumping motorcycles over side-by-side semi-trailers. And he got his publicity. So the stunt

SILENT CITY

by Randall Green

The 49ers on their way to the California gold fields called it the "Silent City." To many Idahoans, it's simply the "City." Congress named it a National Reserve in 1988. But no matter what people call it, this stone metropolis of fantastic structural design and stark beauty, nestled in quiescent repose against Idaho's Albion Mountains, is unlike any man-made urban center.

This city has no symphony halls, theaters, or shopping malls. Instead, coyotes prowl empty passageways in search of food. Mule deer creep out of the shadows to graze in lush meadows at dusk, while turkey buzzards gather on precipitous rock towers to roost for the night. This is a place where the early morning call from a boisterous crow or a meadowlark startles the shy mountain bluebirds, where aspen leaves rustle in the wind like muted chimes. This is Idaho's "City of Rocks." Once it was a place for weary travelers on a tough journey west; today it is an out-of-the-way destination, rich in history and recreation opportunities.

The City of Rocks is located in Idaho's Cassia County, four miles west of Almo and 15 miles southeast of Oakley. The Albion Mountain Range separates it from the Snake River Basin, which forms the northern edge of the Great Basin - the gigantic bowl of high desert that extends from southern Idaho into Utah, Nevada, and eastern California.

Before white travelers ever visited the City, roving bands of Shoshone Indians hunted there. Wildlife thrived until the mass western exodus destroyed adjacent grazing lands and damaged streams and springs. The beaver, bighorn sheep, pronghorn antelope, and gray wolf all disappeared. The Indians came to resent the intruders, but there was nothing they could do to halt the growing stream of wagons.

Mountain man Joseph R. Walker discovered the City when he scouted a new California trail that provided a more direct connection from the Snake River to the Humbolt River. From 1843 on, the City offered thousands of travelers along the California and Salt Lake Cutoff trails a welcome change from the windy high desert of northern Utah. Fresh springs fed by melting snow from neighboring 8,800-foot Graham Peak and 10,000-foot

One of the manmade recreation areas, midway between Sun Valley and Twin Falls, Magic Reservoir provides large lake fishing and boating.

Cache Peak meandered peacefully through the green meadows, and groves of aspen trees whispered among the rocks casting spells of wonder on all who visited there.

Immigration to the West Coast reached its peak in 1852; some 52,000 people found themselves awed by the City's countless granite

---

was a success.

Knevel's daring was merely one of several stupid stunts performed by rash individuals in South Central Idaho over the years. In 1929 a man sailed over Twin Falls in a covered canoe stuffed with inflated tire tubes.

For all the dumb chances taken by wild-eyed ignorants, there have always been more risks taken by romantics. South Central Idaho can seem to have two full moons every month and it clearly has more than its share of lovers' leaps. Marilyn Monroe herself once semi-clothed herself in a Twin Falls potato sack (another publicity stunt). And many a young man has proposed a leap into marriage, while parked in a jalopy on the brink of a precipice.

monoliths, domes and spires. An entry in one of the newcomers' diaries expressed the profound effect the City had on travelers during the mid-1800s: "A most wild and romantic scenery presents to the eye, rocks upon rocks, naked and piled high in the most fantastic shapes. . ."

Spread over more than ten square miles, the jumbled granite rock formations have been eroded by wind and rain for millions of years. The outside of many of the structures, casehardened by minerals such as iron oxide, resisted erosion better than the softer inner layers of rock. The resulting formations resemble bathtubs, toadstools, elephants, dolphins, birds, and dragons. Some structures are more than sixty stories high.

Located at 5,000 to 6,000 feet above sea level and sandwiched between mountains and desert, the City's climate is often extreme. It is not uncommon for temperatures in July and August to either surpass 100 degrees or fall below freezing. Storms in September sometimes cover the City in a blanket of snow that lasts until May. Winds that have lashed at the stone monuments for eons can strip the region of life-giving moisture, yet clouds hanging on the nearby mountain peaks may pour down torrents of rain and hail on short notice.

It's not unusual, in this seemingly isolated terrain, to hear the lowing of cattle grazing on nearby rangeland or the whoop of a rock climber joyously announcing a successful ascent. Ranchers such as Wally Taylor, a third-generation native from nearby Almo, have been trailing their cattle through the City since the 1940s. "We used to hunt in there," Taylor says. "There were lots of deer, sage hens, and nobody around." But as more people began discovering the City's recreation potential in the 1980s; it became evident that there was a need for the implementation of a cooperative management plan to protect the area for future generations.

Manager Ned Jackson says that the City of Rocks was managed minimally before Congress set it aside as a National Reserve in 1988. Until then, the City was a landmark because of the significance of its relationship to the California Trail and the history of American westward migration. Several federal and state agencies collaborated with private land-owners to manage

UPPER SALMON FALLS   BISBEE-1000

the area until a growing interest in camping, sightseeing, hiking and climbing spurred the need for a comprehensive management plan. Now the National Park Service is coordinating a three-phase plan designed to strike a balance between users and management groups.

The peculiar texture of the rock and overhanging cliff faces present world-class challenges for technical climbers. Almost all the national and international climbing magazines have run articles about the City - many ran cover features. As a result, most of the park users are climbers and about 15 percent of the total park users are foreign.

The City's relatively close proximity to large airports in Boise and Salt Lake has contributed to its popularity with foreign climbers, and since most climbs are accessible by road or a short walk, some of the best climbers from all over the world have made the journey, establishing some of the hardest climbs in the country. Even so, the City is uncrowded compared to other popular climbing centers, and is still a place where both beginners and expert climbers can enjoy the copious supply of rock. The park also offers other recreational activities, such as camping, hiking and mountain biking.

Although campsites are primitive, without picnic tables or permanent fire pits, there are sites to pitch a tent or park a camper and have spectacular views of the park. Pines, juniper and aspen trees provide shade and protection from the wind. The limited number of campsites guarantees plenty of space between neighboring campers. New restrooms have been constructed at eight locations, and drinking water is available on the Emery Canyon Road on the northeast side of the Bread Loaf formation.

Most of the park's prominent features can be seen without leaving the comfort of an automobile, but hiking through the park can be

The Thousand Springs area of the Snake offers boating, a huge "Balanced Rock" still perched above a country road, sturgeon fishing, cajun food, and several family hot spring spas nearby.

educational and rewarding for the naturalist or history buff. Wildflowers abound in the spring and early summer among the sage and service berry bushes; lodgepole pine, douglas fir and mountain mahogany trees provide cover for deer and elk that migrate through the region. You may even be lucky enough to encounter other residents of the City - mountain lions, coyotes, and raptors such as red-tailed, kestrel and marsh hawks. Those interested in the area's history may want to locate the portions of the old wagon trails that are still visible, or the rock formations that display "historical graffiti" - names of emigrants applied in axle grease. Take care to acknowledge No Trespassing signs and keep gates closed, since some of the historic signatures are on private land. All the roads through the reserve are improved dirt and gravel, suitable for riding mountain bikes. ◅

And all this is just along the Snake River, the part of South Central Idaho that Oregon Trail and modern highway travelers have come to know best. For those who would rather "romance the stone," two of the finest experiences in Idaho lie north and south of the Snake. In the north, the Gooding City of Rocks presents a menagerie of whimsical rhyolite rock forms. To the southeast, the Silent City of Rocks has built a metropolis of granite. This area so impressed the Oregon and California Trails immigrants that they often wrote their names on the rocks, using axle grease for ink. Every Idahoan certainly — and probably every tourist — needs to stand among these silent stone sentinels.

Shoshone Ice Cave, north of Shoshone, has a sparkling ice floor one thousand feet long. It was formed

THE TWIN FALLS STORY

The thousands of emigrants that traveled on the Oregon Trail, over the rich volcanic soil of the Snake River plains, showed little interest in stopping. For those travelers, the area was one of frustration. The Snake River, bisecting the dry desert, was inaccessible because of the deep canyon.

Twin Falls today is but one fall, the other sacrificed to the electric power god.

The emigrants were forced to make long daily marches or spend a night without water. It didn't help that they found themselves crossing this hot, dusty desert during the hottest part of the summer. In an attempt to find forage for livestock and access to water, trails were made on both sides of the river. Two routes of the Oregon Trail went through the future site of Twin Falls. One crossed Blue Lakes Boulevard near Pole Line Road. The other crossed Rock Creek near the sugar factory, then through South Park and the Municipal Golf Course. One unique reminder of the Oregon Trail is the Rock Creek store southeast of Twin Falls. Built in 1865 near Ben Holladays stage station, it was the only place between Fort Hall and Fort Boise where travelers could obtain supplies. The store was a focal point for the valley before the irrigation system was built. Three major roads met there: the Oregon Trail, the stagecoach road, and the Kelton Freight Road. Today the store and nearby Stricker home, constructed in 1900, are being preserved by the Idaho State Historical Society.

Two stagecoach drivers, on a day off in 1869, panned some gold at Shoshone Falls and started the rush to the Snake River Mining District. The only problem was that it was fine flour gold requiring a lot of work by the placer miners to recover it. By 1873, three thousand persons were estimated to be involved with the placer mines in the canyon. Mining activity continued well into the present century although the quality washed down the river each year decreased significantly after the dams were built on the river.

by a lava tube which emptied out as it cooled. Now, heavy cool air remains in the cave winter and summer, preserving the anomaly of ice in the desert.

The history of South Central Idaho is one of getting things done. After all, this country isn't going to do it for you. For the Shoshone Indians it was usually meager pickings, especially above Salmon Falls, which stopped the anadromaus fish. For the first Euro Americans there was "not much of not much" except right along the Snake River, where hand ditches could be dug for irrigation.

But things changed when the 1894 Carey Act opened up desert lands for agriculture and provided the framework to finance and construct dam and irrigation projects. Idaho — and South Central Idaho in

For more than a century, the cattle industry has been important to the area. Thousands of cattle ranged from the Snake River throughout the Great Basin before the construction of the Twin Falls irrigation project. The Twin Falls townsite was a round-up site for the cattle companies on the south side of the Snake River.

From the beginning, the builders of the Twin Falls irrigation project knew a town was a vital part of their endeavors. The plan for Twin Falls was a model used for some of the other towns in the valley. Thousands of trees were planted on the barren townsite, and the town grew rapidly even though all materials and supplies had to be hauled thirty miles from the railroad at Shoshone across the desert and the Snake River until the railroad reached the town in August 1905.

The Snake River's swift waters and deep canyon were a troublesome barrier until the second decade of the this century. Many ferries operated on the river before any bridge was built. The first was the Blue Lakes bridge which was completed in 1911. It was a toll bridge built by Mr. Perrine, which operated for ten years. It is now used by the City of Twin Falls to hold a water pipeline. Several other bridges have come and gone. The present Perrine Memorial bridge was completed and opened to traffic on July 3, 1976.

Courtesy Rock Creek Restaurant

This record crop of seeds (17 bushels to an acre at $21 per bushel in 1916) from the Twin Falls tract helps record the impact of irrigation of southern Idaho.

CALLING THE COYOTES IN
by Kim Barnes

Dark green ravines run like lava
through the canyon's fissured humps,
and it is here they come, late
in winter's good cold, to find
the seventy-dollar pelts.
Crouched in a shadowing hedge
of sumac and sap-leeched syringa,
she waits. Five nights
they have worked the ridges, calling
the coyotes in. From the camouflaged recorder
cries of a dying rabbit play
again and again, a chant
she rocks to, feet numbed to stone.
Beside her, the man squats trigger-ready,
the white orbit of his eyes blueing
in half moon light.
He's been in Nam, and though she won't say it,
there's an enemy somewhere. Even his breath
seems cloistered, the way his jaw slacks
to quiet the rush of air.
This time, two split
from the tangle of brambled cottonwood,

particular — was the big beneficiary of the Carey Act: over 600,000 acres were planted by 1930. Near Twin Falls, the Milner Dam was completed in 1905. Now the area is an agricultural leader.

Twin Falls is the cultural and commercial capital of South Central Idaho. It has wonderful parks and delightful old buildings. Its location however, will forever be its most famous aspect. It is perched on the edge of the Snake River canyon. The College of Southern Idaho presents a beautiful campus, and one of the top small college basketball programs in the nation.

trot forward, high-stepping the snow
He signals for her to take the right one.
Raising the rifle, liquid from knees to cheek,
she shoots easy, good at limiting damage:
behind the ear, a finger-sized hole.
The man stands, the blue flame
he holds to her blinding
as she draws the smoke deep.
Kneeling at the first belly, he begins
the skinning, cigarette clenched
between his teeth.
She'll take her time with hers
slip the knife between muscle
and hide, follow the leg's curve
to cobbled spine.
There's a moment when he'll call her, in his hands
a bundle rolled tail to nose, and she'll see
how his lips have tightened to hold
the last biting fire, how he hasn't moved
to stop the calling, and neither has she,
knee-deep in dark dappled snow,
Feeling all around them the closing eyes. ⊸

The other South Central Idaho towns — like Burley, Buhl, Gooding, Shoshone, Jerome and Wendell — have their own special charms and histories. These communities are both a part of this area and unique in their own ways. And lest the traveler think this area is too tame, Jackpot, Nevada, sits right across the border, drawing gamblers with its neon lights and games. ⊸

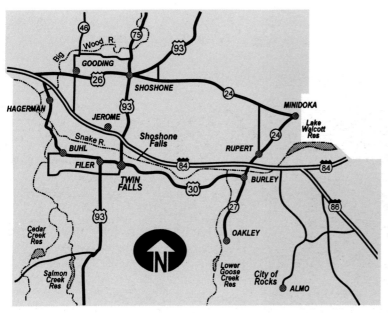

CALENDAR

Buhl Sagebrush Days, Buhl, July 4: A down-home summer celebration with the works (fireworks, too). Contact: Buhl Chamber of Commerce, (208) 543-6682.

Rupert July 4th Celebration, Rupert, July 4: A traditional summer gathering including a rodeo, concessions, fireworks, and fun. Contact: Rupert Chamber of Commerce: (208) 436-4793.

Old Time Fiddlers Jamboree, Shoshone, second week in July: Come enjoy some of the best fiddlin' around anywhere. Contact: (208) 733-3974.

Pioneer Days, Oakley, July: Pony express ride, barbecue, dutch oven cook-off, gymkhana, rodeo. Contact: (208) 678-1575 or (208) 862-9255.

Art in the Park, Twin Falls, last weekend in July: Homespun crafts and other works of art are for sale in the City Park. Contact: (208) 733-8458.

Cassia County fair and Rodeo, Burley, second week in August: A six-day event packed full of daring cowboy action, exhibits, carnival rides and plenty of food. Contact: Burley Chamber of Commerce, (208) 678-7230.

Twin Falls County Fair and Rodeo, Filer, first week in September: In addition to the agricultural exposition, exhibits and carnival, the rodeo is a P.R.C.A. points gathering event, where Miss Rodeo Idaho is crowned. Top name entertainment performs. Contact: Twin Falls Chamber ot Commerce, (208) 733-3974

Oktoberfest, Twin Falls, early October: October wouldn't be the same without this two day extravaganza. Contact: (208) 733-3974.

TIPS: FOOD & SHELTER

Rock Creek Restaurant in Twin Falls choices from steak to fresh oysters, and offers a great mini menu in the comfortable bar area. Good prices, excellent food, good service -one of the top picks in Idaho!

The Wood River Inn in Gooding is another choice for quality beef, Idaho baked potatoes & trout.

Catfish, hush puppies, and homemade pies are the fare at the **River Bank** in Hagerman.

Hamburgers and beer, and host Tom and his friendly staff at the **Oasis** attract locals and visitors alike - from lunch on.

Locals time their travel to get a cheeseburger and milkshake at the **Shoshone Snack Bar** (opposite the school), and **Conner's Cafe** in Burley.

Francisco's Mexican is an old standby in Twin Falls.

Locals in Twin Falls find breakfast at the **Buffalo Cafe** or **The Depot**.

The Loading Chute in Carey draws its customers from the South Central area as well as Ketchum & Hailey.

The Sandpiper in Twin offers a wide menu and entertainment many nights. ✍

Southeast Idaho
Region 5

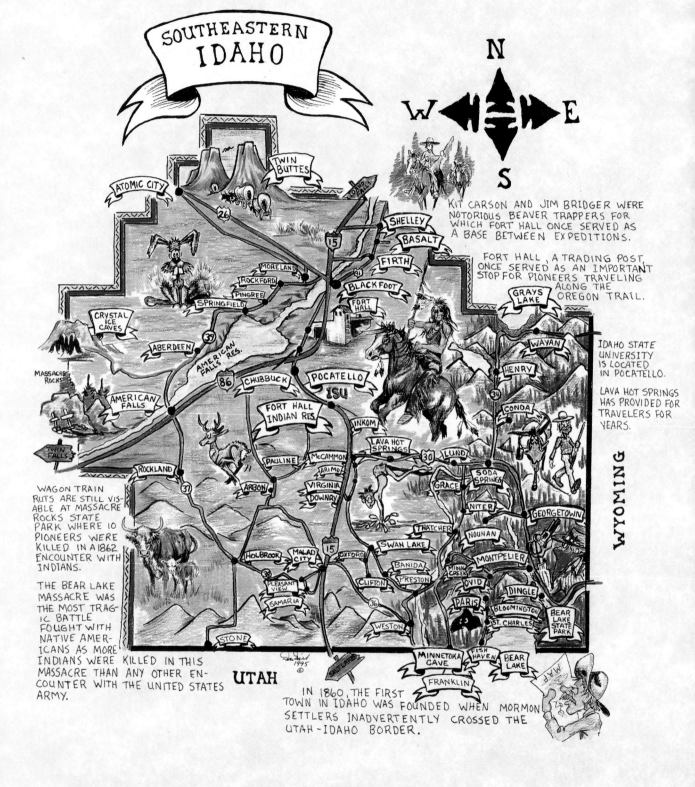

SOUTHEASTERN IDAHO

N
W   E
S

ATOMIC CITY
TWIN BUTTES
26
IDAHO FALLS
SHELLEY
BASALT
FIRTH
MORELAND
ROCKFORD
PINGREE
SPRINGFIELD
BLACK FOOT
FORT HALL
15
91
CRYSTAL ICE CAVES
ABERDEEN
37
AMERICAN FALLS RES.
MASSACRE ROCKS
86
CHUBBUCK
POCATELLO
ISU
AMERICAN FALLS
FORT HALL INDIAN RES.
INKOM
LAVA HOT SPRINGS
TWIN FALLS
PAULINE
McCAMMON
ARIMO
VIRGINIA
DOWNEY
ROCKLAND
37
ARBON
30
LUND
GRACE
SODA SPRINGS
NITER
NOUNAN
THATCHER
SWAN LAKE
MONTPELIER
HOLBROOK
MALAD CITY
15
OXFORD
BANIDA
PRESTON
MINK CREEK
OVID
DINGLE
PLEASANT VIEW
CLIFTON
PARIS
BLOOMINGTON
BEAR LAKE STATE PARK
SAMARIA
36
ST. CHARLES
WESTON
STONE
MINNETOKA CAVE
FISH HAVEN
BEAR LAKE
MAP
FRANKLIN
SALT LAKE
GRAYS LAKE
WAYAN
HENRY
34
CONDA
GEORGETOWN

UTAH

WYOMING

KIT CARSON AND JIM BRIDGER WERE NOTORIOUS BEAVER TRAPPERS FOR WHICH FORT HALL ONCE SERVED AS A BASE BETWEEN EXPEDITIONS.

FORT HALL, A TRADING POST, ONCE SERVED AS AN IMPORTANT STOP FOR PIONEERS TRAVELING ALONG THE OREGON TRAIL.

IDAHO STATE UNIVERSITY IS LOCATED IN POCATELLO.

LAVA HOT SPRINGS HAS PROVIDED FOR TRAVELERS FOR YEARS.

WAGON TRAIN RUTS ARE STILL VISABLE AT MASSACRE ROCKS STATE PARK WHERE 10 PIONEERS WERE KILLED IN A 1862 ENCOUNTER WITH INDIANS.

THE BEAR LAKE MASSACRE WAS THE MOST TRAGIC BATTLE FOUGHT WITH NATIVE AMERICANS AS MORE INDIANS WERE KILLED IN THIS MASSACRE THAN ANY OTHER ENCOUNTER WITH THE UNITED STATES ARMY.

IN 1860, THE FIRST TOWN IN IDAHO WAS FOUNDED WHEN MORMON SETTLERS INADVERTENTLY CROSSED THE UTAH-IDAHO BORDER.

Chapter VI
SOUTHEASTERN IDAHO
Region 5

SPRING IN POCATELLO

by Harald Wyndham

NO. 24 ADMINISTRATION BUILDING, I.T.C.
POCATELLO, IDAHO.

In Pocatello, popular wisdom holds that "spring is a Thursday in June," and some years it certainly seems that way as the ground stays frozen and the ice storms howl through the end of April. Other years the folks who watch for the snowdrift shaped like a "seven" on the left ridge of Kinport Peak are worried to see it appear in February, meaning an early spring and a dry summer. In recent years there has been no "seven" at all. Spring is anticipated with an eagerness born of the cold, wet, gray, dark, smoke-smudged, ice-edged weeks at the end of March when one aches to tear down the plastic tacked up around the windows and let a fresh, clean wind purge the house of five months' stale air. And when it arrives, hopefully it is Saturday, because nobody is going to stay inside a moment longer.

Idaho State University's lovely shady campus has provided a welcome respite from the heat of summer since 1901.

Southeastern Idaho illustrates how difficult Idaho can be to describe. Bear Lake seems to glow an incredible, almost impossible blue. This blue catches the eye and then captures the brain. Then the sunset adds pinks, purples and oranges to the lake's turquoisey pallet and destroys people's powers of description. All they can say is, "Will you look at that . . . ?" No, postcards don't do it justice.

Carbonates in Bear Lake's water account for its mystical blues and indicate the great mineral wealth of the region. The abundance of wildlife and waterfowl demonstrates its biological importance. Several species of fish can be found nowhere else on earth, including the Bonneville Cisco, also called the Bear Lake sardine.

Pocatello is a city of neighborhoods. The railroad switching yards divide the older west side from the upstart northeast neighborhoods which were built without much evident planning so that the neighborhoods resemble garden patches of wildflowers with brick homes, wood-frame cottages, roofed basements, tract homes, and the occasional trailer all living side by side. Rich and poor are scattered through each of these gardenplots with the same democracy that they are buried in the Mount Moriah Cemetery. It is part of the charm of a western community that we grew so quickly there wasn't time for class or caste to separate us. Only in the more recent bench subdivisions will you find those homogenous groupings of next-to-identical houses that surround most cities -and even they are sprinkled with families of various income. The city, therefore, has no obvious areas of "urban blight," but rather a multiplicity of colorful neighborhoods. In fact, it feels less like a city and more like a big small town.

With spring weather, the diversity of culture blossoms also in Pocatello. Strong ethnic communities - Japanese, Greek, Italian, Spanish, Basque, Chinese - flavor the atmosphere with their cooking and festivals. Poets and writers gather at the Walrus for evening readings, and several of the watering holes feature local musicians. The University Theater and Symphony bring their seasons to dramatic finale, and each weekend in May one sees bouquets of young people in pastel gowns and elegant tuxedo's clustering into restaurants, auditoriums, and school gymnasiums to perform those rites of spring that usher them from adolescence into the big, scary, grownup world. Though thunderstorms are rare, one can generally count on a "gullywasher" to hit one hour before commencement ceremonies at Holt Arena.

In a year of good rain, the mountains that surround our valley will be lush and green through June. The hiking enthusiast can be on the trail in less than half-an-hour, climbing City Creek to the top of Kinport, or Gibson Jack Creek clear to Elk Meadows. After five minutes you are in the wilderness out of sight and sound of the city. Wildflowers poke through the crusts of shaded snowdrifts. The streams surge down the canyons driven by snowmelt. The beaver are busy with aspen logs they gnawed off and dragged to the pondside in February. On opening weekend many a local fisherman will escape the crowd of Utahns by testing these unassuming streams and ponds and be rewarded by cutthroats and browns worth bragging about.

The first "blue" days arrive when the sky is so clear and stunningly cobalt it almost blinds you. The air is rich with sage and the first hint of powdery dust from the trail. You treasure the beauty that surrounds you in such abundance - treasure it for being close to hand, uncrowded, isolated, wild and free to wanderers like so few places left on earth.◄

Southeastern Idaho's high fertile valleys are its dominant feature. Most lie at over 5000 feet elevation. Mountains here reach to 10,000 feet. Many are Precambrian sedimentary formations, laid down by lakes and seas before animals appeared, more than a half-billion years ago.

Shallow seas of about one-quarter billion years ago laid down the Phosphoria Formation which supplies Southeastern Idaho with some of the world's largest phosphate deposits. Phosphate is used in fertilizers, explosives, match heads and detergents, and even in soft drinks like the cherry phosphate.

"Overthrusting" is an interesting and promising characteristic of Southeastern Idaho's Rocky Mountains. As the main part of the Rockies rose in the east, beginning about 90 million years ago immense slabs of

THE POCATELLO LAND RUSH

The date was June 17, 1902. The time was just before twelve noon. A reporter described the scene: "From Butte and Boise and Salt Lake, and even as far as Cheyenne, have they come: prospectors looking for mines, cattlemen for cattle chances, lawyers expecting to make their wits do the work of legs, aimless young men scenting from afar the savor of excitement and adventure."

The men were there for the Pocatello land rush—a time when over 400,000 acres of reservation land was opened for settlement. All you had to do was wait outside the reservation boundaries, then run for the land you desired at the stroke of noon, post up your notice of possession, then rush back on foot, by horse, on bicycle, or by train to the land offce in Blackfoot. If you were among the first in line, you could buy the land at bargain prices.

But there would probably be a number of "sooners" ahead of you. Sooners were men who would sneak onto the reservation at night to post land, getting a head start on the competition. More honest men ran horses into the ground, scrambled onto moving trains, and otherwise risked their lives for a chance at cheap land, only to find a sooner had beat them to Blackfoot. The quickest of the land rushers that day posted his notice on prime reservation land, rushed to Pocatello, then an additional 24 miles to Blackfoot to be first in line, all in just over an hour—a feat that would be difficult today in a car.

---

rock slid off them toward the west, sometimes on top of younger rocks. This created a situation where sometimes the rock gets younger the deeper one digs. It also created the necessary formations for the creation of oil and natural gas. Little gas or oil has been found in Idaho, but if it is found, chances are that it will here be in the southeast.

Basin-and-range faulting continues to pull at Southeastern Idaho's mountains. Stand in one of the high grassy valleys and imagine that the wide sky above is getting wider. Slowly, slowly it is.

Southeastern Idaho is also the origin of the great Bonneville Flood. Enormous Lake Bonneville once covered much of Utah and Nevada, and filled some of Southeastern Idaho's valleys. Some 15 thousand

THE FORT HALL LIQUIDATION SALE

More Idaho sand dunes -these near Franklin.

Fort Hall. That name has a safe, substantial sound to it. But did you know that the famous stopping spot on the Oregon Trail started out as a liquidation sale?

In 1834, Massachusetts businessman Nathanial J. Wyeth brought several wagon loads of merchandise to the Green River Rendezvous in what is now Wyoming. He had contracted to supply the Rocky Mountain Fur Company, but when he arrived he met new owners who had no intention of buying from him.

Rather than cart everything back East, Wyeth decided to continue west and set up an outpost where he could sell his goods. He picked a spot about 20 miles northwest of present day Pocatello, and named the new trading post Fort Hall, after the eldest of his business partners.

Although it wasn't yet a military outpost, Fort Hall was a sturdy stockade built of cottonwood trees sunk two and half feet into the ground and extending above ground 15 feet.

On August 5,1834 Wyeth and his men dedicated the outpost by raising a United States flag they had stitched together from unbleached sheeting, red flannel, and blue patches. It was probably the only U.S. flag to fly west of the Continental Divide that year.

The British Hudson Bay Company, which owned Fort Boise, didn't want the competition from Fort Hall. They undercut Wyeth's prices, forcing him to sell out to them at a substantial loss in 1836. Though Nathanial Wyeth's operation was not a success, Fort Hall became one of the most important supply points on the Oregon Trail in later years.◈

---

years ago it eroded an outlet at Red Rock Pass, south of Pocatello. Then all heck broke loose. Lake Bonneville broke free and roared down Marsh Creek to the Portneuf River and on to the Snake River, scouring out canyons and strewing boulders and great gravel bars clean across southern Idaho.

Other recent geologic activity is evident at Hell's Half Acre Lava Field, about ten miles north of Blackfoot. Here, an unweathered 28,000-year-old lava flow covers 180 square miles. But one needs not be content with geologic relics. Both boiling and freezing geophysics exist here.

Lava Hotsprings is a world famous spa. Some 200,000 people visited it in 1924. Here, mineral laden water of 110° bubbles up between bathers' toes. Another fountain, the Soda Springs, have been famous —

No longer beer in Soda Springs, and Main Street isn't the same either.

~~BEER~~ SODA SPRINGS

The only man made geyser in the world is in Soda Springs. Soda Springs has always been a "curiosity". When emigrants on the Oregon Trail saw something new or unique they would call it a "curiosity", such as the landmarks of Chimney Rock and Courthouse Rocks in what would become Nebraska or Independence Rock in Wyoming. But, Soda Springs was one of the greatest of the "curiosities" that they would see. Soda Springs was a thermal area with geysers and hot pools that bubbled up out of the ground. This was a special area for the Indians and the mountain men too. The mountain men called the area Beer Springs, because they thought the bubbly water tasted like lager beer. They would drink a gallon or two of the effervescent water and act drunk. I guess if you drink a gallon or two of any thing you would act drunk. When the emigrants come through it was a place to stop and wash their clothes, taste the waters and enjoy the "curiosities", including Steamboat Spring, a hot three foot geyser. It was named Steamboat because of the subterranean sound it made. If you read the journals of the emigrants you would find that they would stick their heads down the vent holes and make bets on who could keep their heads in the hole the longest before the geysers went off. One fellow even sat down an one of the geyser holes thinking he would stop it from going off. Well, it went off with him sitting on the spout of water and it splashed him all over the place. With the Indians watching these antics, you don't have to read their journals to know what they thought was a "curiosity".

and enjoyed — since the days of the mountain men. Captain Bonneville's noted that in 1834, "The most noted curiosity . . . of this singular region, is the Beer Spring, of which trappers give wonderful accounts. They drink of its waters, with as much eagerness as the Arab seeks some famous well of the desert. . .

"In a few moments every spring had its jovial knot of hard drinkers, with tin cup in hand, indulging in mock carouse: quaffing, pledging, toasting, bandying jokes, singing drinking songs and uttering peals of laughter, until it seemed as if their imaginations had given potency to the beverage, and cheated them into a fit of intoxication."

The geyser is now regulated by city officials, not to curb imaginary drunkenness but to provide photo

Today, same road, great grandchildren drive this land in a different vehicle. All once under the water of Lake Bonneville.

When the Mormons settled there years later they didn't think Beer Springs was a good name for their community, so they renamed it Soda Springs. Then Soda's neighboring community of Lava Hot Springs started developing a good tourist business, with people soaking in it's natural hot springs. So the citizens of Soda Springs thought that if they would drill down, tap into the thermal waters and could fill a swimming pool in the natatorium that they wanted to build, the tourist would visit their community. Well, when they drilled down, they did hit natural hot water, and it was under pressure. But they had a problem, the water stank so bad you couldn't get close to it, let alone in it, so they capped it off. Then somebody had the great idea of putting it on a timer and having it go, off like a geyser on the hour every hour. They thought that tourists would come and see their geyser, and not go to Yellowstone Park and see Old Faithful. But they had a problem with that that too, the geyser was right in the downtown area, and it stank so bad when the wind was out of the west no one would shop, and it etched the windows so bad you couldn't see out of them. So, they put a weather vane on the geyser, and now it goes off on the hour every hour if the wind isn't out of the west. ↝

THE BONNEVILLE FLOOD

When the Teton Dam failed in 1976 it created a devastating torrent that killed several people and left millions of dollars of property damage. Yet, it was barely a trickle, compared with the Bonneville Flood.

About 14,000 years ago Lake Bonneville covered much of Utah, Nevada, and parts of southern Idaho. It was really an inland sea, comparable to one of our modern Great Lakes.

As the lake level rose, the water began to spill over Red Rock Pass near Preston. The water eroded the pass until it cut through the hard rock and into a layer of softer soil. Once the softer material was exposed, the flow became a flood.

The torrent crashed down the Portneuf River to where Pocatello is today, then sped downstream along the Snake. In the 300-square-mile Rupert Basin the water averaged 50 feet deep. It filled the entire Snake River Canyon where Twin Falls and Shoshone Falls are today and still spread out across the Snake River Plain.

The flood ripped chunks from the walls of the canyon and carried boulders the size of cars along with it, rolling and polishing them as they tumbled. Giant gravel bars 100 feet high and a mile long are common in the canyon. There are hundreds of acres of melon-sized boulders left behind by the flood from Hagerman to Swan Falls.

At its peak, the Bonneville Flood rushed down the Snake River at a rate five or six times the flow of the Amazon. About 600 cubic miles of water passed through Idaho on its way to the Pacific, all in a matter of weeks. The Bonneville flood was the second largest in the geologic history of Earth. ↝

BEAUTIFUL CACHE VALLEY

by Daniel Roberts

Franklin County, nestled in the northern end of Cache Valley, and between two mountain ranges of the Cache Mountains, boasts of one of the most delightful climates in the inter-mountain area.

Preston, the county seat, established in 1877, is centrally located at an elevation of 4,700 feet, has an average of 16.5 inches of rainfall annually, a 123 frost free day growing season, which makes the area an ideal place for diversified agricultural and livestock raising.

The Cache Mountains on either side of the fertile valley rise to heights up to ten thousand feet providing clear mountain streams, from the year round snow capped peaks.

Cache Valley, originally named Willow Valley, was given its present name because it was used as a hiding place for fur taken from the Bear River and its tributaries. William Sublette, Jim Bridger and other fur traders entered the valley in 1824, from the Yellowstone Park region.

To the north twenty miles lies Red Rock, the divide between the Snake River and Columbia Basin, and Bear River and the Bonneville Basin, of which Franklin County is a part. This area has no outlet to the sea but ends in the Great Salt Lake.

Franklin City is proud of being Idaho's first permanent white settlement. Thirteen Mormon pioneer families arrived by covered wagon and settled at Franklin, Idaho, on April 14, 1860. Idahos first reported irrigation took place that year with waters from Spring Creek near the town of Franklin.

It was not until 1872, when the U.S. Government survey was completed, that this group were aware they were north of the 42 parallel and in Idaho and the Oregon country and not in Utah and the Mexican or Spanish territory.

For the visitor, Franklin County's many irrigation reservoirs offer boat fishing and water skiing. Bear River, Cub River and Mink Creek offer camping and stream fishing. The mountains are a haven for the deer hunter and horseman. Everyone attends the Famous Preston Nite Rodeo the last week in July. U.S. Highway 191 leads to and from Logan, Ogden and Salt Lake City to the south and Pocatello, Idaho, and points west and Yellowstone Park and points north.

Highway 34 leaving Preston leads you to the Blackfoot River, Star Valley, the Palisades and the south fork of the Snake River and Jackson, Wyoming and the south entrance to Yellowstone Park.

Now a junction on I-15 between Pocatello and Salt Lake, this was Malad City on New Year's Day in 1906.

opportunities that fit tourist schedules.

After hotsprings, tourists and locals can still "chill out" at Minnetonka Cave, west of St. Charles. This year-round, 40-degree, constant-climate cave offers a half-mile long cavern with nine separate chambers and walls of shining ice crystals and banded rock.

History began in Southeastern Idaho in 1811, when the Astorian expedition made the first transit of southern Idaho by EuroAmericans. At that time, Shoshone and Bannock Indians were the dominant tribes. They had adopted a plains-style culture, after receiving horses from their cousins to the south, the Comanches. The present-day Fort Hall reservation may comprise one-half million acres, but it is a small fraction of what

The Round House in Pocatello, a Western railroad landmark.

FRANKLIN

The oldest town in Idaho is Franklin, named for Franklin Richards. And we got it by default. What happened was that the Mormons were prospering in Salt Lake City and started sending folks out to start other communities. They started Franklin on April 14, 1860 in Cache valley, not realizing that they had crossed the Utah border into what was at that time the Washington territory. But, nobody noticed that until a lot later, not until that part of the country was surveyed in 1872, and by then it was in the Idaho territory and had been since 1863. Even though Franklin had been incorporated as a Utah town since 1868, they had to wait until 1897 before the Idaho legislature granted them a new charter. It must have been hard for kids growing up there not knowing where they were. If Franklin didn't get its Idaho charter until 1897, was Franklin a Utah town in Washington and Idaho or just a town with a Utah charter in Washington and Idaho? I wonder how those people got their mail? It probably was a good thing that they didn't have zip codes back then. ◄

the Indians once called home.

Like much of Idaho, the first history of Southeastern Idaho concerns the competitions and capers of the wild and woolly mountain men, against a background of international intrigue. The U.S. claimed the Northwest, but so did Britain and Russia. Idaho's southern border (now Utah) was then with New Spain. Southeastern Idaho was full of beaver. Peter Ogden wrote, "a finer country for beaver never seen." The area became a commercial battleground between British and U.S. trapping interests.

In 1824, the Hudson's Bay Company knew that American trappers were coming into the country and they determined to trap out all of southern Idaho in order to make it a barrier against the Americans' Rocky

THE YELLOWSTONE LEAGUE:
PROFESSIONAL BASEBALL

In 1920 a professional baseball league was organized in southeast Idaho. It was named the Yellowstone League. St. Anthony, Rexburg, Rigby, Idaho Falls, Blackfoot, and Pocatello each sponsored a team.

Professional ballplayers were hired to play in the Yellowstone League in 1920. Chick Gandil had been hired to play first base for the St. Anthony team. He had recently been released from the Chicago White Sox. Rexburg secured the services of Dave Davenport a 6 '4 " pitcher, who had played for the St. Louis Browns, and Tub Spencer who had played in Seattle in the Pacific Coast League. Each team was com-posed entirely of paid professional ballplayers.

To watch the Rigby Bears in action cost twenty-five cents for children and thirty-five cents for adults. The opening game of the season netted gate receipts of $975.

The climax of the ball season occurred in Rexburg, on August 19, 1920. The game was between the Rexburg and Rigby teams. Each community had raised a purse of $3,500. The winning team would receive the entire $7,000. Rexburg won the game five to three.

The Yellowstone League lasted only from May until August, 1920. Southeast Idaho did not have resources to sustain professional baseball. The Rigby team alone cost over $11,000 to maintain, and it was reported that Rexburg's Dave Davenport was paid $500 for every game he pitched. But, while it lasted, the Yellowstone League provided a level of baseball never before seen by most of the people living in southeast Idaho. ✄

Pocatello, Idaho, continuing to grow up and upwards.

Mountain Fur Company. The names of the trappers — both for Britain and the U.S. — who came into Southeastern Idaho in 1825, read like the cast of the best mountain man movie one could ever hope to see: Jedidiah Smith, Peter Ogden Alexander Ross, Francois Payette, Jim Bridger, Joe Meek and John Weber.

A great cast of Indians was here, too. Shoshone Snakes and Sheepeaters, Nez Perce, Flatheads, and Blackfeet supplied excitement and danger. After Francois Payette was surprised by Blackfeet, Ogden wrote that he "arrived naked . . . he had a most narrow escape . . . he *escaped* in the bushes . . . then left his Horse & traps & Swam across the River."

From then on, the Indians both helped and resisted the EuroAmericans. The British finally won out — at

MOUNT HARRISON AND LAKE CLEVELAND

Most people think patriotic surveyors named the mountains and lakes in southern Idaho because of Independence Peak, the Independence Lakes, and Mount Harrison and Lake Cleveland being named for presidents. Now there may have been patriotic surveyors in southern Idaho, but what happened is local settlers from Utah named Independence Peak and Lakes for Independence, Missouri. I don't know why people from Utah would name a mountain in Idaho for a town in Missouri.

In 1888 the heated election campaign between President Grover Cleveland and Benjamin Harrison for President of the United States was in progress when some picnickers decided to name the mountain and lake. They decided to name the mountain for the winner of the election and the lake for the loser. Harrison won, so the mountain was named for him and the lake was named for Cleveland.

Some people think that Harrison messed up the numbering system of the presidents by winning that election. Grover Cleveland is the only person elected twice without serving consecutive terms. He was our 22nd and 24th President, the only one to have such designations, with Benjamin Harrison being the 23rd President. No wonder people have a hard time remembering the Presidents and some people wonder why we didn't name the mountain and lake the other way around.

from: TAKING ROOT
by Karen Finnigan

How do you take root in Idaho? If you stake your claim with an Idaho birth certificate, roots just come naturally, I expect. But for us transplants, it is a more gradual process, about as elusive as watching a tree grow.

After all, putting down roots is not as obvious as marking pencil lines on the wall to see how tall we have grown. Becoming an Idahoan, like taking root, is a downward process, something that happens inside, below the surface.

The chance to take stock of our transplanted roots happened unexpectedly, a couple of seasons ago. Oh, we didn't plan on any introspection. In fact, we had planned no more than a carefree drive up in the high country to show off our acres of private forest. The place: somewhere beyond Bone, up where the sage and potatoes and wheat of the Snake River Valley give way to indigenous aspen and evergreen. Just this side of the Wolverine Canyon Ridge, in Bingham County, in case geography buffs want to pin this tale to a map.

We are a family to whom southern Idaho is our adopted home. Less than a score of years have passed since we moved here with two small boys and a love of big skies in tow. Our first impression: this was a wonderful place to raise a family — if the wind didn't get you first. And fragrant though the sage was, it made shade a veritable vanishing species. We craved trees, longed for a wooded place all our own, something more than merely an Idaho Falls address for our mail.

How do you take root in Idaho? For us it was forested land. Eighty acres we bought our first summer here, as if that would more quickly make us Idahoans. When we drove into our

least until the end of the Idaho fur trade. American Nathaniel Wyeth established Fort Hall near Pocatello in 1834, the same year that the Hudson's Bay Company established Fort Boise. Wyeth wrote that "the fort looks quite as warlike as a pile of ice but not quite so profitable."

Mr. Wyeth's comparison derives from his earlier profession as an ice merchant in Boston. But whatever he exactly meant by it, a fine whitewashed replica of the Fort Hall is available for touring in Pocatello's Ross Park. The original site is on the Fort Hall Reservation, near the American Falls Reservoir.

Wyeth's venture failed, and he sold out to Hudson's Bay after two years. But Wyeth had brought with him Jason Lee, a Methodist missionary. Lee's arrival announced both the beginning of religious missions

forest, 80 acres of green enveloped us. Aspen green. Douglas fir green. Lodgepole pine green. Grass green. Nettle green. Moss green, sage green and the leaf green of wildflowers too abundant to count.

My husband, Frank, and our two sons pitched our tent down in our little canyon, out of the wind, back amidst adolescent evergreens. Our door afforded a view of one of two beaver ponds ringed with aspens. While Frank hammered together a rustic table from windfall, the boys and I collected rocks to ring our campfire. Behind our tent, up above our secluded canyon, sloped a fair-sized hill, steep enough to wind me on the climb to its peak. A miniature mountain it was, marbled with thick high woods, acres and acres of lodgepole pine and Douglas fir. If the boys strayed too far up into those woods, the wind chased them back into camp, and then we would set them to work slashing nettles to clear a path to our natural spring.

For us, life didn't come any more primitive, especially after the last marshmallow dropped off its stick and melted into the embers. At night we lingered long around our campfire watching the stars come out, listening to the wind ruffle the aspens, dreaming about the cabin we might build here someday, and telling stories to camouflage the occasional coyote howl.

How do you put down roots in Idaho? By summer after summer of camping on this land, searching the borders of our acres, living out our version of the pioneer experience.◅

JIM BECKWITH'S RUN

Jim Beckwith hung around various trappers including Jim Bridger and Kit Carson. One day while outfitting at Fort Hall, he met up with a man named Reese and a friendship rapidly developed. Reese talked Beckwith into accompanying him to the headwaters of the Snake, about 100 miles from Fort Hall, where beaver lodges were extremely abundant. Being in hostile Blackfoot and Crow territory, few trappers dared the region. But the Indians only occupied the area from spring through fall.

The two men spent the winter gathering pelts. As spring approached, they were reluctant to leave the rich beaver area, so they tried to stretch the spring a little. It didn't work. In late April, as the two were finishing breakfast, they were rushed by a large group of Blackfeet Indians. Reese was killed immediately.

Beckwith looked at the horses still grazing in the meadow, glanced at the massive mound of furs gathered during the cold winter, then bid both horses and furs a silent farewell. His feet hit the dirt and Beckwith sped off with the agility of a jackrabbit. He heard the hooves of Indian ponies pounding after him as he darted in and out among the trees. Soon he heard nothing but his own heavy breathing and the pounding of his heart. The veins in his legs burst and the limbs swelled painfully. Still he raced on, making Fort Hall late that same night.

Beckwith's run made him a cripple for life, but he never complained. Being crippled was a damn sight better than being dead.◅

---

from the United States and the opening of what was to be the Oregon Trail. Lee drove the first herd of cattle along the trail across Idaho, on his way to his destination on the lower Columbia River. After 1840, a flood of immigrants traveled the Oregon Trail, and Fort Hall and Fort Boise became two of the most important stopping places. Indian hostility forced Hudson's Bay to abandon Fort Boise in 1855 and Fort Hall in 1856.

Except for passing wagon trains each summer, the Indians had all of Idaho to themselves for a few short years. Then in 1860 gold was discovered in North Central Idaho, and the "Indian summer" was over. Also in 1860, Mormon pioneers staked out the first town in Southeastern Idaho. Franklin was the first of many Mormon settlements, and with it they established a dream and a life style.

IDAHO'S LAVA HOT SPRINGS

by Elizabeth Rose Bell

Idaho's famous Lava Hot Springs have been used for over a hundred and fifty years. Now State-run, the facilities includes swimming pools, hot baths, sun rooms, and a camp-ground and golf course for summer use.

The scenic gems, the memorable spots, are not always emblazoned on a map. Sometimes you arrive on them unexpectedly, or a casual tourist acquaintance will give you the tip, or sometimes, if you stop to read a State Historical Monument sign, you will find that unforgettable place that lifts you out of a tiring day of traveling.

The sign on Highway 30 North, part way across the broad desert country of southern Idaho, says "Lava Hot Springs," and the historical legend following can only be read by pulling off the highway into the small parking area.

Then comes the surprise. Opening up at your feet is a V-shaped cleft in the lava rock, and planted in every nook and cranny of that area, a cave whose roof has long-since fallen in, are trees and shrubs and vines and flowers of every hue.

At the bottom of the canyon where the Portneuf River cuts a wider valley are the main buildings of the Lava Hot Springs Foundation, run by the State of Idaho. In 1902 the Federal government granted 178 acres on the north side of the river to the State of Idaho. This included a large mineral hot springs which welled up from the mud at the base of the lava formation.

The springs had been known and used by the Indians. The Wilson Hunt party of white men came through the area in 1812. John C.

The Franklin settlers first lived in their wagon boxes and then in crude cabins, but they got a sawmill operating by 1861, supplying lumber all the way to Salt Lake City. Life improved quickly. By 1870, stone homes were being built in the Greek Revival style. Several historic buildings still stand in Franklin. Nearby Preston, Paris, Malad, Montpelier and Soda Springs are also full of pioneer history. The 1889 Paris Tabernacle is built of red sandstone brought by sleds from a quarry 18 miles away. Montpelier's bank earned lasting fame by being robbed by Butch Cassidy's gang, in 1896.

Idaho's bloodiest battle occurred northwest of Franklin, on the Bear River. Here in 1863, a federal force of California Volunteers attacked a Shoshone encampment and killed 400 Indians. The Mormons had refused

Fremont's surveying party of 1843 came this way searching for a way through the mountains to the far west. In 1860 the Hudson Bay Company had a fur post here.

Today the residents of Idaho and of the neighboring states of Wyoming and Utah, and the tourists traveling Highway 30 North can stop to enjoy the area.

They can bathe in the open-air health baths, enjoy private hot baths and sun rooms, or swim in the huge enclosed natatorium or the newer outdoor swimming pool.

They can stroll the paths in the sunken garden or rest on green shady lawns beside the river and feed the rainbow trout which will rise to bread crumbs or popcorn. They can picnic in a pavilioned, shady park.

A beautiful rolling golf course marks the western boundary of the State of Idaho property, and a modern trailer park nestles in green lawns and trees beside the quiet river at the eastern end. These, too, are state-owned and operated.

The town of Lava Hot Springs has motels, hotels, and restaurants, but reservations are advisable after June 1.

In the winter the area will be blanketed with snow, and the gardens dormant until the coming of spring, but the health baths will still be providing their warm, soothing water for all comers, and the pavilion will be an ice-skating rink. The state keeps these facilities open all year.

*Beautiful Bear Lake.
No reports of the monster since Thursday last.*

to help the soldiers, and after the massacre, they took in wounded orphans. The Bear River battlefield remains undignified, but east of American Falls, Massacre Rocks State Park commemorates an attack by Indians on Oregon Trail immigrants, in 1862.

Pocatello is the crossroads and keystone city of Southeastern Idaho. Much of its surrounding area was purchased from Shoshone tribe, and in 1902, it opened to settlement in an Oklahoma-style land rush. It has been a major center for Union Pacific Railroad and was once the largest "train town" west of the Mississippi. The Bannock County Historical Museum and the Short Line Depot offer railroad history. Idaho State University, one of the three sisters of Idaho higher education, serves all of Idaho with academics and athletics.

THE BEAR LAKE MONSTER

In 1868 Joseph Rich owned a spa on Bear Lake in the southeast corner of Idaho. He wrote to the Deseret News in Salt Lake City and told a story he said he'd heard from local Indians. According to their legends a serpentine monster prowled Bear Lake. It had short, stubby legs it sometimes used to scurry onto shore and snatch away maidens in its terrible jaws.

After the letter appeared, people all over the valley began seeing the monster. One said it was 40 feet long and swam faster than a horse could run. Another claimed it was 90 feet long and swam faster than a locomotive.

This astonishing creature had everyone in an uproar The Salt Lake newspaper carried many accounts of monster sightings, and efforts to trap the beast.

—Except this sighting yesterday morning.

Then, Joseph Rich wrote another letter to the paper expressing his sorrow that some didn't believe in the monster. He said "they might come up here someday and through their unbelief, be thrown off their guard and gobbled up by the Water Devil." There was a tone to that letter though, that not everyone caught. Mr. Rich was writing tongue in cheek and having a wonderful time with the tale he had invented to attract customers to his resort.

Many more people claimed to have spotted the Bear Lake Monster over the years, and they started seeing monsters in other nearby lakes... which must have been an endless source of amusement for the monster's father, Joseph Rich. ⌐⌐

IGNACE HATCHIORAQUASHA

Ignace, a half-Iroquois Canadian trapper of the Hudson's Bay Company, shortened his name to John Grey. It brought fewer snickers from his comrades, and lessened the fisticuffs which resulted when individuals, unable to pronounce Hatchioraquasha, would address Ignace as "Hey, Breed!"

There's a lake north of Soda Springs which should rightfully bear the name Hatchioraquasha. Or at least Ignace. It is, however, called Grays Lake, named after alias John Grey .

The lake was discovered by "Grey" between 1818 and 1820. He was one of the 55 fur trappers with Donald ("Perpetual Motion") Mackenzie's Snake River Brigade of the Northwest Fur Company.

That southeastern section of the future state of Idaho was a paradise. "Grey" saw deer grazing in vast herds, grizzly bear, eagles, otters and wild horses. There were also wolves, foxes, raccoons and badgers. The animals exhibited little fear of man.

Grays Lake has since become a wildlife refuge - a nesting ground for Sandhill cranes and Canadian geese.

As for Ignace Hatchioraquasha, he died in Kansas City in 1844 at the hands of an angered Indian woman.

Thus, we are left with his legacy - a lake bearing the name which wasn't Ignace's name at all. ⌐⌐

This was Montpelier shortly before Butch Cassidy and his wild bunch rode down this street and robbed the Montpelier Bank. Old timers still argue over how much they got away with, and great grandchildren still hunt for the never-recovered loot hidden somewhere in the Wind River Range.

BUTCH CASSIDY HITS MONTPELIER

He went as far north as Idaho Falls and then down to Blackfoot Pocatello, and made his way over near Bear Lake. Of all prospects he had looked over he considered the best was a small thriving town near the head of Bear Lake. The chance of a get away from there appeared good and the bank seemed to carry plenty money. He returned to the gang. They considered the trail they would take for their get away and studied landmarks for they would need plenty of land marks to make speed in a get away. They made camp at the point where they would leave the relay about fifteen miles out of town at the head of a creek where there was plenty of food and water for the horses. There was no fire built. In the morning they wrapped a light supper of food in there slickers and tied them behind the saddles. It was planned to stick together across the Green River valley also across the Wind River range of mountains and down through the Sweet water country if possible.

About one o'clock they rode leisurely into town. One stayed with the horses and Butch took the lead in the bank. It was a matter of a few seconds to line up the customers and bank employees. Maxwell stood at one end of the line while Butch transferred the cash to a sack he carried. First the money in the vault & then the cash behind the counter. Coming from behind the cage, he noticed that one man in the line up had a small boy on the floor beside him. He put the contents which was currency into the bag and then examined the customers and found two six shooters. He told them to hold their hands up. They made for the door and their horses & were gone. The whole thing took about ten minutes.

The alarm was set off and a posse arranged immediately. The delay gave the Wild bunch a three minute head start. They reached their relay. Changed horses and were off again. Owing to the relay being a little way from the main trail, the posse did not discover a change of horses had been made and continued to follow until nearly dark and their horses played out. They were forced to abandon the search until the following morning. The bandits finally stopped to rest and divided the cash which was about 28 thousand dollars. They parted again to meet later.

A legend persists in Wyoming that Cassidy and Elzy Lay, being hard pressed by posses, buried some of the Montpelier loot in the Wind River Mountains. Cassidy dug a hole in the sand at the base of a large, lightning-struck stump with the butt of his revolver and deposited the money, figuring the snag to be a good enough land mark to guide them back to the cache. The same old-timers who tell the story talk in terms of $30,000, which is similar to the $28,000 figure claimed by Cassidy, but is substantially larger than the $7,165 reported by A. N. MacIntosh, the Montpelier bank's teller.

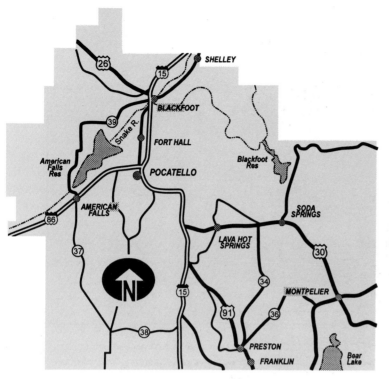

CALENDAR

Dodge National Circuit Finals Rodeo, Pocatello, March: The second largest points qualifying rodeo in the U.S. Only the top two qualifying cowboys from each of twelve circuits nationwide are allowed to compete. Contact: Pocatello Frontier Rodeo Association, (208) 233-1546.

Massacre Rocks Rendezvous, American Falls, June: The lifestyle of the past is relived by rugged mountain men. Some features include a tepee village, traders' row, black powder shoots and a knife throwing contest. Contact: Massacre Rocks State Park, (208) 548-2672.

Oregon Trail Rendezvous Pageant, Montpelier, July: Dutch oven supper, musical entertainment, live action pageant and dancing on the Oregon Trail. Contact: (208) 945-2333.

Mountain Man Rendezvous-Pioneer Days Celebration, Lava Hot Springs, July: A celebration of Idaho's history with many fun events. Contact: Lava Hot Springs Foundation. (208) 776-5221.

Famous Preston Night Rodeo, Preston, Late July: Three nights of PRCA rodeo featuring top rodeo performers and a carnival. Contact (208) 852-2703.

Shoshone-Bannock Indian Festival, Fort Hall, August: A celebration of Indian culture. Festivities include traditional Indian dress, dances, games, and art. Also featured is an All-Indian Old Timer's Rodeo. Contact: Blackfoot Chamber of Commerce, (208) 785-0510.

Eastern Idaho State Fair, Blackfoot, first week in September: Top name stars, a rodeo, horse and pig racing, and a demolition derby are just some of the atractions. Contact: Blackfoot Chamber of Commerce, (208) 785-0510.

Idaho Spud Day, Shelley, September: The Annual Idaho Spud Day is a country-style gala celebration of the Idaho potato that offers events and attractions for visitars of all ages. Contact: (208) 357-7662.

Festival of Lights, Preston, late November through December: Opens with Veteran's Day Parade, musical, and the lighting of the best light display in Idaho: Contact: (208) 852-1969.

TIPS: FOOD & SHELTER

In Pocatello the **Sandpiper Restaurant** provides consistent good food and selections.

The pastrami burger at **Tom's Gyros** in Pocatello, and good shrimp is available at the **Press Box**, which is the favorite local sports bar. For almost half a century locals stop by **Brown's Store & Bar** which boasts the coldest beer in Idaho.

Two very popular Italian restaurants are **Remo's**, also serving steaks and great prime rib, and **Buddy's**, with salads a speciality (they distribute their own salad dressing brand).

East Idaho
Region 6

Chapter VII
EASTERN IDAHO
Region 6

The Grand Tetons from the Idaho side –outside of Driggs. A half million tourists a year pass through on the way to Jackson Hole, Yellowstone, or Grand Targee. Many visit Driggs for their famous July hot air balloon show or bluegrass festival every August.

THE SUNRISE SIDE OF THE TETONS

by Patti Sherlock

When the pre-dawn sky whitens, granite spires loom in the east. A layer of red seeps up behind the famous mountains and turns them a profound purple. Then a yellow-balloon sun floats up from jagged peaks, and day has begun in Idaho's Teton Basin.

Indians, who watched the sun come up over the 13,700-foot Grand Teton and its companions, Mount Owen and the Middle Grand, thought the "sunrise mountains" held a mystic sanctity. Today, those who live in Idaho's Teton Valley still glory in their western-side view of the range.

Yet it is not this view of the acclaimed

They call Eastern Idaho, "Rendezvous Country," because here the mountain men gathered to trade furs for provisions. Today, this is where one can rendezvous with one's freer spirit and trade the doubts in the brain for a certainty in the heart.

This is the heart of the heart of the West. That may sound redundant, but it can't be repeated enough. This is it: the inner sanctum, the sunrise side of the Tetons. Here, the mythical meaning of the word "Idaho" best matches "the sun shining on mountains."

The Teton Valley. The Yellowstone. Henry's Fork. Island Park. Famous names and famous places for two very good and opposite reasons: Eastern Idaho is a great place for a person to enjoy alone, and it's a won-

mighty Tetons was the Idaho view. In 1872, William Henry Jackson, official photographer of the Hayden survey party, hauled in 100 pounds of primitive photography equipment on pack mules. One of his favorite spots for shooting was near the present-day Grand Targhee ski area. Sometimes he camped alone all night to be in an advantageous place to shoot a perfect picture in the morning. Jackson, who later painted excellent watercolors of his Teton Basin adventures, regarded that time in his youth as the highlight of his long career.

However, people had been enchanted with the basin long before Jackson arrived. Blackfoot, Nez Perce and other western tribes hunted game and camped in the Teton Valley. As early as 1808, mountain men arrived to trap beaver. Many of the mountain-man legends - John Colter, Jedediah Smith, Jeremiah Johnson, Jim Bridger and Kit Carson - plied their trade in Teton Valley.

The valley took on the name Pierre's Hole after a French trapper, Vieux Pierre. The Pierre's Hole Rendezvous became a summer event where trappers gathered with their families and friendly Indians to sell furs, trade and often drink up and gamble away their year's earnings. In 1832, a famous battle erupted between Blackfeet Indians and trappers. After that, the valley was abandoned as a rendezvous site. Nowadays, the Pierre's Hole Rendezvous is commemorated each August with black powder shoots and log rolling while modern mountain men roam Driggs' streets in authentic garb.

The mountain man era faded when beaver prices fell. Others came - drifters, horse thieves, fleeing polygamists. Serious settlement started in the late 1880s with an influx of Mormon pioneers from Utah. The valley remains 80 percent Mormon.

Getting to the valley and its extraordinary

Tetons America sees on calendars, posters and paintings. The Idaho side is second choice for artists and photographers. In Wyoming, viewers get a closer look at the range. Climbers prefer to scale the Tetons from the less difficult Wyoming side. Jackson Hole, which lies at the base of the peaks in Wyoming, is renowned, while Driggs, Idaho, nestles obscurely under the range on the west. Jackson lures millionaires and recreationists, hosts an international music festival and beckons artists by the wagonload. The Tetons mean big money in Wyoming.

But residents of Driggs, population 939, do not mind saying others are wrong. A row of foothills does alter the Idaho view, but in their opinion, only for the better.

Doris Moss, a member of the Teton County Historical Society, believes the Tetons were named from the Idaho side. That's where the early exploration was and besides, she points out, "The name in French means breasts, and the resemblance to a woman's breast is greater from our side."

Interestingly, America's first glimpse of the

derful place for people to enjoy together. Moose, deer, elk, bear and wolverine share this biological Shangri-la. Great waves of waterfowl wash across its skies. It is world-famous for its production of fighting trout.

Geographically, Eastern Idaho can be called the Tail of the Snake: the headwaters of one of the grandest rivers of the West. Here — and on the eastern side of the Tetons —the great Snake begins its journey toward the sea.

Geologically, Eastern Idaho is at the head of another kind of stream, one called a "heat flow" from deep within the earth, which has been moving "upstream" across the continent's drift for millions of years. This geologic hotspot is perhaps a hole in the earth's crust punched by a giant meteorite 17 million years ago.

views is pleasant business. From Idaho Falls, two routes go to Driggs. Both take about 1 1/2 hours. I-15 North is a straight, four-lane road; then turn onto Idaho 33 just past Sugar City. Idaho 33 goes east through hilly farm country and small towns like Newdale and Tetonia. The drive offers graceful farm scenery - silos reaching into blue skies, green pastures enclosed with rail fences and antique farm equipment rusting in gullies. But it's the expanding view of the Tetons that makes the route stunning.

East from Idaho Falls, U.S. 26 passes rolling dry farms and Garn's Mountain, then drops into picturesque Swan Valley beside the Snake River. Idaho 31 climbs through the Targhee National Forest along Pine Creek and hugs the Big Hole Mountains to Victor.

Tourists from Wyoming come into Victor over the Teton Pass. With 10 percent grades and no guard rails, Wyoming 20 is an acrophobic's nightmare. But the locals take it in stride. "The pass tells you something about the people," says Ira Koplow, former director of the Teton valley Chamber of Commerce.

In the days of buggies and sleighs, it was an overnight trip to get over the pass. W. Leigh Fullmer, 89, who has been in the valley since 1918, recalls the road had six horseshoe bends on one side. Snowslides sometimes blocked the

Pierre's Hole was the annual July meeting place for the fur trade in the 1820s and 1830s. Trappers (every nationality, every color of skin) were joined by Nez Perce and Flathead Indians to defeat the Blackfeet in the bloody 1832 Battle.

Beginning in southern Oregon and arcing across southern Idaho, the course of the hotspot is marked by the sequential eruptions of enormous volcanoes.

The last few volcanoes appear plainly on relief maps. The 20-mile diameter Island Park Caldera may be the largest circular caldera on earth. It is the remains of a volcano whose eruption about two million years ago covered 6,000 square miles of Idaho and Montana with white hot ash. The Island Park Caldera is now extinct. The Yellowstone Caldera, just next door in the national park, will likely erupt again.

Big Springs is the outlet for great volumes of subterranean water which has percolated from the Yellowstone Plateau. This water is the major source of the Henry's Fork flow and provides even-temperature

way for weeks. In 1923, Fullmer and his wife Addie ran a boarding house at the top of the pass. Mail carriers, tourists and teamsters were their guests.

"We had only one bed, but we had a big floor for sleeping, and Addie kept a fire going to warm it," Fullmer said.

Sometimes, poachers dropped in. Until a law forbade the use of elks' teeth in jewelry, poachers sometimes killed dozens of elk at a time, only for the teeth.

Back then there was talk of putting a road through the mountain, but counties did not have money or equipment for tunneling like the railroads did. Since then, Fullmer said, attempts to provide an easier road between the two sides of the Tetons have gone nowhere. "Jackson is too important to Wyoming, economically, and Wyoming opposes any plan to bypass it," he said.

The geologically rich valley has at various times attracted gold prospectors and limestone, Gilsonite, lead, copper and phosphate miners. Coal mining gave birth to Sam, a town only a shout from Driggs that boasted 40 families, a schoolhouse and a post office. Teton County holds a large, undeveloped body of coal, but recovering it economically is an unsolved problem.

Though slower to gain fame, the valley isn't undiscovered either. Some 400,000 to 500,000 visitors pass through Driggs each year. About a fifth of tourists are winter skiers going to Grand Targhee Ski Area. The area is located just past the state boundary by Driggs. Grand Targhee enjoys 500 inches of snow per year, world class powder and a season extending from Thanksgiving to April.

The hot air balloon races in July, a four-day event, attract national participation. "Can you imagine, from a pilot's view, a greater place for competition?" Ira Koplow asked.

The Driggs airport can land business jets owned by wealthy summer residents who have built homes in scenic canyons close to town.

The influx of newcomers, land speculators and the rich has brought with it what Leigh Fullmer politely calls "contentions." "I'm for growth, yes," Fullmer said. "But I'm not for dirty water. At one time, there wasn't a stream in this valley you couldn't lie down and drink from. You can't do that now."

The Teton River, which snakes through the valley, is attracting development. Formed by springs, some of which are hot, the river holds rainbow, brook and cutthroat trout. The Soil Conservation service has started preservation programs to slow down erosion. Ira Koplaw sees the river as the valley's great untapped resource.

Fishermen, hikers, canoeists and peak watchers enjoy the "other side" of the Tetons in relative seclusion. The only crowding is in the meadows, where yellow mountain laurel, rosy shooting stars, violets, larkspur, phlox, sunflowers, columbines, pansies, Indian paintbrush, wild roses and yarrow vie for a place to bloom.

Do lovers of the sunrise side concede sunsets to Wyoming? They do not. When the setting sun reflects off the jagged range, it turns it vivid pink. Leigh Fullmer recalls when his niece Sarah wrote an essay about sunsets in Teton Basin for an English assignment.

"She wrote about the pink mountains. Her teacher failed her. He said, 'Mountains can't be pink,'" Fullmer remembers.

Addie Fullmer, who has watched six decades of valley sunsets, likes the giant bear who appears on the mountain. "When conditions are right, a shadow, shaped like a bear, appears at dusk on the Grand." Her eyes twinkled. "Only on the Idaho side." ✍

water for the magnificent trout habitat. The Henry's Fork of the Snake River also provides the most important habitat for trumpeter swans in the United States.

In 1809, Andrew Henry established a fur trapping outpost on Henry's Fork of the Snake River, near Egin. He and his men spent a rough winter here. Snow fell deep. Temperatures fell deeper. Wild game disappeared. So did the expedition's horses, as they had to be eaten. It is too bad that Henry did not comprehend the meaning of the Shoshone word, "Egin." Egin means "cold." The next year the Astorian Expedition left their horses here and began their disastrous voyage down the Snake River.

Shoshones were the most numerous Indians in Eastern Idaho, but this was rendezvous country for

BATTLE NEAR PIERRE'S HOLE

The junction town of Victor as it appeared in the last century, now a picturesque stopping spot for experienced travelers.

The July rendezvous of 1832 began calmly at Pierre's Hole. The Nez Perces had erected 120 of their lodges There were 80 Flathead lodges. A company of 90 trappers under the firm of Drips and Fontenelle, connected with the American Fur Company, were present, as were many independent hunters and about 100 of the men from Sublette's Rocky Mountain Fur Company.

Amid the shady nooks, tree-lined streams and grass plains, alcohol flowed freely and wild spirits went rampant.

On July 17th, Milton Sublette and his men, and another small party, broke camp to head westward. As they were approaching the south side of Darley Creek, they saw a Blackfoot chief, advancing singly and unarmed, bearing a peace pipe. Antoine Godin, a half-breed with Sublette's party, accompanied by a Flathead, rode to meet the Blackfoot chief. Upon grasping the chief's extended hand, Antoine ordered the Flathead to shoot. The chief fell dead.

Warriors, who had been watching from the distance, came swooping down upon the trappers. One of the trappers high-tailed it back to Pierre's Hole and, within a short time, returned with Nez Perce, Flathead and white reinforcements.

The Blackfeet warriors fortified themselves in the timber. They were under continuous attack throughout the day. Under the cover of darkness the defeated Blackfeet slipped away, leaving their lodges and twenty of their dead.

Three whitemen had been killed in the battle. William Sublette and eight others had been badly wounded.

IN THE SHADOW OF YELLOWSTONE

by Mario P. Delisio

In my many years of travel throughout Idaho, I have found two places that appear similar to Switzerland - the Stanley Basin area of central Idaho and eastern Idaho's Island Park region. Each encompasses a region of towering landforms, lush vegetation, clear-cold lakes and streams as well as wonderfully clear air - all reminiscent of Switzerland. Although both display an outdoors American West lifestyle complete with wildlife that variously includes moose, elk, deer, antelope and trout, a Swiss would feel pretty much at home in either place. In fact, several years ago a native Swiss named Robert Wutrith did live in Island Park, Swiss chalet and all! He was known throughout for his excellent photography and smiling demeanor. A true Swiss!

Less than a day's drive from Treasure Valley, Island Park is adjacent to the east entrance to Yellowstone Park. U.S. 20-191 passes north-south through the heart of it. Because of its proximity to Yellowstone, Island Park is heavily traversed by Park visitors but little experienced by them. Except for the requisite fuel and food stops, travelers often pass through, having little knowledge of the grandeur they are missing.

One of those best kept secrets in Western skiing -the Grand Targee resort outside of Driggs, in the shadow of the Tetons and Yellowstone Park.

Geographically, Island Park is unique in that it sits primarily in the crater of an extinct volcano. Known as the Island Park Caldera, the feature encompasses such places as Henrys Lake - famed as an outstanding trout lake, Island Park Reservoir, Harriman State Park, Upper and Lower Mesa Falls, Big Springs and 9,902-foot-high Sawtell Peak.

Calderas are formed when the top of a volcano is blown apart, such as in the Mt. St. Helens eruption or in the blast that created Crater Lake about 6,500 years ago in Oregon. Calderas can also be formed when the crater of a volcano collapses because of the lack of internal support. In either case, the effect is to form an enormous cavity-like depression which often looks like an extremely large crater. Calderas can be many miles in diameter.

My continuing images of Island Park are that of lush vegetation, myriad water features and rugged terrain. The lush vegetation consists of fields of wild flowers and stands of evergreen trees, mainly lodgepole pines. These are traversed by cold, clear, trout-filled streams such as the Buffalo River and the Henrys Fork of the Snake River, which in places has cut two spectacular waterfalls - Upper and Lower Mesa - of 105 and 65 feet through sheer, spray-filled canyons. The two dominant lakes, Henrys and Island Park Reservoir, add to the aura of water-bounded landscape.

The area is well served by a variety of lodges, restaurants, guest ranches and other travel services. Virtually all display a down-home charm of hospitality, good food and the aesthetic warmth of log construction.

Henrys Lake is known as a premier trout fishery. Surrounded on three sides by the towering mountains of the Continental Divide, the lake is an outdoorsman's delight with its natural yet varied scenery. At one end is a spring

Indians, too. Frequent Indian visitors to the area included Nez Perce, Flathead and Blackfeet. Crows probably entered from the other side of Yellowstone. The Shoshones often fought the Nez Perce and Flathead. Everyone often fought the Blackfeet.

One of the most famous rendezvous was one held in 1832 in the Teton Valley, which was then called Pierre's Hole (in honor of a trapper felled by the Blackfeet). Nathaniel Wyeth reported over 200 mountain men, many Iroquois trappers, 120 Nez Perce lodges, and 80 Flathead lodges. After the rendezvous, as one small group of trappers was breaking camp, a war party of Blackfeet approached. The Blackfeet possibly had no idea how many other trappers and their Indian allies were nearby. But the trappers knew. A Flathead

around which the fish congregate in the springtime while later in the year they disperse throughout the lake.

Island Park Reservoir, meanwhile, features both trout fishing and water skiing. With its broad, open surface and five boat ramps, a wide range of boating activities is possible.

Certainly one of the most unique spots is Big Springs, headwaters of the Henrys Fork of the Snake River. The Springs appear full force at the base of the encompassing mountain with a flow of 92,000 gallons of water per minute at a year round temperature of 50 degrees Fahrenheit. The sight is made even more impressive by the clusters of large trout which feed in the rich waters or from the handouts of bread from visitors. Sorry, no fishing here. At

Big Springs, in addition, is the John Sack Cabin, on the National Register of Historic Places, noted for its many unique hand-crafted features.

Towering over all this majestic landscape is Sawtell Peak. The 9,902-foot mountain is accessible by automobile throughout the summer months. The view, as expected, is awe-inspiring:you can see parts of three states, Yellowstone National Park and the panorama of Island Park! Wild flowers in profusion during the spring add to Sawtell's color and drama.

Fall and winter in Island Park present many opportunities for outdoor enthusiasts. Fall offers regal hunting-elk, deer, moose and black bear plus geese and ducks. Big game animals drift out of nearby Yellowstone and into Island Park on their migration to lower elevations.

Fall fishing for trout and kokanee is another facet of Island Park's recreational activities. With the cool days and sparkling skies, it is a refreshing time. That, plus the lack of crowds, allows one to truly get back to nature and in touch with oneself.

shot a Blackfeet who had come forward bearing a peace pipe. Before the smoke had cleared, the dead numbered 26 Blackfeet, six trappers and seven Nez Perce.

The big fur trapping years lasted another decade in Eastern Idaho, then Mormon settlers began to turn the rich soil to agriculture. "Famous Idaho Potatoes" are more famous when they're from Eastern Idaho where the high-elevation, volcanic soil grows perfect tubers within view of the Tetons. Schools still let out students during harvest in the fall (although often the students are more interested in harvesting deer). Late in September, the Annual Spud Day is always celebrated in Shelley.

Brain power also grows in Eastern Idaho's farm fields. Early settlers believed in the ethic, "Don't fight it,

Highly recommended is an exploration of Harriman State Park. Named after the Harrimans of Union Pacific fame, (see Governor's Message, page 7), the Park lies in the heart of the Harriman Wildlife Refuge. Known as "Railroad Ranch" throughout its history, the site traces back to 1902 when several officials of the Oregon Shortline Railroad, the predecessor of the Union Pacific in Idaho, purchased the lands that now comprise Harriman State Park. The property was the private retreat of the Guggenheims as well as the Harrimans. Charlie Jones, once president of Richfield Oil Company, also held a share in the ranch at another time. The ranch was a working cattle operation besides serving as a respite for the wealthy owners.

The Railroad Ranch Historical Area within the Park retains many of the original buildings and all the charm of days gone by. Guided historical and nature walks, horseback riding, bicycling on the meadow trails (old ranch roads) and fly fishing along Henrys Fork make a full day of it.

Winter transportation by dogsled. When the mail absolutely, positively, did not need to be there overnight. Spencer is known for its opal mines, Monida a contraction of Montana/Idaho. Note the "paymaster's tree" to save extra employee trips to town.

if you can figure it," and they figured out ingenious irrigation and cultivation schemes. The most famous of Eastern Idaho's farm boys is no doubt Philo Farnsworth, of Rigby, who invented the cathode ray tube, making modern television possible. As a teenager, Farnsworth drew out plans for the picture tube on his high school blackboard. Today, the majority of employees at the Idaho National Engineering Laboratory live in and around Idaho Falls. Surveys have shown that Eastern Idahoans are among the best read in the nation.

Idaho Falls serves as Eastern Idaho's hub. It was always an important crossing of the Snake River, and was first called Eagle Rock. In 1891, Citizens changed its name to Idaho Falls, even before there was a falls,

There are 16,000 acres of forests, meadows, lakes and streams within the Island Park region. The refuge protects a diversity of birds and mammals similar to those found in Yellowstone National Park. Perhaps chief among these are trumpeter swans found on the gently

"Spud Day" in Idaho Falls. Since then they have added the Great Snake River Duck Races to their repertoire of celebrations.

flowing Henrys Fork of the Snake River. Kept ice-free by springs, the Henrys Fork provides an excellent environment for 300-400 trumpeters by mid-winter. This is one-third of the Rocky Mountain population.

The total effect of the Park is one of peaceful solitude. Harriman, however, is day use only, so plan your Island Park stay at any of the numerous lodges or campgrounds. Be sure to bring your camera, plenty of film and binoculars!

Winter in Island Park is a snow encapsulated wonderland. It is a mixture of solitude and dynamic action depending on the time and place. For those who like the enchantment of quiet peace there is a choice of cross-country skiing at its best or ice fishing on Island Park Reservoir. For those who thrill for action there is snowmobiling.

Winter in Island Park is also a great time to savor the rustic lodges that line the highway to Yellowstone. My own experience includes Ponds Lodge, Macks Inn and Island Park Lodge. Food, lodging and good cheer are all a part of the experience. Besides these, there are a number of other lodging, food and service providers. The Island Park Chamber of Commerce at 208-558-7783 can provide all the information needed.

In many ways, Island Park is a microcosm of Yellowstone without the thermal features. It has the majestic landscape of mountain, forest, meadow, stream and lakes, spectacular waterfalls through carved canyons, a diversity of animal life and a significant historical heritage without, however, the overwhelming crowds that plague Yellowstone much of the year. That is why I like the area so much and that is why I keep going back.

Altogether, Island Park, in many ways, is one of Idaho's best kept secrets. Nestled next to Yellowstone National Park, it is often by-passed and overlooked, except by those "in the know."

---

which was constructed as a dam in 1911. Talk about positive thinking. Today, Idaho Falls is one of Idaho's most attractive cities — and third largest, after Boise and Lewiston.

Idaho's prettiest valley may be the Teton Valley, so beloved by the early trappers. Its view of the Tetons is unsurpassed by the nearby Jackson Hole, Wyoming, whose population exceeds the Teton Valley's by many times and many dollars. For the outdoor enthusiast who does not like crowds, Driggs and Tetonia are too good to be true. The Grand Targhee resort offers incredible snow until early summer and hosts the Teton Valley Hot Air Balloon Races, over the Fourth of July.

Yellowstone National Park extends two miles into Eastern Idaho, and Grand Teton National Park is only

SLEEPING IN A VOLCANO

Would it bother you to sleep inside a volcano? You may have already done so, though you probably didn't know.

The geologic history of Idaho is written in rock. Volcanoes were an important part of what formed our state. That's obvious at Craters of the Moon National Monument, but not so readily apparent in other places.

The Island Park area in eastern Idaho sits right in the middle of an extinct volcano. If you've ever spent a night camping on the shores of Henry's Lake, you've slept inside that old volcano, or caldera.

Geologists call volcanoes that blow apart - as Mount St. Helens did a few years back - calderas. Calderas can also be formed when a volcano collapses. Either way, calderas are huge crater-like features that can be many miles wide

The Island Park Caldera is one of the largest - perhaps the largest - symmetrical caldera in the world. It's about 16 miles wide and 23 miles long.

Inside the ancient crater are Henry's Lake, Island Park Reservoir, Harriman State Park, Sawtell Peak, Big Springs, Upper and Lower Mesa Falls, and Island Park itself, the long, skinny community that is scattered out for miles along highway 20.

Now, if you do decide to spend the night inside the Island Park Caldera, what are your chances of getting a rude volcanic awakening? Slim to none. The volcano hasn't been active in several million years. ∾

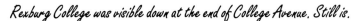

Rexburg College was visible down at the end of College Avenue. Still is.

six miles inside Wyoming. However, the Idaho say into these national jewels is not by motor home cruising on paved highways, but by foot; hiking on forest trails.

Most of Eastern Idaho is a natural park, with everything ranging from the 150-square-mile St. Anthony Sand Dunes to thousands of square miles of forest and stream. Moose love this country for what the U.S. Geological Survey has been forced to label "numerous small lakes," because there are too many to name. Upper and Lower Mesa Falls strike one with fear, love and awe, at the same time. Wallace Stegner wrote, "I gave my heart to the mountains the minute I stood beside this river with its spray in my face and watched it thunder into foam, smooth to green glass over sunken rocks, shatter to foam again. . ."

Main Street, USA, early this century. Happens to be Rigby, Idaho, where a 14 year old boy named Philo invented television in 1922.

ANDREW HENRY

A ndrew Henry was born in Pennsylvania around 1775. He developed into a tall, dark-complected man who enjoyed the finer things in life. He wore the latest fashions, dined in the finest homes and played the violin. Henry kept himself active in various organizations, often holding high positions within their structure. He was also civic-minded, serving as election judge and juryman. Andrew Henry had been born to a life of affluence and social prominence, and untill he reached the age of thirty-three, accepted that existence. But something was missing. Adventure.

In 1808, he joined Manuel Lisa and eight others in organizing the Missouri Fur Company. Not content to operate behind the scenes from an office in St. Louis, Henry donned buckskins and headed to the Rockies. Off and on throughout the next sixteen years, Henry was involved in the fur trade, for here he found the adventure he had missed during early adulthood.

In the Rockies he contended with the hardships of the trade. Grizzly bear attacks. Fighting Blackfeet warriors. Hunger. Cold. Thirst. Exhaustion. Henry retired in 1824 at the age of fifty and died ten years later.

Andrew Henry could have lived and died a very wealthy man. He didn't. He had chosen adventure instead. He once told a friend that he had suffered a great deal and had met with many misfortunes. But he left a legacy which must certainly have eased some of his losses - the establishment of Fort Henry, in present-day Idaho, the first American fur post erected on the Pacific side of the Rockies. ⚓

Harriman State Park is a 10,000-acre wildlife park, donated to the State of Idaho by the famous New York railroad family. The old ranch buildings are maintained for visitors, and the meadowlands harbor migrating swans and cranes. North of the park, through the Island Park area, Henry's Lake has delighted everyone since Andrew Henry camped here in 1810. Its trout Fishing has long been world-famous.

So far, the picture of Eastern Idaho has been painted as bucolic. Which it is; it is natural, peaceful and serene. But those who think nothing much happens in Eastern Idaho, except for the glories of nature, need only to remember June 5,1976.

Geologically, Idaho is famous for great floods. The Spokane Flood emptied Glacial Lake Missoula and

IDAHO FALLS
AND THE UPPER
SNAKE RIVER VALLEY

If you have an appreciation for hunting, fishing, park trips, winter sports or the scenic beauties of unspoiled nature, then there is a place in your heart for that Outdoor Eden of America found in the Upper Snake River Valley and the adjacent valleys of the Lemhi, Salmon and Lost rivers.

Captains Lewis and Clark paid a newcomer's call to the Salmon Valley in 1805 but it wasn't until September 1808 that John Colter dropped over the Continental Divide for a white man's first look at Yellowstone Park (which he named "Colter's Hell") into the Teton Basin and scored a double by being the first white man to lay eyes on the fertile valley of the Upper Snake River.

In 1810 Major Andrew Henry established the rendezvous of Fort Henry, a few miles down the Snake River from the falls of St. Anthony. The Redman's name for the water course was Pohogava, or Sagebrush River. Early settlers opined that inasmuch as it was as crooked as a snake track and home of the Snake (Shoshone) Indians, the Snake River it should be.

Although Captain Bonneville had made some sketches, maps and notes of the territory in 1832 it continued to be the domain of the fur trappers and mountain men who traded with the Indians from their trading centers at Market Lake, Pierre's Hole and Fort Henry. Many fortunes were made in furs through this area until the silkworm challenged the beaver for the high hat market.

The first colonization in this area (or any part of Idaho) was established on the Lemhi River near the present site of Tendoy by a colony of Mormons from Salt Lake in 1855. This outpost was maintained for three years through the protection of adobe walls three feet thick and nine feet high which resisted the sporadic attacks of the Bannocks and Blackfeet.

In 1863 when a brisk traffic to the goldfields of the "Grasshopper Diggin's" in Montana showed no signs of abating, a reformed gold-seeker named Mat Taylor left Missouri, outgrew Denver and decided to make his pile by building and operating a toll bridge across the Snake at what is now Idaho Falls.

In 1880 the terminal of the Utah-Northern Railroad Company was built to the Snake River Junction, then known as Eagle Rock, and the age of progress had overtaken and vanquished the pioneer era.

It was in the succeeding decade that the far-sighted settlers foresaw the value of the Snake River as the primary artery of Idaho and from this time on the life-blood of the stream has been, tapped throughout the upper Snake River Valley.❧

Another invention, the rotary snow plow, kept trains running in deep and drifting snow throughout the Rockies.

roared across North Idaho. The Bonneville Flood emptied Lake Bonneville and scoured the Snake River Canyons. But those floods happened thousands of years ago, before there were people here to watch them. The Teton Flood happened when thousands were living in the Upper Snake River Valley and it's a wonder so few were killed.

Construction on the Teton Dam was almost completed when two leaks were reported on a Saturday morning. Before noon, the dam gave way. Eighty billion gallons of water broke through and devastated Wilford, Sugar City, Rexburg, Idaho Falls, Shelley and Blackfoot, forcing 25,000 people from their homes, drowning 18,000 stock animals and causing nearly one billion dollars in damage.

"AGENTS" VANDERBURGH AND DRIPS

The American Fur Company, under John Jacob Aster was new to the game of "find and skin the beaver," so who did such an infant company choose to be its mentors? None other than the experienced trappers of the Rocky Mountain Fur Company - much to the later's infinite vexation.

W.H. Vanderburgh, Andrew Drips and, on occasion, Lucien Fontenelle were sent into the Rockies to find the trapping location of the competitors. Vanderburgh and Drips, in particular, got caught up in the sport. They relentlessly followed such experts as Tom Fitzpatrick, Milton Sublette, Henry Fraeb, Jean Baptiste Gervais and Jim Bridger.

It seemed that each time these men of The Rocky Mountain Fur Company went to their favorite beaver haunts, they'd find Astor's spies hot on their trail. To add to their mortification, Vanderburgh and Drips were seen hanging around Pierre's Hole waiting for the rendezvous so that they could sell packs of beaver pelts pirated from the ponds once trapped solely by the Rocky Mountain crew .

At the 1832 rendezvous, an offer was made to divide the trapping territory with these devious members of Aster's company. Vanderburgh and Drips declined.

So when again the newcomers showed up in a favored trapping ground on Jefferson Fork, Tom Fitzpatrick and Jim Bridger reached the end of their rope. They resolved to lead their tormentors on a chase which would put an end to their exasperating methods. Fitzpatrick and Bridger plunged into the heart of Blackfoot country with Vanderburgh and Drips hot on their trail. Sure enough, the Blackfeet rallied to the occasion, slaying Vanderburgh.

Jim Bridger was also attacked and carried an arrowhead in his back for two years - a constant reminder of the escapade.

FORT HENRY

During the spring of 1810, Andrew Henry and his men built a fort on the Three Forks of the Missouri. However, a little over a month later the fort came under attack. Eight trappers lost their lives fighting the territorial Blackfeet. Many other were seriously wounded.

Knowing that the attacks would continue, Henry abandoned the fort. He and his company ascended the Madison River, crossed the Continental Divide and came upon a lake (Henry's Lake). The group continued on until they found a well-watered district with numerous tributaries. Here he erected a fort (in the vicinity of the present city of St. Anthony). Three log houses were built to serve as temporary winter quarters for his men.

The area seemed ideal for such a post. There was an abundance of game, wood and grass. Streams crisscrossed the area and beaver ponds were common.

The Shoshoni called the area "Egin," meaning cold. Its elevation was 4,600 feet and had heavy snowfall. Below-zero temperatures often persisted for weeks during the winter months. Had Henry known this, his fort would probably been moved seventy miles farther south to the bottomlands by the Portneuf.

Poor planning, said the experts. A bad day, said everyone. But most people rebuilt, without thinking twice. All of Idaho pitched in. By the Wednesday after the flood, semi-trailers were rolling into Eastern Idaho, filled with relief food and clothing from nearly every town in the state.

TELEVISION

Modern television was invented in Idaho! It was invented in 1922 by a young fellow going to school in Rigby. And at that time, there was only one radio station licensed in the whole Mountain West, and none had been licensed in Idaho yet! It wasn't until later in that year, 1922, that Idaho's first radio station, in Boise, was granted it's license.

The name of the inventor was Philo Taylor Farnsworth. Some people think that is a great sounding name for an inventor. And I suppose that if you are going to invent something, you might as well invent something big like TV, but I think he must have been very bored in Rigby to invent something like television!

What he did was to figure out how to make an cathode-ray tube that became the basis for a practical way to utilize images and radio by transmitting them electronically. No matter what you think of television, it's a pretty amazing invention . . and Philo had done it when he was only fourteen years old!

Some of the best duck hunting and trout fishing in North America is at Henry's Fork, while the grand Tetons watch westward from the horizon.

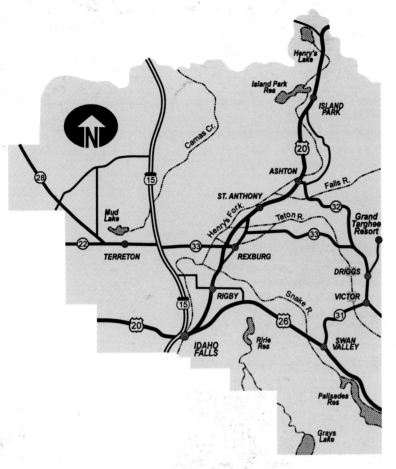

CALENDAR

St. Anthony fishermen's Breakfast, St.Anthony, May: This annual event marks the beginning of fishing season. Many activities follow the free breakfast from 6:00 a.m. to 2:00 p.m. Contact: South Fremont Chamber of Commerce, (208) 624-4455.

Pierre's Playhouse, Victor, June-September: The Teton Valley Players present excellent old fashioned melodrama. Theres also a taste of Pierre's famous Dutch Oven chicken dinners. Contact: Pierre's Playhouse, (208) 787-2249.

Teton Valley Hot Air Balloon Races, Driggs, July 1-3: A festival which features 30-40 hot air balloons in a race overlooking the Grand Teton Mountain Range. Contact: Grand Targhee Resort, (800) 443-8146.

Idaho Falls Snake River Settlers, Idaho Falls, July 4: A day Filled with exciting activities: Start out with the July 4 parade, then step back in time at the Snake River Settlers activities at Tautphaus Park. Fireworks explode at dusk and is the perfect ending to a perfect day. Contact: Idaho Falls Chamber of Commerce, (800) 634-3246.

River Park Festival, Idaho Falls, last weekend in July: Arts and crafts displays and the third-annual Great Snake River Greenbelt Duck Race. Contact: (800) 634-3246.

Idaho International Folk Dance Festival, Rexburg, July 29-August 5: A spectacular cultural event that features dance troupes from around the world. Contact: Rexburg Chamber of Commerce, (208) 356-5700.

Bluegrass festival, Driggs, mid-August: Chairlift rides to a spectacular view of the Grand Teton Mountain Range and top name musical talent highlight this three-day event at Grand Targhee Resort. Contact: Grand Targhee Resort, (800) TARGHEE.

TIPS: FOOD & SHELTER

The South Fork Lodge in Swan Valley is on the Snake, and the **Swan Valley B&B** offers a full continental breakfast, has a hot tub, barbecue area, and other extras.

The North Highway Cafe in Idaho Falls boasts prime rib that customers drive miles for. **The Sandpiper** and **Jaker's** are also found here for their usual good beef, seafood, and salad bar offerings.

The Pine Inn's chef in Victor draws loyal customers from Jackson Hole, Wyoming, and is a must stop for anyone going or coming to Grand Targee.

Central Idaho
Region 7

N
W E
S

93 GIBBONSVILLE
CHIEF JOSEPH
SHOUP
NORTH FORK
MONTANA
SALMON
TENDOY
MIDDLE FORK
SALMON RIVER
LEMHI
MT. BORAH
12,662'
MAY

LEWIS AND CLARK
BECOME THE FIRST
WHITE PEOPLE TO
ENTER IDAHO WHEN
THEY PASS OVER THE
LEMHI PASS IN
1804.

CHALLIS
PATTERSON

75

Sacajawea with
Lewis and Clark   MT BORAH
RISES TO AN ELEVATION OF
12,662 FT. MAKING IT THE
STATES HIGHEST PEAK

STANLEY
CLAYTON
93
BIG LOST RIVER

28

THE BIG LOST
RIVER DISAPPEARS
UNDERGROUND ONLY
TO READPEAR 150
MILES AWAY AT THE
THOUSAND SPRINGS
OUTLET OF THE
SNAKE RIVER CAN-
YON.

21
REDFISH LAKE
75
MACKAY
LESLIE
DARLINGTON
MOORE
HOWE
LITTLE LOST
RIVER
SUN VALLEY
ARCO
BUTTE CITY

KETCHUM
HAILEY
LITTLE WOOD
RES.
CRATERS
OF THE
MOON
World's
First Nuclear
Plant

FAIRFIELD
BELLEVUE
20
MORMON
RES.
MAGIC
RES.
CAREY

IN 1951 ARCO BECOMES
THE FIRST TOWN IN THE
WORLD TO RECEIVE EN-
ERGY FROM A NUCLEAR
POWER PLANT.

CRATERS OF THE MOON NAT-
IONAL MONUMENT CONTAIN
SOME OF THE MOST INTERESTING GEO-
LOGICAL LANDSCAPES IN IDAHO WITH
ITS VOLCANIC FORMATIONS.

CENTRAL
IDAHO

IN THE 1930'S
RAILROAD EXECUTIVE
AVERELL HARRIMAN
FOUNDS AMERICA'S FIRST
DESTINATION SKI RE-
SORT IN SUN VALLEY
AND IT BECOMES
THE FIRST RESORT IN THE WORLD
TO USE CHAIR LIFTS.

THE CAMAS
PRAIRIE, WHICH
ONCE SERVED AS
A SHORT CUT FOR
WAGON RIDING
PIONEERS
FROM FORT
HALL TO FORT
BOISE, NOW
SERVES AS AN IM-
PORTANT SOURCE OF
ALFALFA, WHEAT, AND
BARLEY.

Chapter VIII
CENTRAL IDAHO
Region 3

from:
ON GOING BACK TO SAWTOOTH VALLEY
by John Rember

L ast year I cashed out of the ski resort of Sun Valley, Idaho, and came back to my family's place in the Sawtooth Valley to build a house. I did so out of deep instinct - the same 40 acres that has sustained our tiny herd of horses every summer for 35 years has sustained for me, summer and winter, a vision of a right place in the world, a place I belonged, where I could get up in the morning, step out the door and catch dinner from the Salmon river. Or simply step out

to watch the sunrise light up the Sawtooths above dark foothills. And then - depending on my horoscope in a week-old *Idaho Statesman* or the shape of the morning's clouds - I could fix the avalanche holes in the fences, cut firewood, change the water on the pasture, plant trees, or just do more fishing.

It was a vision of a place of healing, of life not alienated from its roots. I think now it was engendered by memories of our horses, brought up from winter pasture every June, whinnying and bucking around the fence lines, biting into the spring grass, running full-gallop through the shallow water on flooded river-islands, home at last. Such memories become metaphors, and metaphors become compelling calls to action, at age 37.

Tall Central Idaho roofs the state with snowy gables. And although it is the toughest part of Idaho to travel through, it is also one of the easiest to love. It is here on its own terms — mostly vertical, often mystical — and its invigorating beauty is too big to stay mad at. Climb a mountain, take a deep breath, then try to count to ten. This cleanest air in the U.S. is also some of the thinnest. It makes you dizzy and happy, as though you've climbed into heaven.

Just like getting into heaven, Central Idaho presents a big challenge. And that challenge is often accepted, albeit not always met. Central Idaho is where Lewis and Clark first stepped into the Pacific Northwest. They found it too tough to traverse and almost too tough to describe. When William Clark remarked that these

So when I found myself in the unexpected condition of being able to come home, I did. The house is finished now, and I'm sitting at my desk, warm and comfortable, the nearby cold of a Sawtooth Valley spring held harmless by thermopane windows and six inches of

Papa Hemingway helped make the resort of Sun Valley famous, and both his family lineage and literary heritage remain present in his beloved Wood River Valley.

fiberglass. If I look up from my computer screen, I can see grim towers of stone, blue-grey and white, their ragged edges smoothed here and there by thick drifts of snow. The willows in the river bottom are skeletal and frosted, but every bit as beautiful as they will be when the horses hide in them to escape the flies and - for maybe three days in late July - the heat. At least once a day these days, I'm out wandering the fence lines, or sitting on the melted-off river bank watching the fly-overs of returning geese, or skiing the hill behind the house, or running to the mailbox when I hear the mailman accelerating towards his next target, my neighbor's

mailbox a mile up the road. Home at last. Home at last. Thank God Almighty, home at last.

But it isn't home. I'm finding that what once was familiar is unfamiliar, what once was real is no longer real. Everything may look the same to the horses this spring, but things are more surface than substance to me, and the house I've built has not freed me from the indenture of memory.

Last fall the power crew spent a few days digging trenches and driving a pipe under the highway in order to run power underground from the pole on the other side of the road to the house. There are no wires in the air outside the windows.

The Forest Service wanted it that way. That agency is charged with maintaining the pastoral values of Sawtooth Valley as part of its larger mission of overseeing the Sawtooth National Recreation Area, a central Idaho enclave of fun that includes the Sawtooth, White Cloud, and Boulder Mountain Ranges, and the small patches of flat ground between them. Forest Service agents were authorized to purchase land and easements on land under the act that established the SNRA, and while my family was lucky enough to be allowed to stay, the Forest Service tells us what structure we may build and where they may be placed. It wanted the wires buried.

I wanted them buried too. A wire running into a house looks ugly to me, as do the strung-together lines of great steel crucifixes stretching across formerly pagan western deserts. They are associated, for me, with the wires that run above, say, any of the intra- Boise strip cities, wires that power neon signs, the flash-fryers of franchise restaurants, the glittery lights of automobile show-rooms, and the hundred hanging ceiling

weren't like any mountains he had seen, he quoted a local Shoshone Indian, who said that here the country rose "like the Side of a tree Straight up."

Central Idaho offers wild lands, ranch lands, badlands, and a play land for the rich. It is rich in minerals, and it serves as a recreational haven for many Idahoans. It is also important environmentally, as the headwaters spawning grounds for ocean-going salmon and steelhead trout and as the new home for wolves recently transplanted from Canada.

Central Idaho has always been best known for its mountains. The jagged Sawtooths, Boulders, Pioneers, White Clouds and several other ranges are mainly granite. They were buoyed up from deep within the

fans of home-care centers. I didn't much want those associations, not here.

But as I was pulling underground cable along the bottom of the trench that lead to the house, I was visited by a memory, one ironic and disturbing. I remembered the summer of 1956, when we watched with something like patriotic awe as the Rural Electrification Administration planted the first power poles in the soil of Sawtooth Valley. I was only five, but I can remember sensing, perhaps for the first time, the great expanding outside nation those poles represented. We had been invited to join it. People outside the valley walls cared about us, we who lived in this most remote place, and were including us in their progress. No longer would we have to use oil lamps for illumination. No longer would our radios run off car batteries. No longer would we be people without power.

The only analogous experience I have had since was watching the now also ironic ending of *Dr. Zhivago*, where the image of the hydro-electric dam clears away messy images of human tragedy and replaces them with clean and impersonal concrete and Soviet light. At age five, in wonder and delight, I switched the newly-wired lights of our little cabin on and off and on again. At five I would not have cared to bury the power lines.

The next year a substantial section of the sixty-mile highway between Stanley and Ketchum was paved, including the section in front of our place. This, too, was welcome.

My father was a fishing and hunting guide, and the better road meant more tourists, and more tourists meant better business. People would come to the house at four A.M. for sour-dough pancakes and strong black coffee. After breakfast, my father would take them back through the willows to the river and hook a big fish and hand them the pole, all for $10.00 per person, per day. Always a metaphorical thinker, he didn't guarantee them a fish, just a fish on the line.

In the spring, before the salmon runs, he and his clients would fish in the inlets of Redfish Lake for bulltrout, and I can remember days when a limit of trout, spread out on the grass at home for a photo opportunity, weighed more than a limit of salmon.

"Once you have entered the world of mountains, you will look forward with joy to each successive return, as one looks forward to a return home. For you return to a clean, simple world, in which the race was born and your ancestors grew to fit and came to love." -Russell Harrison Varian

It was a kind of paradise we lived in. We had electricity, paved roads, a new '56 Ford, and an endless string of professional visitors - doctors, lawyers, CEOS, politicians - who assured us we were living the kind of life they would live if only they could break free from their responsibilities to live it. I took every yearning word they spoke literally, even when the snow drove us out every fall, and we moved over Galena Summit to Wood River, where my mother was a nurse at Sun Valley and where my father drove a ski bus. By winter, our southern freezer was full of venison and elk and the french-bread shapes of salmon, and you only had to look at your plate to realize where you were based, where your sustenance lay. Every May, we returned, over the still frozen Galena, to a valley mirror-bright with water and new willow leaf, noisy with the sounds of returning birds and the roar of rapids.

This world lasted longer than it had any right to. It lasted long enough for me to be raised in it. It lasted, I suppose, from our '56 Ford to our next car, a '65 Ford.

SAWTOOTH NATIONAL RECREATION AREA

The 756,000 acre National Recreation Area is part of the publicly-owned Sawtooth National Forest. It is managed by the Forest Service, part of the U.S. Department of Agriculture. The Sawtooth NRA is one of the largest and most magnificent National Recreation Areas in the United States. Four mountain ranges, the Sawtooths, Boulders, White Clouds and Smokys provide scenic landscapes every direction, with 40 peaks 10,000 feet or higher. There are more than 300 high mountain lakes here, as well as the headwaters of four of Idaho's major rivers, the Salmon, Payette, Boise, and Big Wood. Summer and fall activities within the Sawtooth NRA include fishing, hiking, camping, horseback riding, picnicking, mountain climbing, nature trails wildlife viewing, interpretive programs, mountain biking, motor-biking, hunting, off-road vehicle travel, bird watching, airplane tours, llama trekking, lake canoeing, swimming, kayaking, waterskiing, and whitewater rafting. During the winter and spring, popular activities are cross-country skiing, sledding, snow-mobile snowshoeing, ice skating, steelhead fishing and winter camping. The Sawtooth NRA was established by Congress in 1972. These lands were set aside ". . . in order to assure the preservation and protection of the natural, scenic, historic, pastoral and fish and wildlife values and to provide for the enhancement of the recreational values associated therewith . . ." At the same time, the 217,000 acre Sawtooth Primitive Area was designated as the Sawtooth Wilderness Area.

YOUR OWN PRIVATE IDAHO

Excellent skiing, No Lift Lines, Await The Sun Valley Visitor
by Rick Sylvain

Ketchum, Idaho - In the Marlboro fog of the-Dyn-o-Mite Lounge, the Accelerators are doing a bluesy set for the Friday night crowd. "Anybody ski Sun Valley today?" asks the very recognizable lead singer. Dressed in black wool cap, black shades, tank-top undershirt and black Levi's, Bruce Willis is one bad blues brother.

"YEAH!" roars the crowd.

"Or did you just cocktail all day?"

A louder "YEAH!"

Maybe answer No. 2 is closer to the truth.

Must be, because Sun Valley skiing is so un-crowded all these people have to be some place.

Sun Valley's Bald Mountain boasts no lift lines, an easy pace and some of the best, most challenging skiing there is.

And talk about secluded. It may be America's most famous ski resort you can't get to.

No wonder celebrities have gravitated here since the 1930s, when railroad tycoon W. Averell Harriman opened his little vacation retreat in the wilds of Idaho.

Roughing it in luxury was Harriman's dream.

With boutiques and galleries and multi-million-dollar homes, Sun Valley is upscale, all right. But nowhere else do the well-heeled and the merely heeled commingle better.

earth, beginning about 90 million years ago. Because the Atlanta Batholith is older and more eroded, its colors are mainly grays, whereas freshly broken Sawtooth Batholith granites are often pink.

The Challis Volcanics of about 50 million years ago produced many of the multi-colored mountains found in Central Idaho, with their beiges, yellows and pinks. But regardless of color, all the mountains offer art. Here are a myriad peaks, each with its high lakes. Every mountain's face seems to reflect in its own mirror.

In the east, the Lost Rivers, the Lemhis and the Bitterroot ranges form Idaho's rocky "walls." They were formed when the whole of the Rocky Mountains were rising Crustal slabs were forced upon other crustal

Willis owns Dyn-o-Mite in Ketchum and is building another club 10 miles south in Hailey where he and his wife, actress Demi Moore, live.

When he's not watching the kids you might catch Willis wailing on his harmonica at Dyn-o-Mite. Or Arnold Schwarzenegger tooling around in his bright green Hummer. Or Brooke Shields shopping at Atkinsons Market.

In Sun Valley, celebs are "just folks." Have been since those gossamer days when Gary Cooper, Clark Gable, Ginger Rogers and Claudette Colbert made Sun Valley their playground and Ernest Hemingway took himself a room at the Sun Valley Lodge to finish a little tome called "For Whom the Bell Tolls."

Just folks.

At 2,054 skiable acres and 78 runs, Baldy is big mountain skiing. Diverse. Demanding. The timid need not apply (beginning and beginner/ intermediate skiers have their own peak in nearby Dollar Mountain).

Take Warm Springs. This intermediate run free falls 3,400 feet down Baldy in the same unrelenting pitch. Or Limelight - mean and moguled, steep and deep. When fresh snow blankets this expert run, powder hounds are in their glory. With a little pluck, intermediates can tackle the green (easier) and blue (more difficult) runs on Baldy. Just know that about all the greens and blues here and back home have in common is color.

It's tougher out here.

From Warm Springs, a handsome day lodge at the base, Greyhawk chair speeds skiers to Warm Springs' midsection. If you can ski Mid and Lower Springs back down to Warm Springs Lodge, you're ready to go big.

Challenger, a high-speed quad, whisks you to loftier heights. From here at Lookout, blast all the way down Warm Springs. Or do College. Like most of Baldy's runs, College is another

nonstop, thigh-burning fall line with little in the way of natural flats for catching a breather. That makes for fewer bottlenecks. It also makes for a lot of stopped skiers and boarders in a lot of places.

Off College, take the turnoff to two sparkling intermediate runs. Flying Squirrel drops

Skiing is a way of life in this part of the world, and Sun Valley has sent a number of Olympians to claim victory and fame. Picabo Street of the Valley's mining town of Triumph was named after Picabo, Idaho.

slabs, at places creating seeming impossibilities, for example where surface rocks are 200 million years older than the rocks below them. Mt. Borah stands as Idaho's highest peak, at 12,662 feet. A frozen remnant of a glacier still clings to its slopes.

Central Idaho is one of two areas in Idaho at highest risk for earthquakes. The Borah Peak earthquake of 1973 was one of the biggest in North America in the last quarter century. Shaking at 7.3 on the Richter scale, it rolled a 50-ton boulder through Challis, collapsed several buildings, and caused the deaths of two children walking to school.

All this geology has produced great tons of rich mining ore. More tons of molybdenum and other ores

The Sun Valley Lodge and ski area were built in 1937 by Averill Harriman and his Union Pacific Railroad. It stands alone as the grand lady of America's ski reports.

of upper mountain "green" runs they can ski all day. Southern Comfort, Byron's Park and the rest lie just below Seattle Ridge Lodge, an elegant log-and-granite structure with godlike vistas of the towering Sawtooth Mountains.

Typical of all Sun Valley, the log lodge is classy without being pretentious. More hunting lodge than country club in feel. Yellowstone-cozy.

The fireplace dining area is thickly carpeted and the menu caters to discriminating tastes. Breathless skiers order fresh Salmon Normandy, prime rib, swordfish, a $7.50 hamburger. Even the Idaho baked potato comes topped with St. Jacques sauce.

Now, paying top prices on a mountaintop can wreck a budget for a family of four. But this is Sun Valley. "Budget" is not in the vernacular.

When River Run base lodge fully opens next season to join Seattle Ridge and Warm Springs, Baldy will have its tiara of classy new day lodges complete. At 59, Sun Valley is as fresh-faced as in 1936, when Harriman opened Sun Valley Lodge.

steadily to Picabo's Street, named for Sun Valley's home-town Olympics hero. From there it's a straight drop home to Warm Springs Lodge.

Up on Bald Mountain's 9,150-foot summit, advanced intermediates and experts can drop off the ridge for bowl skiing that - when fresh powder has fallen - some skiers rate the best in the West after Vail. Bowls feed to the Roundhouse area midmountain where the truly intrepid can ski Exhibition, a no-guts-no-glory bump run, among Baldy's most challenging.

Less advanced skiers staying up top on the ridgeline can take Broadway down to a six-pack

---

await rising prices. In the late 1800s, gold, silver and lead made millionaires of some boomers. Greed for the same made dead men of others.

Two songs of the times reflect the Idaho of that era. The first reveals how Idaho was perceived by those rushing in:

They say there's a land where crystal waters flow
O'er beds of quartz and purest gold,
Way out in Idaho.

Snowmaking and grooming is art at Sun Valley, a good thing because Mother Nature has been a little stingy this season. Early-season dumpings laid down a good base but much of the rest had been shot from guns until a snowstorm Jan. 7.

Falling flakes blanketed the pines and cottonwoods that day. Slopes got buried in snow - a boon to powder skiers but frightful hard work for the rest of us who, between the hard pack and ski-sculpted drifts, stalled.

A lot.

Fortunately, there's plenty of off-slope diversion. Like shopping, lunching or just sauntering around the old ore mining town of Ketchum. Like hanging out in Sun Valley, at the Sun Valley Lodge and feeling the Tinsel-town history. Like sleigh rides and ice skating and hot tubs in the open air. Like feeling the magic Averell Harriman felt when he opened his little ski mountain - conveniently near his rail line.

For its celebrity roots, Sun Valley isn't the gold lame, in-your-face pretentiousness of some marquee resorts. Heck, banks give out dog biscuits to canines visiting with their owners.

"Sun Valley is good for the soul," said Californian Andre Deklaver, soaking in the heated pool outside Sun Valley Lodge with his wife, Tone. "One of the most wonderful vacations I've experienced."

There are plenty of Bogner ski suits, to be sure. But Sun Valley isn't Aspen, or so comedian Mike Murphy tells the apres-ski crowd at the Ram Bar. "Everybody in Aspen looks the same, high cheekbones and no pores. If you know anybody like that moving here, shoot 'em." ⋙

GOING BACK TO YELLOW JACKET

by William Studebaker

This country is made up of streams and mountains. All except the streams are set up on edge, causing a traveler to go over two sides of it instead of one.
-Colonel E. F. Bernard, 1879

Colonel Bernard, riding into central Idaho from the plains and plateaus, was impressed by the steepness of the mountains. I, driving out of central Idaho and away from the mountains, was impressed by the flatness of the plains and plateaus. The flatland had a strange effect upon my vocabulary. I began to use words like *over, across, beyond,* and *distant.* Where before *up, down, here,* and *close* were adequate. At Yellow Jacket nothing was far away. I could see everything, and if I couldn't, it didn't concern me.

Off and on between 1948 and 1956, I lived at the "Jacket." The Jacket consisted of a campsite at the mouth of Beetle Creek, a ranger station, a small ranch, and a ghost town. What they shared was a creek, Yellow Jacket Creek, that "headed" not far above its confluence with Beetle Creek. My father worked for the Forest Service, and Yellow Jacket Creek was his inland corridor from the Salmon country to the Middle Fork of the Salmon River.

Now, when I go back, I am overwhelmed by the steepness of the hillsides, of the swiftness of the water, of the rugged *gendarmes* jagging out of the slide-rock ridges and breaking the even slide of sedimentary slopes which Doug fir cluster around. I am impressed by the narrowness of the V-shaped valley. Its walls are close, and I wonder at the red-tailed hawk, curving flight

---

The second shows how Idaho was seen as a new start for anyone, be he angel or devil:

Oh, what was your name in the states?
Was it Johnson or Thompson or Bates?
Did you murder your wife or flee for your life?
Say, what was your name in the states?

feathers up, one at a time, just to pull around and swing over me. Down inside the earth like this, I use all of my vision - all 360 degrees. There is just a slit of sky, maybe 20 degrees. The rest of space is occupied by wilderness.

Wilderness now. Again. But once this valley supported a boomtown. The abandoned buildings are strung out across a small and rare alluvial. The town began in 1869, flourished in 1876, again in 1896, and again in 1922, folding finally in 1924. The townsite developed like a gopher colony - people dug in here and there with an odd flare for neighborliness. An old neighbor myself I rummage through the buildings, not as a kid looking for something to pocket but as an adult searching for the loose ends of childhood: odors, places I stood, words

my parents hung in the air, slowness I possessed when my brother and sister left me to scout out the old five-story bunkhouse or mill.

I think of father and his few cronies talking about the "red-light district" just across the creek, and I imagine drunken miners staggering back: some of them making it, a few falling into the cold roar of twisted water beneath the pole bridge. Then I flush, remembering my mother, and wonder what she thought of such talk and of such men.

At night men of such ragtag repute must have spent many cold hours stiffening, their muscles unable to quit work and rest from the drilling, boring, and shoveling that made the tunnels high up on the hillside. They came here to get the gold out and out it came by the millions before the bust that buried some and broke others. Now it's all bust, broken, and pummeled. The days are silent, except for the creek's choleric drone. But the nights are curious. If there is a moon, it passes quickly filling the valley with a translucent, slate-gray illumination. There is no electricity, no lights other than fire. A small boy, riding through here on a horse, could imagine the fretful hush of slumbering men, of exhausted woman. He could rein his horse through the tangle of log cabins, pass the bunkhouse, round the mill, and saunter into the darkness of the narrow valley

As I scan the area, loading up on images of a place where I can't stay, I feel as though I have been "ghosted," as though my spirit has left my body to frolic on its own. Preparing to leave, I endeavor to compose myself. I think of the house I built in the middle of a distant plain, a place so flat not even the corpses in the cemetery will lie still long enough for me to explain why my house is so far from home. ✍

Today, Challis and Salmon still depend on mining, but most of the little mining towns have died. The ghost towns of Custer and Bonanza in the "Land of the Yankee Fork" still give a good notion of what it was all like. The Yankee Fork gold dredge is a rusty and weathered monument to hard work and hard times. Remember that early Idaho towns often looked almost this old as soon as they were built out of unpainted timbers and iron.

The very name Yankee Fork carries history all by itself. Much of the big Idaho gold rushes occurred during the Civil War, and the rushers came from both North and South. The Southerners were generally the loudest sympathizers; the Unionists quietly marked their time. Civil War place names in Idaho include their

INCIDENT AT LEADORE

by Ron McFarland

The town of Leadore, about fifty miles south of Salmon and eighteen from Lemhi, might be described as a gap in the fences. What is it about a town (population 114 in this case) that makes you look twice or that stops you dead in your tracks and causes you to make the utterly irrational decision to eat breakfast there? And even before you think about stopping, your mind is spinning. You're taking temporary possession of the place, or perhaps it is taking possession of you, and in a way you will always belong to it, even though you've never really lived there. It becomes what the late Washington / Montana poet Richard Hugo called a "triggering town." Your imagination knows there is something here in all this apparent nothing. What the eyes fail to see, the imagination will provide.

The large, fairly new school gives you a certain feeling of confidence. It is flanked on one side by an almost equally large and even newer Church of Jesus Christ of the Latter-Day Saints and on the other side by a very small white frame church that seems deserted. In front of the school lies an empty lot with about a dozen humps of dirt, what looks like a bad dream of a baseball diamond. Irrigation pipes lie all around watering hay out of the Lemhi, which drops down here from the mountains, but not much water is spent on Leadore, which is largely given over to sagebrush. Small, square houses squat under the sun along with trailers (nothing here as impressive as a "mobile home" so far as I can see), and in the winter, the imagination whispers, they all shrink in the bitter cold and snow.

Leadore possesses two Main Streets. The new one runs along the highway and is dominated by the two-story, red, galvanized steel-sided Leadore General Store. The old one meets it on the perpendicular and consists of a half dozen deserted stores, including the former post office and McRea's Grocery. These have the old high, false frames, paint flaking away, windows revealing emptiness, a city waiting for an excuse to go up in flames. And as if in response to that threat, a forties vintage fire engine sits fading and rusting in the intense glare of the late morning sun.

Nostalgia yields, however, to the present demands of the stomach. In Leadore the choice is simple: either the Sagebrush Saloon or the Silver Dollar Bar, both equally unimposing from the outside. Both claim to double as cafes. For no reason I can think of, I opt for the Silver Dollar, which turns out well. On another day, visiting this very temporary hometown, I'll try the Sagebrush.

The picturesque historic town of Hailey produced poet and writer Ezra Pound, and used to house miners, ore wagons, and horses. Today the county seat hosts a rodeo, popular nite spots, and hollywood actors.

Dixie, Leesburg and Atlanta. The Secesh River was named for the Secessionists who mined there.

Mining created most of the early towns in Central Idaho. Hailey, especially, became a prosperous berg. Hailey had the first telephone service and electric lights in Idaho. The Oregon Short Line railroad arrived in 1883. Hailey now caters more to tourists and "second-homers," like its Wood River neighbor, Ketchum, just to the north.

As late as the 1930s, Ketchum was hardly a village. Indeed, it barely clung to one side of the road. Then, in 1936, the Union Pacific Railroad sent Austrian Count Felix Schaffgotsch to search its vast rail area for a site to establish the first European ski resort in the U.S. The Count loved Bald Mountain. Union Pacific named

The little town of Mackay anchors the magnificent Lost River Valley.

NO. 12. MAIN STREET, MACKAY, IDAHO.

"When're you leaving?" the old man's wife asks.

"Next week," the waitress says.

"Going to Alaska," she tells me, to work on a ferry. She was up there for a couple years after high school and loved it. They'll live in a town about twenty miles from Anchorage. She pours everyone another round of coffee.

The fact that she can hardly wait to get out of Leadore saddens me. I see no future for the town that I seem to have adopted in some odd fashion, and I struggle against a rising tide of nostalgia. Yet what could there be for her and her husband here? I try to imagine the two of them living in Alaska. Maybe he gets a place on a salmon fishing boat, or mayhe he makes big money working for Exxon. Maybe he starts to drink too much, begins to abuse her. They split up and she comes back to Leadore. I shake this story from my head as she pours me another cup of coffee and asks how I liked my breakfast. "Julie," an old man calls from the counter. I suppose he's been there all along, but he just now makes his way into my consciousness.

"The usual, Dad?"

Her father? A little elderly, but quite possible.

"I don't know. Let me think." He seems melancholy, no doubt bothered by this talk of his daughter's departure, probably a bit offended by her cheerfulness.

"He always has one egg over easy and one pancake," she announces.

The cook comes out. She could be Julie's sister, a few years older and several pounds heavier. A young man in shorts and wearing a Tigers baseball cap comes in with some invoices for her to sign. Then an attractive girl in bright blue shorts and a T-shirt that reads "Alive with pleasure!-Newport-." The demographics are changing before my eyes. It's a youth movement. "Washer's broke down," she says happily as she slaps a small stack of towels and aprons on the counter. "Hope this'll do ya."

"Should," says Julie. "Who's with Billy today?"

"Tanya."

"She's nice. You and Rob going up to Salmon tonight?"

"Went last night. Nothing going on."

I get up and head for the cash register, still feeling, but vaguely, a part of the life of Leadore. Life is a long conversation, some philosopher said, and the dialogues of Leadore are resuming as if I had never tried to impose myself on the place. It leaves me feeling a little melancholy.

"How was your breakfast?" thc cook asks pleasantly.

"Great," I say, "just fine."

"Glad I did *something* right today," she says. "Yeah. I heard about the eggs."

"How'd you hear about that?"

"News travels fast in a small town," I say. We laugh.

And that's Leadore. We part amicably, another loose end raveling somewhere among the sagebrush. ᔐ

---

their venture Sun Valley. And the place is still making history.

Bald Mountain is one of the best ski mountains in the world, featuring dry Idaho powder snows, high-speed quad lifts, and exhilarating, challenging runs. Even the man- made snow — used to ensure late autumn openings — is among the world's best. And of course below Baldy lies picturesque Ketchum with its classic view back up at Baldy. They combine to create an alpine-and-urban version of a mutual admiration society.

The admiration is deserved. And many are moving in to join in the marveling. They are building the fine homes that make the Wood River Valley the highest priced real estate in Idaho. Architecturally, "Sun Valley"

CRATERS OF THE MOON

It seem like in the early days people kept moving places around or changing the names. When the emigrants traveled the Goodale Cutoff on the Oregon Trail they were traveling what had been originally called Jeffery's Cutoff. As they crossed the Little Lost River they went across what the mountain men had called the John Day River. But now the John Day River is in Oregon, and Idaho has the Little Lost River, and the Lost River that used to be called Godins River. I don't know where Godins River went. As the emigrants traveled south from Root Hog, later renamed Arco for a visiting count from Europe, they passed the incredibly tortured landscape of what became Craters of the Moon National Monument. The emigrants didn't call the miles and miles of the black lava flows "Craters of the Moon". They called the area "Devils Vomit". Well, It's probably a good thing that they changed that name, so Idaho isn't known for Devils Vomit National Monument.

THE ROOF OF IDAHO

By: Greg Koller

It's the highest point for hundreds of miles around. Below stretches a domain of smaller mountains, farms and ranches, narrow canyons, natural wetlands, and a powerful river that later disappears into the southern Idaho desert floor.

Antelope, deer, elk, hawks, cougars, and bobcats play and hunt at its base; forests of spruce, Douglas fir, and white bark pine cover its flanks. But despite its splendor, Idaho's Mt. Borah is a virtual stranger in its own land.

Although neighboring states Washington and Oregon have turned high points Mt. Rainier and Mt. Hood into popular symbols of their respective states, Mt. Borah, sometimes called Borah Peak, is not widely associated with Idaho. And, while many Washingtonians and Oregonians are intimately familiar with and even boastful of their highest peaks, only the most avid climbers can easily recognize Idaho's 12,662-foot high point.

"It's because Mt. Borah is really one in a series of peaks. It's not distinctly visible from 60 miles away, like those other mountains," explains Keith Tondrick of Boise, former president of the Mountain West Outdoor Club. "It's also

Explorers were not sure what to make of the other world-like "Craters of the Moon" National Monument.

is becoming known as a building style that combines the Northwest's traditional use of logs with the white stucco walls of the Desert Southwest.

Central Idaho's southwest is cowboy country. Cattle and sheep ranches spread across camas prairies and up into high grasslands, to create a perfect remnant of the Old West. Or even of the West before the Old West. The Camas Prairie Centennial Marsh gets so flower-full in spring that it looks like the Garden of Eden.

Close-by to paradise, one can often find a hell. And Central Idaho has its own hell — a hell of a strange and fun place to visit. The Craters of the Moon volcanic region gives the feeling of a frozen inferno. Geologically, it's an infant; some of the lava flows may be less than 300 years old. This place is as weird as

remote, has few glaciers, and isn't in a national park or near the state's premiere hiking spots, which are in the Sawtooth, White Cloud, and Pioneer Mountains."

Mt. Borah is located far from Idaho's population centers and resorts, in the Lost River Range in east central Idaho. Even considering its relative remoteness, surprisingly little has been written about it, and geologists and mountaineers are still learning about the peak. It was only a few years ago that geologists from Idaho State University discovered that, contrary to earlier belief, the mountain actually does have a glacier on its north face.

Until 1929, popular thought had it that 12,078-foot Hyndman Peak (in the Pioneer Mountains near Ketchum) was Idaho's tallest mountain. That year, while Lee Morrison of the US Geological Survey's Sacramento office was mapping an area near Challis, he measured several high points to the east, and found three loftier than Hyndman. Subsequent surveys by the USGS confirmed his findings

The highest of Morrison's peaks was officially unnamed, although a survey team dubbed it Mt. Beauty and a map accompanying a 1917 USGS paper had labeled it, along with some adjacent ridges, "Chilly Mountain." Suggestions for an appropriate title were quickly submitted, including one in honor of Idaho's internationally known statesman, Senator William E. Borah. At that time, Borah was chairman of the Senate Foreign Relations Committee and the most visible and quoted member of Congress. The US Board on Geographic Names approved the new name on December 4, 1929.

Overlooked by Mount Baldy's ski runs, hundred year old buildings of Ketchum have been turned into restaurants, shops, art galleries, and bookstores.

it is wondrous. And it's absolutely stunning. In spring when the flowers bloom from a million cracks in the lavas, one can imagine the beginnings of life on a young earth. In winter when the white snow contrasts the black, one can picture a planet first burned and then frozen.

To the east of the Craters there are rivers that lose themselves into the earth. Their waters re-emerge — perhaps thousands of years later — as the bountiful springs of the Snake River cliffs. To the east of the Lost River country, in what appears desolation, the Idaho National engineering Laboratory employs thousands of people working on energy research projects critical to the nation.

Central to Central Idaho is the Stanley Basin. It is the pastoral calm eye in the veritable hurricane of

LILIES OF THE FIELD
by June Johnson

A sea of blue camas lilies offers magnificent vistas as you travel Highway 20 near Fairfield in the springtime, through one of the sites in Idaho where Indians historically gathered the nutritious camas roots for food. A sense of history, thousands of wildflowers, and the hundreds of birds beginning to raise their young make the Camas Prairie a beautiful and interesting place to visit.

An unusual feature of the prairie in the spring is the huge moving lake formed by snow melt. Up to 35 miles long from east to west and up to 12 miles wide from north to south, the lake ranges from six inches to two feet deep. This large body of water, estimated to cover anywhere from 5,000 to 6,000 acres after a winter of good snowfall, moves slowly across the prairie. This can be especially scenic in the first few weeks of May, before the snow is completely melted off the mountains. There is an excellent area to photograph just south of the small town of Hill City, located to the west of Fairfield on Highway 20.

As time passes, the lake slowly recedes and only a few streams, ditches and potholes remain filled with water. It is estimated that by mid-June only 100 acres of permanent water remain. In

The forks of the River of No Return – the Salmon. Salmon run up it, whitewater rafters run down it.

May and June, acres and acres of beautiful purplish-blue camas lilies pop up. From a distance it looks as if the lake is still there. The lilies in full bloom are such a spectacular sight that it is hard to do them justice through description. It is well worth a drive in June to experience the area for yourself.

Wildlife abounds in this lush setting. The prairie is a refuge and breeding ground for many different birds, as well as home to countless mammals. The stately sandhill cranes can be seen tossing a stick to their mates as they dance in their mating ritual, which commences at the beginning of spring. Other birds present on the prairie are willets and yellow-headed black birds; swallows on fence posts; and ducks, geese,

mountains. Hudson's Bay explorer Alexander Ross once thought this basin was so remote that he didn't have to post a sentry at night (He should have.). The town of Stanley now stands as an outpost in the wilderness. Folks are as warm as the nights are cold, often the coldest in the United States.

Central Idaho's northeastern portion is mainly basin and range: spring-fed grassy basins edged by towering mountain walls, wonderful ranch lands and far-fabled hunting lands for deer, antelope and elk. Both Challis and Salmon are famous as headquarters for backcountry outfitters and guides. Salmon is the jump off spot for the many vacationers who float the Salmon River.

Central Idaho's northwestern flank is a pristine wilderness, the rocky and riverine spirit heart of Idaho.

snipes, phalaropes and advocets in the waterways. Sandhill cranes and curlews inhabit the upland areas. The unusual warbling whoop of the sandhill crane and the honking of Canadian geese greet visitors as they emerge from their vehicles to admire or photograph the abundant wildlife and spectacular scenery. The Idaho Department of Fish and Game is trying to make the area, recently named the Camas Prairie Centennial Marsh, even more attractive to wildlife.

The Camas Prairie is rich with Indian history. Bands of Bannock Indians would camp on the prairie from June to September to dig and cook the camas lily bulbs, which taste sweet after baking. The large bulbs were carried to camp, cleaned, and then cooked in earthen ovens. A pit was built in the ground to heat rocks. The camas bulbs were put over the rocks between layers of grass, covered with soil and left for days. For winter food, the bulbs were either baked, mashed and shaped into loaves, or boiled and patted into cakes to be dried in the sun. The camas bulbs were the Bannocks' winter food staple. If they didn't prepare enough to eat, they would go hungry that winter.

The Bannock War erupted over the issue of this particular food supply. The Camas Prairie was designated for use by the Bannock Indians in the Treaty of Fort Bridger. When the government failed to prevent white men from working the Camas

Pettit Lake is the one of the more popular recreation lakes of the Stanley Basin.

Prairie valley, the Indians became restless. The stockmen were beginning to take it over. In May 1878, when the Bannocks went into the area to harvest their camas roots, they found a band of hogs digging up the bulbs, and cattle and horses grazing. The Indians left the site and retaliated by raiding King Hill and Glenn's Ferry, continuing across the Snake River. The Bannocks fought all the way to central Oregon before returning, defeated, to their homeland. After this incident, they were restricted to the Fort Hall reservation in Pocatello.

The Camas Prairie Centennial Marsh is an area that has something to offer almost everyone. It is rich in beauty, wildlife and history.✍

HUNDRED DOLLAR JIM

Unusual among the characters of southern Idaho was Hundred Dollar Jim, an old prospector who for many years lived in the Hailey area. Neither the man's name nor the location of his mine was known. Periodically he came to town and stopped at the general store to buy supplies, and at the Northern Star Casino where he always placed a hundred dollars in gold dust on a number of the roulette wheel. Win or lose, he never wagered twice in the same day. One December, when the snow was deep, it was remembered that Jim had not come to town and a searching party set out to find him and his treasure. They went up Warm Springs creek; and after they had gone a few miles they saw Jim across from them on a mountain flank, drawing a laden sled through the snow. A few minutes later, a thaw loosened the deep snow into a slide and they saw Jim carried downward and buried. So far as is known, he was pitched into Dollar Lake, a very deep body of water, and both Jim and his treasure are still there.✍

Importantly, much of this area is the alpha and omega of the salmon, which swim 600 miles from the Pacific to reproduce and die. They swim past mountain goats, bighorn sheep, moose, deer, elk, bear and wolves — and under the hulls of kayakers and rafters.

Straight as a tree trunk, straight up into heaven soar the Sawtooths, the White Clouds, the Lost Rivers, and innumerable other mountains. Straight up through one's heart rises the spirit of Central Idaho. It needs only to be breathed in to be loved. ✍

DUMARIS AND PLANTE NEVER RETURN

On March 25, 1832, four members of John Work's Hudson's Bay Company expedition undertook a journey down the unexplored Salmon River in search of beaver infested tributaries. The names of the explorers were L. Borsdnt, A. Dumaris, H. Plante and J. Laurin.

The skin canoe was put afloat along a calm stretch of river on a Sunday morning. But before long, it came upon a series of rapids. The small craft filled with water as the four men worked feverishly to maneuver the fragile boat around rocks and boulders jutting out of the frothing river. As soon as it was feasible, the men paddled to shore. It was decided that two would walk the shore and two would man the craft, thus reducing the amount of water taken on while shooting the rapids.

One afternoon the canoe disappeared around the bend with Dumaris and Plante - the two never to be seen again. The two ashore, Borsdnt and Laurin, struggled along the steep canyon goat trails looking for camp the two rivermen were expected to set up. None was found. After an uncomfortable night the two afoot struggled on. Later that morning they found the canoe paddles wedged between some boulders. Further downstream, a scattering of supplies were found.

For days Borsdnt and Laurin struggled along with no food or supplies. Finally some Nez Perce found the half-starved men and took them in.

Four months later the two survivors rejoined Work's expedition with tales of the wild, untamable river. Thus the first trip down Idaho's "River of No Return" went on record.

The Lost River Valley. At the foot of the valley the river disappears into the "sinks", only to reappear as springs into the Snake hundreds of miles Southwest.

ATOMIC POWER DEBUTS IN ARCO

It was a different kind of miracle in the desert. On a quiet Sunday, July 17, 1955, Arco became the first city in the world to be powered by atoms, a key event in the development of the Idaho National Engineering Laboratory.

"One Arco child," reported The Arco Advertiser, "after hearing about the atomic power, wanted to go right home and see if the lights were any brighter and asked his mother if the food would taste any different. (Ed's note: Answer was and is . . .no.)

The event was surrounded by secrecy. But once it was announced, on Aug. 12 at the United Nations Atoms for Peace Conference in Geneva, there were bold predictions about the future of commercial nuclear power.

Not only was there talk of nuclear-powered submarines - which the INEL pioneered - but also of nuclear ships, railroads and airplanes, along with domestic use. The Post-Register of Idaho Falls ran a story headlined "Nuclear Energy Poses Threat to Petroleum," reporting how "anxious" oilmen were about the prospect.

Founded in 1949 as the National Reactor Testing Station, the 892-square-mile federal reservation became the world center of nuclear research in the 1950s. INEL now houses the largest concentration of reactors in the world (52 have operated there), employs 11,000 people, and with a $1 billion annual budget would make the Fortune 500 were it private.

Back in 1955, lighting a town of 1,200 for just over an hour made anything seem possible.

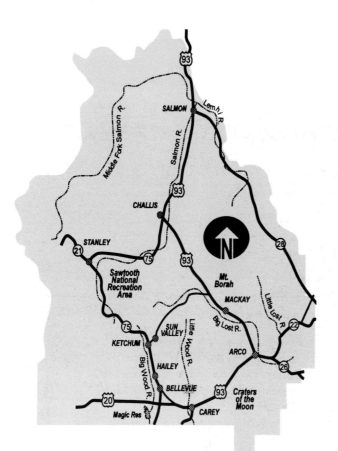

EVENTS

Sun Valley Ice Show, Sun Valley, mid-June through September. The only annual summer outdoor ice show in the United States, featuring world-class Olympic and professional skaters. Contact: (800) 635-8261.

Salmon River Days, Salmon, June 30-July 4. A free breakfast a triathalon, kayak and raft races, an auction, rodeo, parade and a staged bank robbery high-light this five-day event Contact: Salmon Valley Chamber of Commerce, (208) 756-4935.

Sun Valley Music Festival, Sun Valley, July-August. Classical music and jazz performers from all over America are included in this music marathon. Contact: Sun Valley Center for the Arts and Humanities, (208) 726-9491.

Sawtooth Mountain Mamas Arts and Crafts Fair, Stanley, third week-end in July. An annual event in which 80-100 artisans and craftsmen participate. The fun includes old-time fiddlers, a barbecue dinner and a pancake breakfast. Contact:Stanley/Sawtooth Chamber of Commerce, (208) 774-3411.

Salmon Balloon Fest, Salmon, August. Colorful balloons take flight against the beautiful setting of the Central Idaho Rockies. Contact: (208) 756-4935.

Ketchum Wagon Days Celebration, Ketchum, Labor Day weekend. A celebration ot past mining history with the largest non-motorized parade in the West. The fun also features flapjack breakfasts, band concerts and dancers. Contact: Sun Valley/Ketchum Chamber of Commerce, (800) 634-3347.

Swing 'n' Dixie Jazz Jamboree, Sun Valley, mid-October. Featuring twenty-one of the best bands from the United States and Canada, four nights of dancing to the sounds of the Big Band Era and five fun-filled days of ragtime, traditional jazz and swing music. Located at world-famous Sun Valley Resort. Contact: (800) 634-3347.

TIPS: FOOD & SHELTER

The **Pioneer Saloon** has been the most popular prime rib, trout, and baked potato spot in the Sun Valley/ Ketchum area for years. Try the smoked trout and brie appetizer.

Warm Springs Restaurant serves similar fare without the crowds, famous for their honey butter scones, and the **Kneadery** is a world class breakfast spot.

The **Christiana** in Ketchum, now owned by a former Olympic ski coach Michel Rudigo, has tradition and fine continental food.

Desperados has the best mexican food in the area at great prices, but be prepared to wait for a table.

Breakfast in Ketchum has many choices, but Perry's and **Java** are popular. The latter and the **Main Street Book Cafe** serve tasty lite fare with wine or expresso bar offerings. The bookcafe has been written about in national magazines and newspapers for their frequent author readings and poetry slams.

Gurney's in nearby Hailey attracts locals for good standard American food in a pleasant old house atmosphere.

Ernest Hemingway haunts include the Alpine Club (now **Whiskey Jacks**), but the **Casino Club** is still much the same as when Papa held a table there for his friends.

Lodging of every type is available, but the **Sun Valley Lodge** is still a resort in the old European class. **The Duchin Room** in the Lodge still offers light jazz most evenings. The summer outdoor ice shows features most Olympians sooner or later.

Wide selection menu, good food and reasonable prices are the feature at the **Sawtooth Club** next door to the **Book Cafe**.

Chapter IX
IDAHO HISTORY

IDAHO TIMELINE FROM 1805

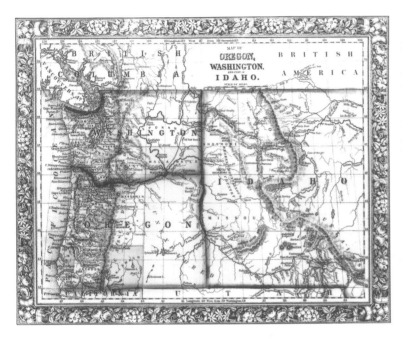

1805   Lewis and Clark discover Idaho at Lemhi pass and cross North Idaho over the Lolo trail.
1809   David Thompson built Idaho's earliest fur trading post-Kullyspell House-on Lake Pend Oreille for the North West Company.
1824   Alexander Ross led the Snake expedition in exploring much of the upper Salmon country, where Jedediah Smith joined him with a band of American trappers. Rivalry between British and American fur hunters continued in Idaho for 14 years.
1832   The great Rocky mountain fur trade rendezvous was held at Pierre's Hole (now known as Teton valley) in July.
1834   Fort Hall and Fort Boise were established as Snake River fur trading centers, but they became important as outposts on the Oregon trail.
1836   Henry Harmon Spalding founded his Nez Perce Indian mission at Lapwai.
1839   Spalding started publishing the Bible in Nez Perce on the earliest printing press in the Pacific Northwest.

History came to Idaho over the continental divide in 1805, when Lewis and Clark entered the Pacific side of their great expedition. That made Idaho the last of the 50 states to be explored by EuroAmericans. Idaho remains unknown to many, today.

Lewis and Clark needed two running starts to effect their transit of Idaho. They first tried going down the canyon of the Main Salmon River, later named by boatmen, "the River of No Return." After seeing the rapids running "with great violence from one rock to another on each side foaming & roaring through rocks in every direction, So as to render the passage of any thing impossible," Lewis and Clark took the local Shoshone Indians' advice. They backtracked into Montana and tried again over Lolo Pass. Until then, they had been following rivers up the long Missouri slope. Now they clung to ridge lines because the canyons were too sheer. Their men began to suffer from hunger and fatigue. When they came upon the Nez Perce Indians an the Clearwater River, they gladly accepted their kindness.

In 1809, David Thompson entered North Idaho from Canada, on a scientific and geographic as well as commercial exploration. He built Kullyspell House, the first log structure in Idaho, near Hope on Lake Pend d'Oreille. The next year, Andrew Henry established the first American fur post west of the divide, on what is now Henry's Fork of the Snake River. In 1811, Nathaniel Wyeth's Astorian expedition first boated, then

1842 The Jesuit Coeur d'Alene Mission of the Sacred Heart was started near Saint Maries. Moved to a site near what now is Cataldo in 1846 (where the old mission church still stands), it now continues at Desmet, where the mission was transferred in 1811.

1846 Idaho, which later became a territory, became part of the United States by a treaty dividing the old Oregon Country with Great Britain.

1849 Over 20,000 emigrants who joined the gold rush came through southeastern Idaho on the California Trail. Heavy traffic on the trail continued for many years.

1854 The Ward Massacre in Boise Valley on the Oregon Trail led to the closing of Fort Boise the next summer and Fort Hall in 1856.

1860 Idaho's oldest town, Franklin, was founded just north of the Utah border, April 14. Gold discoveries at Pierce, September 30, led to the founding of Pierce early in December and to the gold rush in 1861 and 1862.

1863 Idaho territory was established by an act of Congress signed by President Lincoln on March 4. Idaho was organized at Lewiston by Governor William H. Wallace, July 10.

1864 Boise became permanent capital of Idaho, December 24.

1869 Completion of the transcontinental railway at Promentory Summit, Utah, May 10, brought greatly improved transportation to Idaho.

1877 The Nez Perce War broke out in north Idaho in June, with lighting continuing into October in Montana during Chief Joseph's famous retreat.

1878 The Bannock War was started in southern Idaho and moved on into Oregon and back in a summer long campaign.

1880 With discovery of lead-silver lodes around Ketchum, Bellevue, and Hailey, the rush to Wood River transformed south-central Idaho.

1882 Construction of the Northern Pacific across North Idaho commencement of the Oregon Short Line across southern Idaho brought rail service to all parts of the territory.

1884 The Coeur d'Alene stampede, followed by important lead-silver discoveries later in the year, got Idaho's major mining district going in a big way.

1889 In its last session, the territorial legislature located the University of Idaho at Moscow, where it opened in 1892.

1890 Idaho was admitted to the union as a state, July 3.

1891 The College of Idaho opened in Caldwell, October 9.

1892 Martial law commenced in the Coeur d'Alene mines July 14, after the dynamiting of an abandoned mill at Gem.

The University of Idaho opened in Moscow, October 3.

1899 The Coeur d'Alene mine labor war erupted again with the dynamiting of the Bunker Hill and Sullivan concentrator at Wardner, April 29.

---

busted, then blundered their way across southern Idaho, along the course of the Snake River. Idaho still wasn't understood, but at least some of it had been seen.

The fur trappers shared Idaho with the Indians for about thirty years. Much of the state was first explored by these rugged mountain men, who although they spent years alone in the wilderness, have had their names immortalized in history and legend. Donald Mackenzie, Alexander Ross, Jedidiah Smith, Joseph Walker, Jim Bridger, Joe Meek, Peter Ogden, Francois Payette and others all belong to the pantheon of American adventure.

Idaho — then part of Oregon Country — became a commercial battleground between British and U.S. fur interests, with the British trying to "trap out" the Snake River country, so as to create a fur-barren buffer between themselves and the upstart Americans. The British Hudson's Bay Company, a.k.a. "the honorable company," worked hard to run a sensible business operation, maintaining the lonely Idaho outposts of Fort Nez Perce near Lewiston, Fort Boise near Parma, and Fort Hall near Pocatello.

Hudson's Bay's various "Snake expeditions" were big time affairs, often accompanied by wives and children, and bringing in Iroquois Indian trappers from eastern North America. In contrast, the American fur trappers lived lives more like those of the Indians themselves, and gathered at annual rendezvous in Eastern

1901 The Academy of Idaho (now Idaho State University) was established in Pocatello.

1902 After concluding that Diamondfield Jack Davis had been convicted by mistake, in a case growing out of the most notable incident in the Idaho sheep and cattle wars, the State Board of Pardons turned him loose.

1904 With the beginning of irrigation in the Twin Falls country, the city of Twin Falls was started.

1905 Former Governor Frank Steunenberg was assassinated, December 30.

1907 William E. Borah was elected to the United States Senate, where he gained an international reputation during thirty-three years of service.

William D. Haywood, charged with conspiracy and the assassination of Frank Steunenberg, was found not guilty at the end of an internationally celebrated trial.

1910 Idaho's worst forest fire burned over a large tract in the northern part of the state.

1919 Boise's Music Week began.

1920 Whitebird hill grade connecting north and south Idaho was opened.

The State Capitol was completed.

1924 Craters of the Moon National Monument was established.

1931 A large primitive area was established in the mountains of central Idaho.

1932 Boise Junior College was established.

1933 North Idaho Junior College was established in Coeur d'Alene.

1936 Sun Valley was established as a ski resort by the Union Pacific.

Left: A giant red cedar dwarfs more than the lumberjack. Idaho's forests today make the state the most forested in the West.

Heavy snow did little to slow the boom town growth when gold or silver was struck —as this photo of early Wallace attests.

"Tiny"Roy Bowers and his dependable mare Molly.An assistant putting snow-shoes on Molly. Then off over the deep

Idaho, to exchange their pelts for supplies and whisky, and the freshest old news. The British "won," but it really didn't matter. Indian displeasure had increased. High fashion in the East gave up beaver hats for silk, and the bottom fell out of the fur trade.

The Indians got back Idaho for a few short years. Then came the Oregon Trail. U.S.-British competition had been evolving from fancy hats to actual territory. James K. Polk campaigned for the Presidency on the slogan "fifty-four forty or fight." Had we fought — and that latitude been made the border — Idaho's panhandle might have stretched north another 300 miles. But it was the Columbia Basin part of Oregon Country that the U.S. most coveted. The Oregon Trail's great immigration gave it an American population.

The longest stretch of the Oregon Trail looped through southern Idaho. Fort Hall and Fort Boise were the most important resupply stations along the entire route. After seeing much of the West, the immigrants could still marvel at the Silent City of Rocks. They then had to make two memorable crossings of the Snake River, at Three Island Crossing and at Farewell Bend. Several were killed by Indians along the way. Of the thousands who were not, few broke down for long enough to have to settle in Idaho. The immigrants had their sights set on the more tempting and temperate Willamette Valley in western Oregon.

Indian resentment continued to build. The Whitman massacre in 1847 led to the abandonment of the

Stage transportation took people the places trains couldn't go —like up and down the Snake River canyons.

1938 Paving of the north and south highway finally was completed.

1942 Farragut naval training station was established on Lake Pend Oreille, a Pocatello army air base and a Pocatello gun relining plant were established, and a Japanese relocation center was built at Hunt.

1968 Hell's Canyon Dam was completed on the Snake River.

1972 Sunshine Mine disaster.

1976 Teton Dam collapses, Rexburg, Blackfoot and other towns almost destroyed.

1981 Claude Dallas kills two state Fish & Game Wardens.

1982 Dallas arrested, convicted of manslaughter.

1983 Earthquake near Mt. Borah measures 7.3, kills two Challis residents.

1984 Harmon Killebrew of Payette inducted into Baseball's Hall of Fame in Cooperstown.

1986 Claude Dallas escapes from prison, arrested eleven months later in Riverside, California.

Barbara Morgan, a McCall teacher is named by NASA as their Teacher in Space.

1990 Idaho Celebrates its Centennial.

1992 Largest snowmaking system in the world opens at Sun Valley.

1994 Huge forest fire near McCall closes roads.

1994 Picabo Street of Sun Valley takes Olympic silver medal.

1995 Street wins skiing's world cup in the downhill.

1995 Gary Stevens of Boise rides Thunder Gulch to victory at the Kentucky Derby. ✍

Spalding mission at Lapwai among the Nez Perce. In 1854, the Ward party was massacred in the Boise valley. Reprisals against the Indians caused further animosities, and Hudson Bay abandoned Fort Boise and Fort Hall. The Mormon were establishing a farming colony in the Lemhi Valley, but Indian hostility forced them out in 1858.

Gold was what got EuroAmericans to come to Idaho in great numbers, much to the Indians' misfortune. French trappers had already found gold in the North Idaho, but not in exciting quantities. In 1860, E.D. Pierce entered the original Nez Perce reservation, disguised as a trader because prospecting was forbidden on Indian lands. Pierce made the first big gold find at Orofino and after that it was "Katy, bar the door." Unlike most of the U.S., Idaho was not settled from the east. Idaho's settlement was more like a backsplash from the West Coast. Miners flooded in from California, Oregon and elsewhere. They came over land and up the Columbia river, some on a steamboat named "Idaho." A San Francisco reporter wrote, "All Willamette Valley seems to be here. I do not know who will take care of the crops in Oregon. . ."

It was a stampede of high hopes and greedy dreams. An example of the misinformation prevailing in those days is an 1885 encyclopedia entry stating that Florence, near Riggins, was the highest town in America at an elevation of exactly 11,100 feet. By 1862, 10,000 miners had ascended to Florence. Some struck it big;

GHOST TOWNS

Idaho's landscape is dotted with historic places . . . the ghost towns of yesteryear.

Idaho has a rich heritage in these slumbering ghosts of glory. As one walks down shabby, dusty streets, imagination can recapture the past . . . a gun battle over a gambling debt . . . the stage arriving with the mail . . . horses straining to pull the load of ore.

ROCKY BAR

At Dixie, on highway 22, the road to Rocky Bar winds through towering forests, along meandering streams abounding with fish. It is truly a ghost-town of tumbling buildings, rusting machinery, century-old cemeteries.

WARREN

Warren, located 44 miles northeast of McCall might well have been named "gambler's luck." Gold was discovered in the vicinity by gambler James Warren. Here, too, was held one of the west's historic poker games with Polly Bemis - a Chinese slave girl as the "stake." Warren "boomed" a second time during the Thunder Mountain gold rush. The road to this ghost town skirts the beautiful Payette Lakes and crosses the alpine Secesh Meadows.

Yep – not much has changed in Idaho City in a hundred years. Still good food, cold and cheap beer. Lodging's more expensive, but a lot more comfortable...and the locals still talk a better game of pool than they play.

most struck out; some froze to death.

Florence, Orofino, Wallace, Thunder Mountain, Roosevelt, Idaho City, Hailey. These were instant towns. At one time, Idaho City was the largest city in the Pacific Northwest. But few of the gold diggers had intentions of staying on in Idaho. Most claims were worked less than three months, but supporting the miners gave the market towns, like Boise and Hailey, the possibility of permanence.

The shape of Idaho and the sound of its name exemplify the mythic qualities of this state. Idaho's shape — a logger's boot, some say — differs from most other western states in that it has a crooked, topographic border. Most western states' boundaries were drawn with an arbitrary straight edge in smoky rooms in Washington D.C. But Idaho's border with Montana seems to make geographic sense, at least for awhile. From the Yellowstone, it follows the continental divide northwest, until the area of the aptly named Lost Trail Pass (lost, for awhile, by Lewis and Clark). From there, it veers west and follows the main ridge of the Bitterroot Mountains north until the Bitterroots begin to peter out. Then it's a 70-mile straight edge north to the Canadian border.

Some, including John Mullan, who engineered the famed Mullan Road across North Idaho in 1861, have said the boundary surveyors were supposed to have followed the continental divide, but they got off

GOLDEN

Golden is situated 35 miles southeast of Grangeville on state highway 14. In the late 1890's Golden sprang up following the discovery of gold on the South Fork of the Clearwater. Difficulty in transportation hampered extensive developments until 1907, when a trail was cut through the mountain wilderness. Mining was profitable for four decades, then the "bust" came, and Golden dwindled into the shadows of its former glory.

ROCK CREEK

Supply wagons and state-lines to Idaho's gold fields gave birth to Rock Creek, 8 miles south of Hansen (U. S. 30) . In 1864, Rock Creek became a "home" station for the Ben Halliday "Overland" stageline from Kelton, Utah to Boise. The first permanent settlement in Magic Valley, Rock Creek is a roadway bordered by a few old weathered buildings. Faded and shabby, it is gateway to the Magic Mountain year-round recreational area.

CUSTER

The General Custer Mill, seven stories high has fallen in a heap of rubble, but the ghost town remains. Eleven miles from Sunbeam (U.S. 93), Custer was but one of numerous mining camps in this sector which flourished in the late 1800's. Flowing through the town is the Yankee Fork of the Salmon River. Located at the edge of a large primitive area, it is not surprising to find a herd of deer standing in the streets of this deserted town. Many beautiful campsites are available.

Coeur d'Alene has grown from timber heritage in the last century to an unrivaled lake resort during this one.

on the wrong ridgeline (hey, it happens in Idaho) at Lost Trail Pass and didn't realize their mistake for over 300 miles, when they stumbled upon the Clark Fork River.

Not quite. Idaho's shape was also determined in smoky Washington D.C. rooms, although a straight-edge didn't fit the politics. After the state of Oregon was carved out of Oregon Territory in 1859, there remained no clearly defined border between the territories of Dakota and Washington (which Idaho was part of). When gold was discovered in what would be Idaho and Montana people realized that further administrative divisions were needed — although not without a fight over where those divisions would go.

Olympia was capital of Washington Territory, but the town of Vancouver thought that it should rule. Walla Walla wanted to be capital, too, but realized it was too far west of the new Idaho gold fields, so it resisted any division. Lewiston then buddied up with Olympia, which wanted division so it could stay capital of at least a smaller Washington. Finally, Olympia's plan succeeded. On the last night of the Thirty-seventh Congress in 1863, a dividing line was drawn straight north from Lewiston, and Idaho Territory was created (Idaho's name almost became "Lafayette," "Columbia," and "Montana."). Idaho was bigger than Texas and stretched clear to Nebraska. In 1864, Congress carved off Montana Territory for the mining interests there, thus giving Idaho its odd but beloved shape. The shape came close to disappearing in 1886, when

YELLOW PINE

Located on Johnson Creek, Yellow Pine lies 63 miles northeast of Cascade (state highway 15). Homesteaded before the turn of the century. Yellow Pine with its sawmill prospered during the Thunder Mountain gold rush. Early discoveries of antimony in the vicinity led to extensive mining. Today Yellow Pine, a "ghost" of mining "booms," lies on the edge of a vast primitive area, where fishing and big game hunting are unexcelled.

PIERCE

Pierce, located on state highway 11, 30 miles east of Orofino grew out of Idaho's first gold strike in 1862. It lies in an area of mountain ranges, expanding and lifting and flowing away in vast forests of evergreen.

In the 1860's, Pierce had a Chinese population which alone numbered nearly 1,000 and a joss house that is said to have rivaled those in the Orient. The first courthouse built in Idaho of hand-hewn logs still stands. Pierce is a vacation wonderland where fishing and big game hunting is good. In recent years this old town has been staging a "comeback" as a lumbering community.

The rotary snow plow helped the railroad change the face of the West — nowhere more than Idaho.

Not that long ago, relatively...while Harriman scoured the West for the "perfect" ski resort of Sun Valley, the National Geographic Society was still trying to plot The River of No Return in 1935.

northern Idaho was almost divided between Washington and Montana, and southern Idaho given to Nevada.

The source of the name Idaho is even more cryptic, perhaps because of the poetry in names. Some people have sworn that "Idaho" is a Shoshone word meaning, "the morning sun shining on the mountains." Others have said that they made up the name themselves, out of whole cloth. Some facts are: the Idaho Springs mining district already existed in Colorado and "Idaho" was one of the first nominees for that state's name; also "Idaho" was the name of the famed Columbia River steamboat, which took miners up to the new gold fields. Idahoans ought to face it: Idaho was probably named after a boat. That's not so unusual — so was the Columbia River. And besides, many an Idaho miner would not have given his real name, anyway.

Name or no name times were wild and confusing. Idaho Territory had no laws at all for almost a year. The judges knew this and sometimes they acted — or didn't act — accordingly. Lewiston, the territorial capital, would not legally be a part of the new Idaho until 1867, because it was on the original Nez Perce reservation. But, before quibbling over that could ever begin, Lewiston lost the capital to Boise in 1865. Then all of Idaho lost the territory's funds to scurrilous carpetbagger officials.

Back east, Idaho was thought of as a place of last chance escape. Idaho's first governor and top scalawag, Caleb Lyons, first applied unsuccessfully for assignments to Constantinople, China, and Bolivia. In his Civil

LEESBURGH

Leesburgh died at the age of 80, when its last permanent residents moved out in 1946. Here, the discovery of gold brought about the settling of eastern Idaho. Once a city of 7,000 with a Main Street a mile long, the town was settled by former Confederate soldiers and southern sympathizers, and was named for Gen. Robert E. Lee. Turn off U.S. 93, two miles south of Salmon to find Leesburgh on Napius Creek.

SILVER CITY

Picturesque patriarch of ghost towns set high in the Owyhee Mountains, Silver City lies 22 miles south of Murphy (state highway 45).

Born out of the "Blue Bucket Legend" of gold, Silver City was appropriately named for the rich silver ore in the vicinity This old town boasted the first daily newspaper in Idaho. Here too, the cattleman's association was organized and each year still holds its annual convention in this ghost town.

Much of the town has been torn down or collapsed with heavy winter snows. However, the famed old Idaho Hotel, the Stoddard House with its fancy gabled roof, the Masonic Hall which spans Jordan Creek and the pioneer church perched on a hill, still fascinate the visitor.⋨

Top: No neoprene waders then. Bottom: This circa 1916 automobile exhibition in Twin Falls might mark the beginning of yet another technology that reduced the size, reluctantly, and transformed the face of Idaho.

War short story, "Jupiter Doke, Brigadier General," Ambrose Bierce had a Union general request the governorship of Idaho so that he could avoid battle. Indeed, enough southern sympathizers declared their own "separate peace" and came out to Idaho right after the war, Idaho's legislature was dominated by "sesechers" (secessionists). Once, Federal troops from Fort Boise had to stop unruly legislators from burning down the Central Hotel, then Idaho's capitol.

But by then, Idaho was Idaho, for both better and worse. The 1870s brought the Indian Wars. Idaho's tribes, — the Coeur d' Alenes, the Nez Perce, the Sheepeaters, the Bannocks and Shoshones — all fought the pony soldiers and inevitably lost. then came the great silver boom and social strife of the north, and the great irrigation developments in the south. Fields were planted; forests were logged; industries developed; tourism grew. Each region of Idaho went on to make its own history, and share a common history with the others.⋨

Chapter X
IDAHO HERITAGE

A FAMILY OF FAMILIES
by Ridley Pearson

The first people to gaze upon the vast deserts and spectacular mountains of what in 1848 became the Oregon Territory, belonged to great "families" with names like Nez Perce, Kootenai, Paiute and Bannock. The Lewis and Clark Expedition spent more than six weeks with the Nez Perce, and from that date onward, Idaho was a melting pot of brazen individualists who came to "conquer" an unpopulated and unexplored territory. Attracted by the gold rush of the late 1800s, the white man flooded into Idaho from all directions hopeful of digging fortunes from the earth. Over the next hundred years, they came for a million different reasons: skiing, timber, rafting, computers, potatoes, insurance and publishing. Idaho is, by the very nature of what brought people here, a state of human diversity. Idaho is American Indian, miner, logger, farmer, quilter, singer, tailor, river guide and marathon runner. She is a vast expanse of land cradling an unlikely variety of adventurous souls who recognized the potential for a new life in an often unforgiving wilderness.

Turn-of-the-century Idaho cowboys on a ranch at Montour, Idaho.

Multiculturalism is word much in fashion today, when the monoculture of television and popular fashions prevails. But Idaho has always been a many cultured place, and many peoples have contributed to its make-up.

Before the coming of the EuroAmericans, the Indians had Idaho to themselves. They lived in it, lived off it, and lived their free lives according to the comings and goings of the resources and the seasons. Borders did not exist, as we know borders today, and the Indians did not think of "territory," in the European sense. Certain places — camas fields, salmon streams, hunting grounds — were useful and spiritual, in their seasons. And at these times and places, the different tribes traded and fought. Some inter-tribal friendships

The reward for the Idaho farmer is not figured on a checkbook nor quoted on a market. The reward is that first shady haze of green as the wet-black pungent earth of spring gives way to the upward struggle of a hundred thousand sprouting plants. Beans, potatoes, hay, corn, grain, beets, garlic, carrots - cash crops for the market and the table. The reward is in the inevitability of growth, of beating the odds, of standing alone. It is silhouetted in the pink stained horizon as the last bale of the year is put to bed and a darkened sheen of sweat is wiped from his brow.

The roots of Idaho's present day economy once grew out of dark holes dug into the earth, and wormed down from tall spires of evergreen that reached their pointed peaks toward the heavens. Mining was Idaho's first industry, and timber remains the state's largest. Both industries once shored up the walls of the state's economy. But an industry is little more than a group of people with a common purpose. Rugged are the men and women who choose this work.

These are the people of Idaho's heritage: the workers of the land. It is from the people who worked raw earth that this state grew.

Given the state's economic beginnings in mining, logging and farming, it is not surprising to learn that sixty percent of all manufacturing employees work in the timber or food processing industries. What might be surprising is that a state which began in the dirt is headed for the circuit board. Machinery and high tech employment fills the second slot of the state's wage earner employment.

Recreation and tourism are quick gainers in this horse race. Idaho is quickly becoming known as the playground of the West, and the economy is curling around this idea like a vine around a stem.

Idaho's great outdoors draw people here like a magnet and iron filings. People are eager to live here, even if it occasionally means a loss in income. The power of this spectacular landscape can change even the most set mind in but a single weekend. Such stories thrive throughout the state; "I came here to run a river for five days - that was eight years ago."

Entrepreneurs find Idaho a place of escape over the weekend, or a place to target a new product, a place to set up shop where employees will appreciate their surroundings.

Educators, faced with a choice between southern California or eastern Idaho, opt for the latter. The beauty of Idaho increases the quality of people who choose to live here, and thus the quality of life.

Unique to the state is a burgeoning industry created around outdoor recreation. River rafting, helicopter skiing, yurt adventures, dude ranches, fly fishing, chariot racing, motocross, gliding, hot air ballooning; the list is growing annually. As professional guiding increases, a more satisfied tourism trade develops, making the state a top pick among vacation spots. Creative and affluent vacationers find the allure of Idaho too tempting and soon bring their positive influences to root here.

Artists and athletes are no strangers here, either. World famous actors, tennis players, musicians, golfers, writers, mountain climbers, painters, skiers, sculptors, poets and filmmakers have chosen Idaho as home or second home.

It is this sense of retreat offers that so many "outsiders" find attractive. And irresistible. It is this magnetism that may prove to be the hub of Idaho's future. A cabin on Henrys Fork or in the snows of the Sawtooths - a place where the only sounds are from birds, rushing water, or the whisper of wind in the treetops. Retreat. Escape. Idaho is a matchless sanctuary in a world quickly running out of such places, and for this very reason it attracts people who seek a reminder of how fantastic a land this country once was.

Idaho is one of the few states of the future. Her people are leaning into the wind.

A state is not built on rivers or mountains, desert or farmland. A state is built on its people-young and old, of various ethnic origins the descendants of pioneers, the high tech immigrants ready to adapt to the future.

These people are not stopped by forty degrees below zero, or snow ten feet high. They are not stopped by grasshoppers or floods or draught. As with the very first Indian inhabitants of this land, they are people who form a large common family out of their smaller families. They are, in the end, a curious collection of individualists, an evolving breed of human spirit determined to hold paradise in their hands and hope in their hearts. They *are* Idaho.⋖

THE MINERS
by William Studebaker

They begin by just walking in
and following the closest
thing to old.

If it's there, they get it.
They have an eye for it
no stone can stop.
They trust it more than love
(a fickle feeling in the bone
that runs hot and cold)

and when the ore peters-out
as a promise whispered in the dark
vanishes in the brain
they take a chance
and tamp their life in-
to another round.

It's a passion
they wholly surrender to
over glasses of disappointment

(like the love-lost and widowed-
a hard guard, an easy knock-out)

or toast with exuberance
and infatuation:
"This time the Motherlode!"

What they risk is limb and dream.
Their heart is a different place
where light is forged to fit the vein.

North Idaho families in the 1800s and early 1900s were either mining families or lumber families...today many still are.

were deep; some enmities were bitter. But the Indians' way of viewing outsiders (both Whites and other tribes) was both more communal and more personal than the way of the nationalist EuroAmericans.

All the Idaho tribes were usually sub-divided into much smaller groupings of families. They periodically gathered together into larger groups for trading, hunting, fishing and war. There were really no "chiefs," in the EuroAmerican sense of the word. At different times and places, some men and women commanded more respect and attention than others, and they became leaders, according to the situations. But not all other Indians had to follow — or even to fight. And any family could leave a group whenever it felt it was correct, or merely convenient.

BUCKSKIN BILLY

I n 1929, Sylvan Hart sought refuge from the oncoming Depression. With a rifle, an ax, some staples and master's degree in engineering, Hart set up housekeeping along a remote stretch of the Salmon River.

With hand-hewn timbers, Hart erected several buildings, then plastered their sides with stucco. One of the buildings bore a sign - "Blacksmithing and Millinery." Here Hart forged copper and steel to produce the necessary tools for his wilderness existence.

Hart adopted the traditional dress of the mountainmen draping himself in tanned hides of elk and deer. Folks who came in contact with the amazing mountain-dweller dubbed the man "Buckskin Billy."

In the 1960s, the U.S. Forest Service decided that it was time to take control of "Buckskin Billy's" homestead and served him with an eviction notice. The modern day mountainman was not about to abandon his home of more than 30 years, so he built a sturdy guntower complete with gunports. He stocked his tower with all the necessities to take a stand - ready to go down fighting for his property.

Oops. The Forest Service suddenly discovered that it didn't own that particular patch of ground. It was part of a patented mine. "Buckskin Billy's" nephew seized the opportunity to purchase the piece of property, and in 1974, gave his uncle the deed.

"Buckskin Billy" was probably the last person to live a mountainman's lifestyle in Idaho's wilderness.

"For the city man, life is just a jumble, like the facts in a college freshman's notebook. But you can ask me about nearly anything, and I can answer because I've had time to think about it." ⤳
-Sylvan Hart, May 10, 1906-April 29, 1980

Significantly, religion among Idaho's Indians was largely a personal matter. Instead of deriving faith from a dogmatic doctrine, Indians drew their beliefs from personal visions and revelations. Every Indian desired personal supernatural power. The quest for it developed a quiet strength and self-control. Even in today's materialistic world, one finds that Idaho tribal members have remarkable discipline and dignity.

While much was similar among peoples living similar lives, each Idaho tribe was in its own way unique. Six Indian tribes lived in Idaho at the time of the EuroAmerican invasion. Several other tribes were frequent visitors. Five tribes live in Idaho today.

In the north, the Kutenai were a plains hunting tribe who had settled around North Idaho's great lakes,

JEAN BAPTISTE CHARBONNEAU

Born of Touissant Charbonneau, of the Lewis and Clark expedition, and of the famous Shoshone guide Sacajawea, Jean Baptiste seemed destined for greatness.

As an infant, he was carried across the continent and back in a cradle board strapped to his mother's back. As a young lad, he was sent to William Clark. Clark saw to it that young Charbonneau received a good education. As a young man, Jean Baptiste rejoined his father and became a trapper and guide on the Missouri River. It was as a guide during 1823 that the young man met Prince Paul of Wurtemberg, Germany, and later traveled to Germany as a guest of the Prince. During a six-year period, Jean Baptiste traveled Europe and North Africa, learning the basic language of Germany, France and Spain.

In 1830, Charbonneau returned to his homeland and the lifestyle he had loved - that of a mountainman. He became an employee of the American Fur Company. That fall he was

Shoshoni Pat Tyhee one day before and after his conversion by the missionaries.

trapping in the future state of Idaho. He and his group became lost in the lava beds around Craters of the Moon. The men were in need of water. Jean Baptiste went to locate some and when he returned, the men were gone. He found his way back to familiar landmarks and soon learned that the other members of his party had been found by their rival, the Hudson's Bay Company, and taken to safety.

Jean Baptiste Charbonneau guided a Mormon battalion from Santa Fe to San Diego during the Mexican War; served as mayor of San Luis Rey (near San Diego); joined the California gold rush; and became a hotel clerk in Auburn. He was heading for new adventures in Montana when he died of pneumonia in Jordan Valley in 1866 at the age of sixty-one.

---

as fishermen. A small group of Kutenai still live on their small "mission" in the Kootenai River valley, near Bonners Ferry. Many more live in Canada and western Montana. The Kutenai never signed a treaty with the U.S. government. In 1974, they staged a brief demonstrational "war" to bring attention to their situation and treatment.

The Coeur d'Alenes live south of the Kutenai and still have a fairly large reservation. They are related linguistically to the Flatheads in western Montana and to the Spokanes in eastern Washington. Like the Nez Perce to their south, the Coeur d'Alenes had adopted the horse and the plains culture before David Thompson's expedition entered their area in 1810. Today, the Coeur d'Alenes are energetically pursuing

FIGHTING THE DRAGON

by Frank Carroll

Idaho wildfires have names, legendary names. The 1910 Fire. The Sundance Fire. Mortar Creek. Long Tom. Anderson. Foolshen. Lowman.

Sleepy, quiet little places most people never hear of until suddenly, grimly, they become cauldrons for the broth of devotion and uncommon valor, forges where endurance and persistence and sacrifice are hammered into men and women alike. Hallowed ground.

United against common foes have always brought people together. In forested Idaho, the foe was and remains fire.

Idaho has no prominent Civil War battlefields, but the men and women who fought and died here in the public service have much in common with their ancestors, North and South: strength, loyalty, a profound sense of personal service and self sacrifice, professionalism, guts.

Idaho firefighters have names, too. Legendary names. Ed Pulaski saved his crew from certain destruction in 1910 and went on to help invent the Pulaski tool, a firefighting tool, part hoe and part axe. The Boise Hot Shots, a professional firefighting crew, are experts in the use of handtools. The McCall Smokejumpers are airborne firefighters who made over 940 airborne fire assaults in 1989. The engine crews of the Bureau of Land Management have saved many homes and lives with their fierce, headlong attacks on fast-moving range fires.

Wildfires have been a part of the Idaho scene forever. However, firefighters are relatively new to Idaho, having been formally organized in 1906. They've had a lot of practice. They've fought fires everywhere in the United States. The Boise Hot Shots have taken their skills to Canada, while others have been to South and Central America, Mexico, Australia, Europe and the Soviet Union.

But they learn the hard lessons here, in Idaho.

Fighters in Idaho are probably tougher than other firefighters. Idaho is tougher country than other places. Every summer, no exceptions, Idaho's range lands and forests burn out of control, pitting highly skilled professional firefighters against the vagaries of nature. Governor Andrus was fond of saying that Idaho is what America was. And he's probably right.

---

various ways to keep their tribe together and vibrant.

The Nez Perce are the largest North Idaho tribe and probably the best know outside Idaho. They are related by language to other Columbia Basin tribes. Tragedy gave them their fame, after their courageous and finally failed 1877 attempt to outwit, outfight and outrun the U.S. Army during their forced march to the border of "Grandmother's Land," in Canada. When Lewis and Clark entered the Nez Perce's area in 1805, it stretched across all of North Central Idaho, south toward Boise, and west into the Wallowa country in northeastern Idaho. Their original "reservation" of 1855 covered 10,000 square miles. It now includes barely 88,000 acres. Their sustenance included the bountiful salmon swimming up the Idaho streams and the

POLLY BEMIS

A romantic tale prevails that "China Polly" was won as a bride in a poker game. Polly herself denied this. She said the credit belonged to an Indian girl living in the same mining camp.

Polly was born in China in 1852. Her parents lived in a poverty stricken area and at the age of 18 she was traded to a brigade leader by her father in exchange for enough seed to put in his next year's crop. From there for a time, she became a slave girl.

She passed through the hands of several owners, and finally found herself in the possession of a white woman. She told Polly that she was sending her to the American gold fields. She assured that girl that she could expect to find gold nuggets laying in the streets of these camps. Eventually she was smuggled into the United States and after a time, she became the slave of a wealthy Oriental who ruled the affairs of the Chinese colony in the rip-roaring mining camp of Warrens, Idaho. She was put to work as a dance hall girl in a local saloon.

Among the patrons of this establishment was a young gambler by the name of Charlie Bemis. Polly was an onlooker one night when Bemis was engaged in a tense card game with a half-breed Lapwai Indian.

The Indian lost heavily, and in a revengeful mood, he approached Bemis the next day, and shot him without warning. The bullet entered his left cheek, proceeded downward through his mouth and lodged in the upper part of his neck. His friends placed him on a table and tried to stop the flow of blood. Polly stepped forward and took charge of the wounded man. He was removed to his cabin. Here she did what she could, even skillfully removing the embedded bullet with a razor. For several weeks, she patiently nursed him back to health. By this time Bemis had fallen in love with her, and took her as a common-law wife.

When the diggings at Warrens petered out, Bemis purchased a small ranch in the depths of the Salmon River Canyon. It could only be approached by a tortuous zig-zag mountain trail, or by a hazardous boat ride on the raging "River of No Return". Here the couple led a peaceful and happy life for nearly 50 years.

Polly was skilled as a goldsmith and often fashioned trinkets out of the gold Bemis sifted from nearby streams. These trinkets were sold for a profit. She also raised a fine garden and had some fruit trees and chickens. This produce had ready sale in surrounding camps and to roving prospectors.

Polly Beamis and a few of her many friends.

great herds of buffalo across the Great Divide in Montana. The Nez Perce developed the famous appaloosa horse, still a highly prized breed because of its looks and intelligence.

When Lewis and Clark arrived, the Nez Perce were at war with another Idaho tribe, the Shoshone, to the south. Today, the Nez Perce work hard to maintain their culture, by preserving their language and taking an active role in natural resources management, like the reintroduction of wolves to Central Idaho.

Another North Idaho tribe was the Kalispell, or Pend d'Oreille. Today they live mainly in eastern Washington and western Montana.

Other Indian tribes were frequent visitors to Idaho. These included the Spokanes, Cayuse and Paiutes,

In 1849, Bemis legally married Polly. If he had not done so, there was a chance she might have had to return to China, due to the passage of the Chinese Deportation Act.

Charlie Bemis died in 1931. Polly was then an old woman. She continued to live alone. Two prospectors had settled across the Salmon, and they took it upon themselves to keep an eye on the little old Chinese woman. They constructed a telephone line across the river, and they communicated daily with her. They picked up her needs at the store in Riggins. They performed her necessary chores. She crossed the river once to listen to their radio. She didn't like it. She thought it was emitting chatterings of evil spirits.

In return for the services of her neighbors, she deeded her property, which would be theirs upon her death.

Late in the summer of 1933, she failed to respond to the telephone. Her two friends quickly crossed the river, and found Polly critically ill. They put her on a horse and traveled the rough trail to a mine where a phone was available. An ambulance was summoned from Grangeville. She entered a hospital there where she lingered for three months. A visitor, hoping to cheer her one day, said "You will be getting well soon". Polly replied, "Me too old to get well—me have to go to a new world to get well". She passed away on November 6, 1933.

She was remembered by old timers for her warm friendly manner and happy disposition. She remains a cherished legend of Central Idaho.◅

Hard working and industrious, many Chinese established roots and prospered in Boise. Boise's Chinatown is gone today, and the culture has blended with others.

from Washington and Oregon, and the Flatheads and Blackfeet from Montana. Iroquois trappers, from New York and eastern Canada, accompanied Hudson's Bay Company expeditions. Amazingly, Hawaiian Island natives also came trapping with "the honorable company." David Thompson at Kullyspell House wrote how much they missed their islands, especially in winter. In Southwest Idaho, Hawaiian trappers left their mark in the form of the name, "Owyhee."

As it does now, Southern Idaho had a drier climate than the north, and the culture of the Indians living here reflected it. These Indians — the Shoshones and Bannocks — speak mutually unintelligible dialects, but both are related linguistically to a large language group which includes the Aztecs of old Mexico.

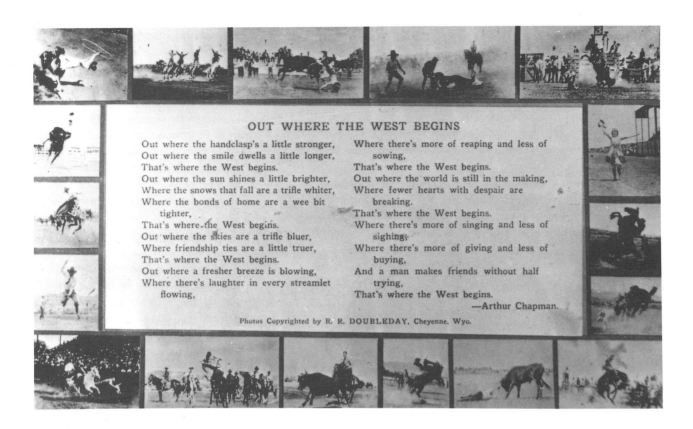

OUT WHERE THE WEST BEGINS

Out where the handclasp's a little stronger,
Out where the smile dwells a little longer,
That's where the West begins.
Out where the sun shines a little brighter,
Where the snows that fall are a trifle whiter,
Where the bonds of home are a wee bit
    tighter,
That's where the West begins.
Out where the skies are a trifle bluer,
Where friendship ties are a little truer,
That's where the West begins.
Out where a fresher breeze is blowing,
Where there's laughter in every streamlet
    flowing,

Where there's more of reaping and less of
    sowing,
That's where the West begins.
Out where the world is still in the making,
Where fewer hearts with despair are
    breaking,
That's where the West begins.
Where there's more of singing and less of
    sighing,
Where there's more of giving and less of
    buying,
And a man makes friends without half
    trying,
That's where the West begins.
                                    —Arthur Chapman.

Photos Copyrighted by R. R. DOUBLEDAY, Cheyenne, Wyo.

MYTHS, BUCKAROOS AND REALITIES

by Scott Preston

"There is an easy comfort given to believers of the Western dream, knowing that cowboys are, at this very moment, galloping around somewhere, roping sick stock, and sleeping out under the stars. Why this kind of trivial knowledge should make a difference in anyone's life is a mystery."

-Kurt Markus, Buckaroo

Deep down the lost trails of history that vein the mind like glitters of fool's gold, the old herds are gathered and led across the land. Dust rises like a storm cloud from the slow movements of hoofprints, and the sound of bone massed against rock is a thunder welling out of the clicking of ten thousand castanets.

On the fringes of this roiling land-cloud, twirling ropes amid sidestepping gallops, ride the Cowboys, lariats flaring halos in the air about their heads, like centaurs executing impossible pirouettes. Forget about the greenhorns riding drag for strays, bandannas plastered over mouth and nose to half-block the lung-drowning dust of the herd's wake. Forget the camp cook, innards rock-jarred in his wagon, watching the mounted through an eye-film of despair, the memory of

These Shoshonean speakers entered Idaho from the south, possibly around the time of Columbus. The Great Basin, which they may have taken generations to cross, had necessitated a culture based on the meagerest of nature's offerings — seeds and insects —and the infrequent feasts on fish, fowl and game. When they reached the Snake River valley, the Shoshoneans found a land of comparative plenty, although meager when compared to the larder of North Idaho. At the time of the arrival of EuroAmericans in 1810, some of the Shoshones in Eastern Idaho had already adopted the horse culture from their cousins, the Comanches. The Shoshones in Southwest Idaho generally depended on the annual salmon runs. Another Shoshonean group — the so-called Sheepeaters — lived in the rugged heart of Central Idaho.

riding now settled on the work of his old age like a shadow of cancer on the soul. Forget the low wages, the isolation, the fact that it ended before it began.

For these images of the West, of freedom harnessed to an inexorable routine, are the seeds of myth that flower on the modern sands of imagination. It little matters that Jesse James was never Robin Hood, that the gunfights and bank jobs and jail breaks of Hollywood legend were, when they happened at all, not the work of men of Ayn Rand's ideal, but of cowards and psychotics and drifters too lazy to bend their backs to the real labor of the West for a ration of beans and salted meat.

The work and the life that did take place in those brief decades after the Civil War was brutally hard and isolated, long on hours and

Many Idaho cowboys made the rodeo circuit, particularly nearby Pendleton and Cheyenne.

short on pay. It was a time and a place where a man had the freedom to quit a job only for as long as his stock of dried goods lasted, only for as long as it took to find the next line shack, the next outfit, the next job. Where a man could go without a woman for years, where the only echo of culture came from songs borrowed or stolen or self-created, where a taste of fresh fruit in the midst of a summer's dust could be more highly valued than either.

Of course they endured, of course there was a keen spark of triumph, anonymous and sun-blistered, glinting at the end of the trail. For they continued to pack their bundles of rags and blankets and head West even into the present day. And sometimes the myths overran themselves, colliding with the modern era in a form of self-ambush as much fantastic as grim. Imagine Claude Dallas alone in his jail cell, haunted for decades by scenes of a few seconds of gunplay, his lost shadow tainting the Owyhee desert like the scent of miles of sagebrush charred by lightning.

The 1870s were the decade of the Indian Wars, in which the tribes were defeated militarily and reduced to the reservations. The last massacre — by either Indians or EuroAmericans — occurred in the Blackstone Desert, south of Bruneau, in 1911. Twelve Shoshones were ambushed in their winter camp. All but four children were murdered.

The first EuroAmericans in Idaho were Scots, English and French-Canadians with the fur trapping companies, and of course the native-born Americans with Lewis and Clark. William Clark's slave York was the first African American in Idaho.

The first EuroAmerican settlements in Idaho were the Mormon colonies around Bear Lake and in the

"The cowboy was just that - a boy who chased cows," one sun-weathered leg-favoring rancher told me. "I always wanted to be a cowboy when I grew up, but what with calving and branding and feeding and vaccinating, bucking hay, mending fence, plugging the leaks in the barn's roof and fixing the windmill, I just never had the time to be a cowboy ."

There are certain distinctions drawn between types of cowboys, although the lines like the horizon, can often blur and elude a final description. In the Great Basin conjunction of Nevada, Idaho and Oregon, the cowboys of classic tradition are most commonly referred to as "buckaroos," a word adapted, like a fascinating range of Western terminology. from elder Spanish sources (in this case, vaquero).

It is a fine yet hazy horizon line dividing skill that separates cowboys from buckaroos. No man wants to be quoted, drawn and quartered in print by defining the boundaries, but a certain unspoken clarity does exist to distinguish the two.

"Well, you won't catch a buckaroo building a fence, for instance," said one source demanding the shield of anonymity. "And a cowboy can do anything a buckaroo can do, but he won't do it quite so pretty. He just wants to get the job done. But a buckaroo, now, he'll maybe put a little underhand toss on his ropin', put a little more of an emphasis on the execution of what he's doin'. Yeah, I guess you could almost call it an art form, though a buckaroo wouldn't. It's something deeper. But it sure is a beautiful thing to watch when it's all happenin' right. That blue smoke starts curlin' up from the rope wound around his saddle horn when he's makin' his dallies, an' he could lose a finger or burn his hand bad makin' a mistake, but he don't. An' that cow'll just lay down like she'd meant to all along. I tell you what, man, it's a

Summer range in the Sawtooths

beautiful sight to watch a good buckaroo workin'
a herd. An' it don't get any better than that."

Spread out like flecks of orange paint on the
rim of a weathered Studebaker wagon wheel, the
clustered buildings and trees of modern ranchlife
look to towns of 400 or less for week to week
existence. Quiet places of two cafes, two bars
and two grocery stores, whose names resound
like mantras in the sweaty heaven of the brow:
Bruneau, Oreana, La-moille, Deeth. Sideyards
full of barking dogs and forever immobile
machinery, scrap lumber and sheet metal, rusting
trucks, bales of barbed wire, stacks of fence
posts, signboards, an out-building fallen or on
the edge of collapse. The paint peels on the
outer walls of houses like aspen leaves shivering
to the ground in November. Then your eyes shift
to the important fences around the stock
enclosures, posts lined up straight as a rifle's
cross hairs, the wires taut, the lines clean and
built with skill and pride. And you realize that
the casual dilapidation of the houses and yards
and trucks is far less a matter of poverty - and
even less of slothfulness- than it is of a lack of
time, of a necessary swerving of attention away
from issues of comfort and aesthetics to those of
the real work.

It's the life that counts more than anything.
When the sun raises a red line at dawn, the trees
of distant ranches feather its edges like small
clumps of fuzz on a great cinema screen. At
sunset, it's the same thing, just the ranches on
the other side of the valley that rest shadows
against the horizon. Either way, the air comes so
cold it brings tears to the eyes, a good excuse for
the tangled emotion of loss and joy at being once
again awake in the new or failing light. It's the
life that counts more than anything.✍

Lemhi Valley. The Mormon church is now the largest in southern Idaho. So many Scandinavians joined the
church and immigrated to Southeastern Idaho that names like Hansen and Larson are common.

The gold rushes brought in EuroAmericans of every imaginable European heritage. Swedes and Greeks.
Spaniards and Russians. Italians and Germans. Many Chinese came from the California gold fields and after
the completion of the transcontinental railroad. From the EuroAmerican miners they received beatings,
swindlings, murders, oppressive laws, and grudging admiration. Often the Chinese worked abandoned
claims.

For a short time, Boise had the largest Chinese community in the Northwest, and Boise treated the

DIAMOND FIELD JACK

The trial of Diamond Field Jack is one of the epic cases of its kind in the history of the State, and marked the last great fight between sheepmen and cattlemen. Jack Davis was a colorful character in the Nevada gold-rush days. A noted gunman, he was also a noted teller of tall tales; and it was chiefly his boasting of himself as a desperate fellow that led to his arrest for the murder of two sheepmen.

At the trial, W. E. Borah and the District Attorney argued for the State, and J. H. Hawley for the defense. There were no witnesses and very little evidence against the accused man; but sheepmen declared that Diamond Field Jack had visited their camps and made threats to kill the whole outfit if the sheepmen didn't clear out of the cattle country.

The trial became a notorious one; feelings ran high. Jack had once worked for the Sparks-Herrel outfit in Nevada; and Sparks, governor of the State, came to the defense of his former employee. Nevertheless, Jack was convicted on circumstantial evidence and sentenced to hang at Albion, though at the last minute Hawley obtained a reprieve.

Of this reprieve, three copies were made, and sent to Albion by three armed messengers, each taking a different route. Jack remained in jail for awhile, but was finally pardoned, whereupon he returned to Nevada and became wealthy. Some old-timers say Governor Sparks of Nevada made two unsuccessful attempts to bribe the court, offering a hundred thousand dollars for the release of the prisoner.◆

Another pack trip to the mountains to hunt.

Chinese with more civility than most places. After the turn of the century, many of the now Chinese-Americans had gravitated to larger coastal communities, like San Francisco and Seattle. But Idaho remained polyglot. As late as 1910, forest rangers complained of not being able to find workers who spoke English.

By World War II, English was it. After the war, many Japanese-Americans, who had been held in the "relocation camps" at Minidoka and elsewhere, stayed in Idaho. Also, Idaho farmers began to hire many Mexican laborers. Again, many stayed, and today the Mexican-American community in Idaho is still growing. Also growing is the Asian-American population in Idaho, especially around the high-tech center of Boise.

Of all the ethnic groups that settled in Idaho, the Basques are probably the best known and best

CLAUDE DALLAS

At a remote campsite in Owyhee County, Jim Stevens stared in disbelief as his friend Claude Dallas riddled two Idaho Fish and Game officers with bullets.

"I heard a loud shot and (Officer William) Pogue said, 'Oh no!'" Stevens testified later. "There was a volley of shots and I saw Claude crouching down with a pistol. I could see smoke coming from Pogue's chest. He stumbled forward and fell face down on the ground."

When it was over, the morning of Jan. 5, 1981, officers Pogue and Conley Elms lay dead. And Dallas began an odyssey that led him in and out of jail and newspaper headlines. To some, he became a folk hero; to others, a reviled murderer.

Dallas shot the officers after they had hiked to his camp on the South Fork of the Owyhee River to question him about poaching. Bobcat and deer skins were found at the camp. Neither

Southern Idaho buckaroo cowboys never could resist roping about anything than ran from them—from bears to porcupines…sometimes even cattle.

game was in season, which meant Dallas faced a possible $300 fine and six months in jail.

After Dallas killed the agents, Stevens walked up to the 30-year-old trapper and asked "Why?"

"I'd swore I'd never be arrested again," replied Dallas, who had served prison time for dodging the draft.

After shooting the men, Dallas dumped Elms body in the river, then loaded Pogue's body in a pickup for 105-mile trip to Paradise Hill, Nev.

He buried the body in the desert, then led state and federal law officers on a 16-month manhunt that ended in the same locale.

Tipped off by an anonymous caller, officers surrounded a trailer where Dallas was staying. The killer tried to escape in a flatbed pickup, but officers chased him down, shot up the truck and wounded Dallas in the ankle. He was arrested and put on trial five months later.

At trial, Dallas claimed he shot Pogue and Elms in self-defense.

The jury rejected the murder charges, finding him guilty of man-slaughter. Judge Edward Lodge imposed the maximum sentence: 30 years.

The case, with its Old West trappings, was made to order for a TV movie. Dallas also was profiled in two books. But the tale wasn't over.

Dallas was 3 1/2 years through his term at the state prison south of Boise when he escaped by cutting through a double chain-link fence in April 1986.

He stayed on the lam for 11 months, undergoing cosmetic surgery in Mexico. He was recaptured coming out of a Convenience store in Riverside, Calif.

Within three weeks, Dallas was transferred to prisons in Nebraska, New Mexico and Kansas, where he is now being held.

---

established, especially in Southwestern and South Central Idaho. While Basques could be called "the original Europeans" because of their presence on the continent since prehistoric times, the Basques speak a language that is unrelated to the others.

The first Basques in Idaho worked as miners and freighters. Later, they became associated with stock raising, and many Idahoans have thought that the Basque country must be a lot like southern Idaho. It isn't. It's more like the rainy coast. The Basques took the herding jobs because they were available. Their industry has made them Idaho leaders in government, business and other areas.

Idaho' s primary culture is, of course, the Western heritage. Great areas of Idaho are still used for range,

RODEO'S SUNDOWN

by Bob Loeffelbein

Culdesac, Idaho, circa 1914 when that part of the West was still wild-was not a lot smaller than it is today. But on or about May 20, the town named from the French cul-de-sac (meaning "bottom of the bag" or "dead-end street") used to undergo a dramatic change.

Each spring, the tiny community hosted a rodeo where cowboys from miles around congregated to test themselves against each other and against the wildest bucking broncs on a horse-stealing raid into the Flathead country. He was about 15 when his family joined Chief Joseph's historic band on its retreat from northwestern Oregon into Montana in 1877. They were, according to Sundown, among those who escaped capture into Canada. Later, his family returned across the border to Nespelum, Wash., and eventually lived on the

and menacing bulls that could be gathered. And the event drew more than 2,000 spectators-at a time when a family had to ride in a wagon one or two days just to get there.

One of the buckaroos billed for the Culdesac Rodeo was Jackson Sundown a Nez Perce Indian who had made a reputation for himself riding in competitions in Montana and winning the big Grangeville, Idaho, rodeo in 1912. Most of the other riders were working cowboys from spreads around the Palouse country and into western Montana and eastern Washington.

The real star of the 1914 show was Jackson Sundown, even though he was 51 years old. Blanket of the Sun (Jackson Sundown's Indian name) was born in Montana about 1863, while his father was away with a band of Nez Perce

Cowboys and Indians became a part of the heritage of the West, and certainly the image to the rest of the World. These particular "cowboys" are Nez Perce "Indians."

Flathead Indian reservation. Sundown did his first rodeo riding there and also married a Flathead maiden, who bore him two children. By 1910 Sundown had married again and was making his home near Jacques Spur on the Nez Perce reservation in Idaho.

Sundown's triumph in the 1912 Grangeville Rodeo cemented his fame as a rider of broncs and bulls.

After his success at Culdesac, Sundown was invited to ride at the biggest event in the West, Oregon's Pendleton Round-Up.

"The year was 1916 and a noisy crowd watched while the only full-blooded Indian ever to compete for the championship of the Pendleton Round-Up rode to victory," according to a report from the association. "Pitted against Sundown in the finals were two of the great bronc riders of the day-Rufus Rollen of Claremont, Okla., and Bob Hall of Pocatello, Idaho. Both made epic rides, but the ride of Sundown eclipsed both, though his competitors were only half his age (he was 53), and well equipped to compete in a young man's game.

Sundown never entered another contest, though he did make exhibition rides at other shows. After 1916, and until the summer before his death on December 18, 1922, he spent much of his time on the Salmon River ranch of Mr. and Mrs. Ben Reeves, where he helped train horses and served as all-around ranch handyman.

A recent cattle drive near Carey.

A few years before Sundown's death, Phineas Proctor, an internationally known sculptor, lived in a tent on the Sundown place for about eight months and produced a statue of the famous Indian rider. The statue stands on the first floor of the RCA Building in Radio City, New York.

Sundown was 60 when he died of pneumonia at his Jacques Spur ranch. He was buried in the St. Joseph's Indian cemetery at Mission Creek, Idaho. But there is no marker on his grave. The greatest rider of his era lies nearly forgotten today.

SNAKE MEDICINE

The cowpunchers of the Salmon River country grew tired of their sowbelly and dough-gods and resolved on a change of fare. With spades they dug for earthworms and filled a tobacco can, and the next morning bright and early they saddled their nags and set out to fish the Middle Fork of the Salmon. On arriving, they learned that they had forgotten their worms, and while looking around for bait one of them saw a bull snake that had partly swallowed a frog and was resting in his labors. The cowpuncher massaged the snake's throat and worked the frog upward and released it but the snake looked up at him so reproachfully that he said, "That's a devil of a way to treat a poor snake what has been out earnun his livun just like us." So he drew his flask of whiskey and opened the snake's mouth and gave the reptile about a half a finger. The snake stuck out its tongue and looked very benign in its eyes and then began to wiggle its tail and roll over as if exceedingly happy. The cow-punchers used the frog for bait; but after awhile one of them was attracted by something that tapped insistently on his boot. He looked down and there was that bull snake, gazing up at him hopefully and holding another frog in its mouth.

IDAHO LORE

A Coeur d'Alene Indian, wishing to comply with the intricacies of civilization, proved himself so industrious a member of the community that the local bank lent him money, taking twenty-two ponies as collateral. When the money was due the Indian paid it. The banker, observing that he still had cash, tried to persuade him to deposit it in the bank explaining to him the advantages. The Indian thereupon laid his money on the desk and asked: "How many ponies you?"

This advertisement appeared in the Idaho World for Oct. 13, 1866: Lost or strade from the subscriber a sheep all over white, one leg was black and half his body. All persons shall receive five dollars to bring him. He was a she goat.

An old-timer in Kootenai Valley says that formerly there was a homesteader in the area whose housekeeping ways were always open to suspicion. The man had a dog which he called Two Waters, and not until after the hound's death could he be prevailed upon to explain why he called a beast so unusual a name. Then the truth came out. When visitors had complained that the dishes and cooking utensils were not very clean, the old fellow had always answered: "They're as plumb clean as Two Waters can get them."

Idaho's towns have always been melting pots. Blackfoot, Idaho in 1900 combined farmers, cowboys, Indians, railroaders —and all the associated combinations of race and religion.

and the preservation of wide open spaces is important to ranchers and city dwellers alike. Legacies of the ranching life pervade Idahoans' language, attitudes and expectations. Even the wealthiest Idahoans often wear Western clothing. Once, when a TV production crew came looking for "the typical Idaho cowboy," they got more than they expected. Idaho's eccentric, brush-popping, individualistic cowboys are a long day's ride beyond Hollywood stereotypes.

Idaho culture is a marvelous mixed bag, whose characteristics have sprung from the livelihoods of its practitioners. Loggers, farmers, miners and cowboys have created many Idaho traditions, such as loggers' fairs, country fairs, square dances and rodeos. Today's livelihoods and personal pursuits might be expected

SOUNDING THE BUGLE FOR THE TRUCE

SENDING FLAG OF TRUCE TO THE INDIAN CAMP

GEORGE A. HUSTON GUIDE

CHIEF JOSEPH'S SURRENDER OCTOBER 5, 1877

"Tell General Howard I know his heart. What he told me before I have in my heart. I am tired of fighting. Our chiefs are killed. Looking Glass is dead. Too-hul-hul-sote is dead. The old men are all dead. It is the young men who say yes or no [that is, vote in council]. He who led on the young men is dead [Joseph's brother, Alokut]. It is cold and we have no blankets. The little children are freezing to death. My people, some of them, have run away to the hills, and have no blankets, no food; no one knows where they are-perhaps freezing to death. I want to have time to look for my children and see how many of them I can find. Maybe I shall find them among the dead. Hear me, my chiefs. I am tired; my heart is sick and sad. From where the sun now stands I will fight no more forever."

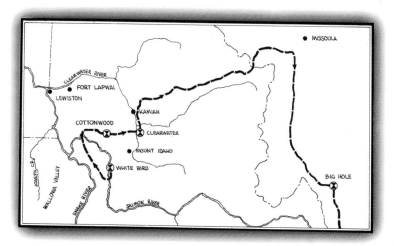

Top: The flight of Chief Joseph from White Bird to Big Hole.

Bottom: Nez Perce war poles.

to create new cultures. Who knows what wonders could spring from the hearts of river guides, mountain bikers, and techno-wonks?

Complicating Idaho's cultural mix, today's Idaho characters often seem to be social crossbreeds, like the cowboy-kayaker and the farmer-hacker. Further, Idaho's combination of a natural resources and high-tech economy has created whole categories of professional hybrids, who combine urban savvy with outdoors experience. Examples include the registered nurse who fights wildfires as a Forest Service smokejumper, the lawyer who flies the backcountry as a bush pilot, the electrical engineer who guides whitewater float trips, and the artificial limb maker who doubles as a rodeo cowboy.

"EUZKERA"

by Roger O. Purcell

The Oinkari Basque Dancers have toured the world. Basque sheepherders today still maintain the nomadic heritage of the grandfathers. Basque bars offer ethnic food & drink and are as popular with non-Basques as Basques.

The dancer's nimble feet traced intricate designs around a full wine glass. Suddenly he sprang, and balanced briefly atop the glass without spilling a drop. This oldest Basque dance, a solo called the "Zamalzian," is one of the spectators' favorites. The unique dance is part of the annual celebration of the culture and history of Idaho's Basque people.

The celebration is a gathering from across Idaho of families with a common origin, a time for remembering ancestors in a renaissance of ethnic tradition.

Everyone is welcome; you do not have to be Basque to attend the festival. It's your opportunity to learn the history of a very unique people to discover the roles they have played in Idaho history, and experience their distinctively flavored food. (The Basque take great pride in their tasty cuisine.)

Young, unmarried Basque men first arrived in Idaho during the 1890s looking for work. Most became sheepherders-not because they tended sheep in the Old Country, but because they were too late for the gold rush and the only work as in the expanding livestock industry. They spoke little or no English, and were sent off alone with their flocks into Idaho's pristine alpine grasslands.

The Basque language (Euzkera) is unrelated to either French or Spanish and is isolated from all other tongues in the world. It is so complex that it is best learned from childhood. As the dialect varies from village to village, one Basque may have difficulty understanding another.

Their folklore says the Devil himself tried to learn "Euzkera" by hiding behind the door of a Basque home: After seven years he gave up, having learned only a single word, "Bai" (yes).

Like most small ethnic groups, the Basques were discriminated against when they first came to America; but by the 1930s and 40s, in addition to being reliable herdsmen, the Basques had become active in Idaho's sports, business and community activities. Today, the Basque are an integrated part of Idaho's culture and work force. Their descendants are found in all economic, educational and social areas.

The Basque represent an ancient culture whose origins have been lost in time. They are considered by some historians to be the oldest surviving ethnic group in Europe. Theirs is a country not of boundaries, but of racial identity. Even their blood is unique: Basque have the highest known incidence of Rh-negative blood type in the world and the lowest frequency of blood type B in Europe.

Europe's first whalers were Basque. By 1550 they were sailing to Labrador, hunting the whale. In 1977 the sunken remains of three ancient Basque galleys were discovered under the freezing waters of the Red Bay.

It is difficult to determine the actual number of Basque in Idaho-estimates range from 10,000 to over 20,000. The Boise area has the largest population of Basque in the world outside of the Pyrenees.

The Basque people played a major role in the drama of the development of Idaho. They brought Old World language and customs to the blending bowl of the state's frontier. Now a part of Idaho's culture, they still maintain their ethnic identity.

Plan on attending a Basque festival this year. Immerse yourself in the culture, enjoy the exquisite food, and absorb the vibrant music and colorful dances.

Take time to visit the Basque museum at 607 Grove Street in Boise. The museum, the only one of its kind in North America, is housed in the oldest surviving brick building in Boise. The home, built in 1864, was a Basque boarding house from 1918 to 1960.

In 1919 the first and only Basque church in America was built at 5th and Idaho. It is an excellent example of the French influence on Basque architecture.

The Basque have made major contributions to Idaho, in the livestock industry, business, sports, and community affairs. Today, their uniquely rich cultural heritage is made available for all Idahoans to share, through their museum and festivals.

Shoshoni tribe leaders with the Fort Hall agent.

A SACRED TRADITION

by Dianna Troyer

There is a hush, a stillness over the land as the dancers stand at the entrance of the circular wooden powwow arena. The golden August sunshine of early dusk waits with them for that first shrill cry of the lead singer.

Then the sense of anticipation breaks. Like a single thunder clap it starts. The emcee calls for the first drum to begin. The lead singer cries out the first notes of the song, the drum echoes his voice and the other singers in the drum group join in.

Some 600 pairs of moccasin-clad dancers' feet begin to move up and down in time with the drums' one-two rhythm. Bells on men's ankles jingle in step like the soothing sound of rainfall. They enter, circling around until the arena is full and all the spectators sitting in bleachers and lawn chairs have seen them.

Two Nez Perce soon after the end of the war, and five North Idaho Indians from two tribes.

The annual Shoshone Bannock Festival at Fort Hall in southeastern Idaho has started-just like it did last summer and just like it will start next summer. The dance is as timeless and dependable as the seasons unfolding and merging into each other.

The powwow circuit is a rite of summer for hundreds of Native Americans who travel to dances from June through September. Families, sometimes three or four generations, pile into a van to travel thousands of miles on the blue highways that connect tiny towns on reservations. A celebration of culture and tradition, the circuit also represents a chance to earn extra income for those who live a nomadic lifestyle by competing for the first place purses reaching as high as $1,000 at several dances.

The Shoshone-Bannock people danced long before fur trappers. Soon after homesteaders came to the Snake River Basin, land was set aside for an Indian reservation with the Fort Bridger Treaty of 1868. Even when their land was whittled away from 1.6 million acres down to its present 543,000 acres, they danced. Today, of the more than 4,000 people on the Fort Hall Reservation in southeast Idaho, more than 3,000 are enrolled tribal members.

The powwow is a convivial affair, where bonds of friendship transcend state borders and strengthen as time and summers pass.

There is an understood open invitation to powwows-Indian and non-Indian alike.

To attend the Sho-Ban festival, just take the Fort Hall exit off Interstate 15 about 10 miles north of Pocatello and follow it west past the huge old elms that border the campgrounds and rodeo area. Look for the tall White teepees, you can't miss them. You might want to bring a lawn chair and a slower time frame, too.

THE RAILROAD COMES TO MOSCOW

by Charles Munson

The road was finished, and the first train arrived on Wednesday, September 23rd, 1885. This great event was advertised all over the country from the limits of the Salmon River, all over the reservation, the Camas Prairie country American Ridge, Burnt Ridge, Little Bear and Big Bear Ridges and beyond. A great crowd was in Moscow that day, and there was great rejoicing. Roman Nose and I left home early. At Lindol Smith's on top of the hill, the G.A.R. cannon was booming; a Zumhof & McCarter's blacksmith shop the anvils, loaded with black powder, were catapulted clear across the street and rang out in salute. The church bells were ringing; whistles were blown. Soon a great crowd, estimated at 10,000 gathered at the depot, waiting for the train that was due in one hour or more.

There were stockmen who had made the trip horseback in five to six days, Indians from the reservation, and people from Camas·Prairie who would take three and four days driving during the horse-and-buggy days; but they were all there. The cowboys in their chaps and regalia were there. The Indians from Lapwai and Kamiah and DeSmet Mission were there, dressed in their feathers and blankets of many colors. Their squaws with the papooses strapped to their backs stood in the crowd to view the great excitement of the big iron horse run by steam, the great invention of the white man. Fifes and drums and the local band made a great noise.

When at last the engine and coaches came in sight, a great cheer rent the air. As the train stopped, the great multitude packed around the engine as tight as sardines. The engine was a very small affair compared to what you see today, but it had a tall smokestack, and it surely could blow a lot of smoke out of the tall chimney and a lot of steam from everywhere. As not more than 15% of the people had ever seen a train, it was great excitement to them. All at once the bell began to ring, and the engineer called out, "You folks will have to get out of the way, for I am going to turn around." He told the truth, for he was going to the roundtable to turn the engine around; but it was misunderstood by the crowd, and they went helter-skelter over each other. The Indian braves stood in front of their klootchmans with their papooses on their backs, and as they stamped over them, it was lucky that they wore moccasins, or there might have been a decrease in the Indian populations.

Next day was the day set for the excursion to Colfax at 10:00 a.m. and return. I put the cayuse in the livery stable that day and walked to the depot. The train arrived. The engineer went to the roundhouse to turn the engine around. Some of the coaches on the track were for children, some for young people, and some for married couples. As I was 24, I took the young people's coach. It was crowded to the limit with these young people. I doubt if a half-dozen ever rode a train before. People will call a ship "she" but they called the engine "he." They would say, "I wonder where he is gone. Will he push us back to Colfax?" After a while the engine came back on another track, and they said, "He is going off and leaving us."

At the fairgrounds there was a sham battle between the settlers and Indians. It was all good, but we had to leave early, so did not know who got licked. There were two trains that would leave for Moscow, one at 4:30 and the other after midnight. The girls would have to take the first one, for their folks would be in Moscow to meet them. We had scant time to make the train. We went on a dogtrot. On account of eating all the candy and all the big popcorn balls, the girls were very thirsty, but we had no time to look for water. There were only a few on the coach, for most of them stayed for the last train after the grand ball that night. I showed the girls how to press down on the "thinking bob" on the water tank that would give them ice-cold water. They camped there and drank glass after glass, and at last the tank went dry. But it did not matter much, for we were then within one mile of Moscow. Their folks were there to meet them, and I took a sad farewell of the girls.

I got Roman Nose out of the livery stable and made for my cabin home, satisfied I had seen something that would not be seen again, and that was the coming of the first railroad into Moscow. The effect of this railroad was great. The farmers hauled their wheat, oats, barley, and flax to be shipped direct to Portland. Groceries, clothing, farm implements, barb wire, etc., were sold at prices the settlers could afford to pay. The inconvenience of doing without those things and cooking on a fireplace was now past. The real pioneer days were gone, never to return again.

– 1885 from Westward to Paradise

CIRCLE OF WOMEN

by Kim Barnes

Mary Hallock Foote's "Afternoon at a Ranch".

Challis women, circa 1903.

*Like an ambush, the forest
rose around the circled trailers.
Wooden and straight and scrubbed
to the splintered floors, they stood stilted
on tamarack and pine. The men every day
off to the woods, the smells of heart-
rot and chain oil, the diesel breath
of machinery. And the women, in days
of long summer and snowed-in winter,
each morning rose to put on
make-up before the bacon and biscuits,
before the gooey-eyed children came
stumbling across the numbing linoleum
to lick the sweet crust of jam jars.
Men gone, children to school,
they nursed the babies and smoked
carefully. They painted their nails,
mending each tear with tissue
and glue. Siren Red and Playfully Pink
flashed like trout through the dishwater.
Wedged in highchairs, the women cut
one another's hair, Sears models
for inspiration, and numbed their ears
with ice before piercing the lobes
with needles fire-blackened.
Denim stained their wash. Pitch
ambered their furniture. Hot mornings,
in meadows of camas and yarrow,
they tanned while brown children in the near
creek clacked stones, and cicadas
whirred away the sound of metal teeth
cutting the fir, the cedar, the very air
the women breathed. Nights, husbands
home and fed, the next day's lunches
packed, they slept in the clean silence
of mountains. My mother, my aunts, acting
as though the men were not intruders
but the very reason, painted
and sweetened their days for greasy touches,
sweet sap kisses, and sawdust sifting their beds
like sand. The men must have thought themselves
lucky then, finding them waiting,
golden-shouldered, hungry for more.* ✒

Chapter XI
IDAHO OUTDOORS

THE ACTIVE FRONTIER

by Ann Vanderbilt

Outdoor recreation is native to Idaho, an inseparable part of an active present and past. Pursuits which a century ago were essential to frontier living-fishing, hunting, hiking, horsepacking, river travel-are still essential in the 1990s, though priorities have changed. Our physical survival no longer

depends on catching a cutthroat or shooting a sage hen for dinner, but our mental well-being has a lot to do with the feel of the fish when it strikes or the sight and sound of the bird when it flushes.

Idaho is gifted with a wealth of natural resources, a diversity of landscape, and the Federal Government (perhaps less a gift than a fortuitous accident), which manages two-thirds of the state's land. In fact, Idaho's mid-section encompasses the largest classified Wilderness area in the lower 48 states. In an era of expanding private ownership, land development and limited access, the existence of public lands- especially two-thirds of an entire state! - is a flashback to the frontier. And it is exactly this hint of the frontier, of the unfenced, the untrammeled and the undiscovered, which lures an ever-growing number of tourists to a state whose celebrity is no longer solely based on spuds.

After all, Idaho is the state where Ernest Hemingway fished, Gary Cooper hunted, Jimmy Carter rafted, and Jackie Onassis skied. Outdoor recreation is the message here, and with tourism firmly settled as Idaho's third largest industry, the message is obviously getting through. A first-time visitor to Idaho from the East Coast, who until recently believed that grizzly bears were a backyard hazard west of the Mississippi, commented last summer, "On a clear day in New York you look across the Hudson and see Hoboken. On a clear day in Idaho you step out your back door and see what America looked like 100 years ago."

It was a rugged land then, and it remains a rugged land. After its neighboring states carved out their borders over a century ago, the familiar wide-based, long-handled wedge of Idaho was left. Deep canyons and needle-sharp mountains scar its face. Fast flowing rivers, quiet streams and Paul Bunyan-size lakes cut through forests where deer inhabit the shadows. Travel by foot, horse, boat, bicycle or four-wheel-drive is *de rigueur*. Yet, a tennis racket and golf clubs are not out of place. Nor is an inner tube for a lazy afternoon of spinning in circles with the current.

Over twenty excellent boating rivers criss-cross Idaho, ranging in difficulty from mellow ripples to world-class whitewater. Each year in downtown Boise over a quarter-million inner-tubers and rafters launch their craft on a 6-mile stretch of the gently-flowing Boise River. In one day alone, 15,000 floaters propel downstream to escape the August heat, while 35 miles north on the North Fork of the Payette the throaty roar of continuous rapids is the *creme de la creme* of kayaking, the spice of life to a select few.

The names of Idaho's white-water rivers and their rapids ring with a magic all their own: Big Mallard on the River of No Return, Velvet Falls and Pistol Creek on the Middle Fork of the Salmon, Wild Sheep in Hell's Canyon, Ladle on the Selway, and the black-walled Bruneau where the rapids are Class IV and the car shuttle is Class VI. Commercial raft trips have

Road and mountain bike competition thrive throughout Idaho, but riders today would still appreciate the Coeur d'Alene bicycle club at the beginning of the century.

become big business in Idaho with all the amenities pre-arranged and pre-paid.

Traditional style dories also drift and spin down Idaho's rivers, as do private parties in kayaks and canoes. Only the jet boats buck the current, traveling up where nature runs down.

Jet boating has a tremendous following in Idaho, as evidenced by the World Championship Jet Boat and Inflatable Boat Races held in 1988 on the Clearwater, Snake, Salmon and Payette rivers in the western part of the state. Jet boats, which are propelled forward by water sucked through the engine, have little draft, making it possible to navigate shallows and rapids impassable to other motorized craft.

While all manner and size of watercraft are plying the surface of Idaho's rivers and lakes, the fish of dreams- a 30 pound steelhead, a 60 pound sturgeon - circles silently below. Asked why he fishes, one Idaho native replies, "Trout take you to the very best places, to some of the prettiest parts of Idaho." And he's right. There's Henry's Lake in the east for rainbows, cutthroats and brookies, and Silver Creek - a fertile, spring-fed creek south of Sun Valley with lots of insects and lots of wary trout. North in the Panhandle, Lake Pend Oreille teems with 14 species of game fish including Kokanee

salmon and a world-record 32-pound Dolly Varden. In the Snake River near Lewiston, sturgeon of mythic proportions patrol the depths.

And of course there's always steelhead. "Dry flies," says one fisherman, "that's the most exciting way to catch them." Other anglers swear by Hot Shots, Wee Willies and Sammies. All seem to be dreaming as they speak, hip deep in the Salmon or Clearwater, an imaginary steelhead on the line. When asked where's the best fishing they've ever had, they answer "Idaho," but not their secret spot, and continue twisting turkey feathers into a Muddler Minnow.

Hunting has its secret spots as well, and like fishing has a mystique which spreads far beyond Idaho's borders. Old photos of Ernest Hemingway and Gary Cooper, their shoulders draped with pheasants and shotguns, build a rough-and-ready image for this rugged state. Grouse-hunting over hills stacked one above the other like sacks of potatoes, or crawling belly-down through the sagebrush "glassing" a herd of

antelope, takes sportsmen back to an earlier era, a wilder time. There are muzzleloader seasons in Idaho and autumn and winter months when bow hunters stalk their prey in full camouflage and blackened faces. There are permits for mountain lion, mountain goats, bighorn sheep and black bear . . . a true sign of existing wilderness, that tantalizing hint of the frontier.

Wilderness has many definitions. One writer, D.J. Allen, has described it as "earth space where it is legal for both land and people to be useless." Idaho, which has over four million acres of legal wilderness (an area larger than the states of Connecticut and Rhode Island combined), excels in this department. Hiking, climbing and horsepacking, all popular Gem State pastimes, don't lead to job promotions or a down payment on a new car. In the Snake River Birds of Prey National Area, eagles, hawks and falcons do nothing more useful than hanging loop-deloops on the desert winds. Squeeze ups, tree molds and blue dragon lava in the Craters of the Moon refer to natural formations, not economic trends. And the only crops grown in the Seven Devils Peaks or the Sawtooth Mountains are boulders, lakes, flowers and solitude.

But solitude is, indeed, a crop, one which Idaho possesses in abundance and markets to a populace up to their ears in bustle and stress. Look for it 9,300 feet down at the bottom of Hell's Canyon, the deepest gorge in America, or 12,655 feet up on the top of Mt. Borah which shot farther into the air after a recent earthquake. Trail a mountain goat up a peak in the Frank Church River of No Return Wilderness and survey two million acres of federally-protected land. Roll down the Bruneau Sand Dunes, lead a 5.10 rock climb in the Silent City of Rocks, horsepack into the White Clouds, ride your mountain bike over the Nez Perce Trail, or for a change of pace, sink a putt for a golfing birdie with a golden eagle overhead.

Golf is a good sport in general for civilized recreation and a great sport in Idaho for uncivilized views. Beyond the well-groomed fairways and manicured greens, a wild backdrop of lakes and rivers, forests and mountains, gives a sense of cosmic perspective to missed wedge shots and bungled drives. Golf courses abound across the state (72 at last count), and carry such evocative names as Shadow Valley, Ponderosa Springs, Hazard Creek and Thunder Canyon. Golf tournaments, with celebrities playing for fun and charity, stud Idaho's warm weather calendar as do an eclectic assortment of other recreational events.

In late spring, the K&K Fishing Derby at Lake Pend Oreille pits man against fish in a week-long quest for the largest kamloops trout and Kokanee salmon. In July, hot air balloonists gather in Driggs on the western slope of the

skating lanes. In many areas trails are maintained by snowcats only slightly less bulky and powerful than those used to groom the downhill slopes.

Without question great numbers of winter enthusiasts have gone to Idaho just because of that heady word, that heady image-skiing. Idaho's romance with the alpine slopes began over 50 years ago when an Austrian count, in search of a location for America's first downhill resort, ended his quest in Ketchum. A half century later not one, but eighteen alpine resorts,

Tetons and launch skywards at daybreak to test their skills as pilots. In October, the International Draft Horse Show in Sandpoint puts horsepower and manpower in muscular perspective.

Speaking of sports on the move and moving into winter, cross-country skiing has exploded in popularity across a state eminently suited in snowfall, terrain and climate to becoming a nordic mecca. Idaho has kept pace with growth and change nationwide; its resorts and recreational hot spots feature telemark skiing, backcountry huts, wilderness touring, and hundreds of kilometers of machine-set tracks and

including Count Schaffgotsch's famous "find," Sun Valley, dot Idaho's downhill map.

Skiing in a state of over 83,000 square miles with a population barely over one million is a powerful draw. So is the amount of snow that falls each winter-500 inches at Grand Targhee in the Tetons, the length of ski runs-up to three miles long at Schweitzer in the Selkirk Mountains, and the maximum vertical drop-3,400 feet from top to bottom at Sun Valley. The reality of these statistics is more skiing and less waiting, uncrowded runs and untracked powder.

Pack trips to the Sawtooths, Smokies, Boulders, or Pioneers are a good choice to explore Idaho's mountains and isolated outback and upback.

Of course, Idaho's astonishing public lands-to-people ratio-35 1/2 acres per person, holds an equal advantage for non-motorized and motorized winter recreation. With so much open territory and such vast expanses of snow-covered terrain, skiing often takes a backseat to snowmobiling. Well-organized statewide with funding for a variety of snowmobile services and facilities, the ORMV (Off-Road Motor Vehicle) recreationists of winter have 5,000 miles of machine-groomed trails to choose from, more than in any other western state.

What it boils down to, this astonishing variety of activities, is a state with an outdoor history, a vigorous tradition interwoven with the land. Idaho is billed as "The Great Getaway." "Discover the Undiscovered" read the tourist brochures, a message not only with a punch but with a hearty dose of truth. Those who live in and visit Idaho are shaped by its spaces. Fresh Idaho air massages away the cares of city living. Fresh Idaho waters provide a panoramic carousel of sun and wind-laundered scenery.

People are exploring new ways to minimize stress and reestablish a balance. The realization is upon us that certain underpinnings of mental and physical well-being have been eroded by conflicting modern-day demands of family, society and career. Out-door enjoyment is not a new but an old way of regaining equanimity, of rebuilding that balance. In Idaho, recreational freedom floats down the Salmon, drives a snow-mobile through Island Park, and shoots a par four over the hill from a browsing elk. Possibilities are not limited by overcrowded camp-sites and liftlines. Big Brother isn't watching from the Bighorn Crags.

Call it escape, adventure, recreational freedom. Call it Idaho: the active frontier.✑

WATER OF LIFE

by Clarence Stilwill

Much of life in Idaho can be defined by her rivers, the type of land they run through and the men and women attached to that land. In the north, large, placid and screened as if for privacy by its border of cotton woods, the Kootenai drops quietly down from Montana, meanders through the Purcell Trench and exits without fanfare into Canada. Dowager Queen of the Idaho Panhandle, serenely beautiful, she treats her neighbors, and they her, with kindly benevolence.

The people who live within sight of this river reflect her characteristics. Here Idaho shelters mostly quiet, hardworking folk who enjoy the same sort of privacy as their tree-shrouded river. They go about their business, mostly farming and logging, with a modest efficiency similar to that with which the Kootenai enters and leaves their valley.

Dammed now in Montana, the Kootenai no longer ravishes the adjacent cropland. The extensive system of flood-control dikes now function mainly as service roads and farm borders, rather than as first lines of defense against the spring floods. Lower yet, where the panhandle becomes the pan, the Clearwater enters the state. Born in Montana as the child of two wild and beautiful parents, the Lochsa and the Selway, this lovely offspring was once a loggers' workhorse bearing a winter's timber harvest to the mills at Lewiston in the spring. It is not hard to imagine the cries and curses of the timber beasts and river pigs who leaped nimbly from log to log. Shod in cork boots, pike poles in hand, they kept the sticks flowing downriver, always working to prevent a jam. Those cries are silent now, yet the river rolls on as if to say, "The lives of men along my banks come and go, but left alone I will flow much the same forever."

To be left alone forever, by law with the nation's blessing, is the mighty Salmon River. Fed by the snowpack of all of Idaho's central mountain ranges-the Sawtooths, the White Clouds, the Lemhi range and the Bighorn Crags among others-this river and her blood-related sister, the Middle Fork of the Salmon, together form part of the Frank Church River of No Return Wilderness Area and have spawned a tourist industry that affects thousands of Idahoans and visitors to the state.

River running, with or without a guide, is a classic way to use a renewable resource without damaging it. Managed correctly, afford a wonderful way of life and enrich the lives of countless numbers of people for as many years as we care to protect it.

Out on the southern deserts of the state there is another kind of river, a different sort of people and different type of protection from encroachment. It's called inaccessibility.

To some, the far southern reaches of Idaho are an inhospitable place, barren, windswept, sparse of vegetation and life. Gazing out from the rim of one of the canyons calls to mind a line from Robert Frost, "not a soul for a windbreak, between me and the North Pole." He could have written it standing in the middle of the Owyhee desert.

A private hot spring break along the Salmon.

The people who have attached themselves to this land seem to share its characteristics. Spare, reserved, they possess an economy of word and motion that stems from living with a land that demands economy just to sustain life.

Though friendly, they have a tighter set to their lips, a deeper squint to their eyes, with the far-off, over-the-horizon look of people used to sensing what is out there, what is coming their way. They are cowmen, buckaroos and dry farmers, with many of the old skills, the old ways. Like the land around them, they live a life of make do, or do without.

Ahh, but the rivers and the canyons. The Jarbige, the Bruneau, the upper Owyhee and the middle, lower and south forks blossom in the spring like desert flowers, passable for only a few short weeks on scant runoff from the desert mountains; some years; not at all.

Not for the faint-hearted floater, some of those canyons require more work than play, just to get through. The weather can drop with startling speed from an eighty-degree spring day to a blinding snowstorm. The rivers can lull you to sleep with hours of lazy drifting and then, within seconds, stamp your boat onto a rock and leave you standing on shore with your gear floating downriver.

The mighty Snake or the legendary "River of No Return", Idaho's rivers inspire and captivate.

Why go? How to get there? I won't tell you, but I will tell you that if you've done what it takes to get there and you find yourself at the bottom of one of those desert gorges staring up at the rim and a private patch of sky, then you will deserve the gifts given to you. You will have earned them.

Finally we come to the mother of Idaho Rivers, the Snake. Beginning at the Idaho-Wyoming border, the Snake describes a large fish-hook through the lower parts of Idaho, curving at the shank at Farewell Bend, parting with the old Oregon Trail on the eastern edge of the State of Oregon. There it heads due north with a vengeance, to be trapped and pooled behind three of the major dams in the northwest's power system before escaping to plunge wildly into Hell's Canyon, America's deepest gorge.

Created by the runoff of the eastern snowpack of the Teton Mountains near Jackson Hole in Wyoming; conjoined and made larger by the Henry's Fork, which drains the western snowpack of the same range; charged by the giant aquifer beneath the Arco and Shoshone deserts and fed by many of Oregon's creeks and

rivers, it is joined by the Main Salmon in the canyon and the Clearwater at Lewiston. It leaves the state quietly, becoming a major contributor to the vast Columbia River watershed.

Wherever the Snake goes she creates a way of life or a livelihood for the people along her banks: river running near Jackson Hole, recreation and power at Swan Valley Dam in Wyoming, fish and bird habitat near the Henry's Fork and power boating at American Falls Dam. This grand river also feeds families many miles from its twisting course; miles of intricate irrigation canals funnel water to thousands of acres of orchards and fertile farmland on both sides of the Snake River Canyon.

Golf courses within the canyon at Twin Falls, fish farms, nature conservancies and

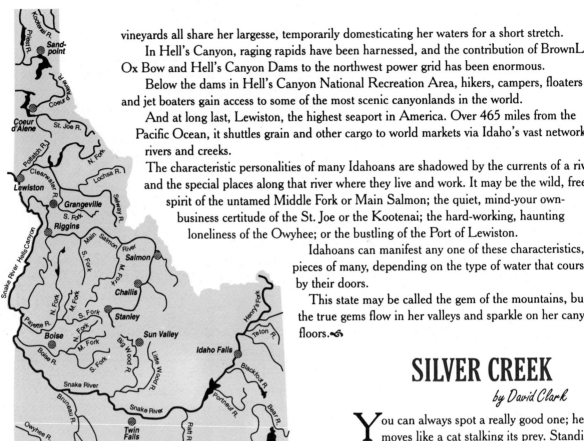

vineyards all share her largesse, temporarily domesticating her waters for a short stretch.

In Hell's Canyon, raging rapids have been harnessed, and the contribution of BrownLee, Ox Bow and Hell's Canyon Dams to the northwest power grid has been enormous.

Below the dams in Hell's Canyon National Recreation Area, hikers, campers, floaters and jet boaters gain access to some of the most scenic canyonlands in the world.

And at long last, Lewiston, the highest seaport in America. Over 465 miles from the Pacific Ocean, it shuttles grain and other cargo to world markets via Idaho's vast network of rivers and creeks.

The characteristic personalities of many Idahoans are shadowed by the currents of a river, and the special places along that river where they live and work. It may be the wild, free spirit of the untamed Middle Fork or Main Salmon; the quiet, mind-your own-business certitude of the St. Joe or the Kootenai; the hard-working, haunting loneliness of the Owyhee; or the bustling of the Port of Lewiston.

Idahoans can manifest any one of these characteristics, or pieces of many, depending on the type of water that courses by their doors.

This state may be called the gem of the mountains, but the true gems flow in her valleys and sparkle on her canyon floors.⊸

SILVER CREEK
by David Clark

You can always spot a really good one; he moves like a cat stalking its prey. Standing completely motionless, he stares hour after hour at his target - a one-foot-square area of water surface. Sporadically, like the nervously twitching tail of a deer, his fly rod flicks backwards and forwards, placing the fly in a slightly different spot each time it rests. Pulling back on his pole, he pounces and sets the hook, sending a rainbow trout into a frenzy punctuated by aerial leaps and splashing water. This is the action of which fly fisherman dream. And it is the reason they seek out Silver Creek.

If you asked any group of fly fisherman to name the top trout streams in the country, Silver Creek would seldom be left out. Many of these fishermen might even list it as the most challenging stream to be found anywhere.

Thousands of fly fishermen make the pilgrimage to this stream, which is known as the graduate school for fly fishermen. He is quick to assert, "The challenge is not just hype. No matter how good an angler you are, Silver Creek will humble you sooner or later."

What makes this stream such a challenge for fishermen? The answer lies in the character of its water. Silver Creek is not the typical Idaho stream. It does not originate directly from the melting snows of the high country. It does not overflow its banks during the spring runoff and drop to a trickle by fall. It does not freeze up with ice in the winter and turn warm to the touch in summer. Silver Creek doesn't do any of these things because it is a spring creek.

Silver Creek owes its origins to the Big Wood River. Ten miles to the north of the headwaters of Silver Creek, a portion of the stream sinks into the ground. This water then flows underground until it resurfaces as a series of springs. When the water from these springs combine, they form Silver Creek.

It is the underground voyage of this water that so drastically alters its nature. Along its subterranean route, the water warms or cools, taking on the temperature of the rock it passes through. When this water surfaces, it has acquired a constant temperature of around 52 degrees. The journey also changes the creek's flow from the rolling, rushing current of a mountain stream, to a steady seep that moves more like the water in a farmer's canal. Because of its gentle flow and moderate temperature, Silver Creek provides near-perfect living conditions for both trout and insects.

Fly fishermen come to Silver Creek because the equation of ideal water conditions plus profuse insect hatches, combined with large numbers of fat trout, equals a potentially incredible fishing experience. But there is one variable that can reduce this equation to zero - "selective trout."

Since the slow-moving water of a spring creek makes it easy to closely inspect anything that floats by, the fish in Silver Creek have become very particular about what they choose to feed upon. Thus, these trout have earned the reputation for being incredibly selective. They have become experts at identifying the feather,

Silver Creek today is maintained by the Nature Conservacy, a non-profit organization dedicated to preserving pristine natural environments around the world.

hair and hook of the fisherman's artificial fly.

The discriminating nature of Silver Creek's trout becomes most evident when the hatch is so thick that a fisherman cannot breath without inhaling an insect, but the fish continue unerringly to ignore his fake offering. It is even more frustrating for the angler when there are so many fish sipping in insects that their spree produces a sucking sound audible thirty feet away, and yet in four hours of fishing, not a single trout can he induced to strike. Not one.

It is this type of scenario that gives Silver Creek its reputation for being tough. To succeed here, the fly fisherman must be perfect. The size, color and shape of the imitation fly must be an exact match of the real insect. Fly line and leader must remain undetectable. The presentation and float of the fly must appear perfectly natural.

Consequently, Silver Creek has become the Mount Everest of fly fishing and every year, over 8,000 fishermen come to see if it can live up to its reputation. ✑

DENIZENS OF THE DEEP

by Andrew Slough

It was late afternoon when the first faint tap echoed through the braided dacron line. In early August the Hells Canyon section of the Snake River is laced with strands of drifting weed, and at first I wondered if perhaps a clump had hit the line. It had been two hours since I lowered the sour chicken leg soaked in coyote musk into the deep hole and by now it would have lost much of its flavor, if it was still attached to the hook at all.

"Probably a weed," I decided, and took a turn on the Penn Senator reel as I watched a trout roll along the edge of the main current. Experience has taught me that fish usually bite when you pay the least attention, so I studied a deer feeding high on the opposite hillside and waited.

I decided to hit the next take. I took a firm purchase on the coffee can-sized reel and braced against the rowing frame. In the next instant the fish saved me the trouble. The line simply went slack while I spun the crank and prayed for weight.

Then it felt as if I'd hooked the bottom, as the tip started toward the water. There was no give in this fish, only the reel's startled shriek as it felt the sting of the hooks and charged downstream. I could not lift the rod tip. The reel was shedding line at an alarming rate and no matter how hard I tried, I could not get the rod tip up.

Sturgeon!

And from the howling reel and straightened rod, a big one.

As fish go, the Idaho white sturgeon is something of a mystery. According to Fred Partridge, a Senior Fisheries Research Biologist for the Idaho Department of Fish and Game, it is almost impossible to draw hard-and-fast conclusions about sturgeon. Though the fossil record dates back 100 million years to the Cretaceous period, sturgeon are docile, reclusive fish, choosing the Snake's deepest holes and swiftest water as their homes.

Sturgeon are bottom feeders, constantly rubbing against rocks, and are therefore extremely resistant to tagging.

Because they are difficult to keep track of, one study will claim sturgeon migrate, the next will insist they are territorial; one says they spawn in fast water, the next in deep eddies; one says they can live to be fifty years old, the next a century. No one disputes, however, that Idaho's white sturgeon can grow to be stupendously big. A sepia photograph taken in 1898 shows a 1500-pound, 20-foot monster being dragged by a four-mule team onto a bank below Twin Falls.

Huge sturgeon have provided fishing challenges along the Snake River for as long as people have fished. The sturgeon have gotten better looking, the men puportedly have not.

The Snake has changed a great deal since the turn of the century. Dams now block upstream migration, limiting both the sturgeon's food base and its ability to spawn. Also, as a practical matter, the Twin Falls monster was caught on a set line (a cable with hooks strung to an anchored barrel, now illegal). The largest sturgeon caught on a rod and reel was 600 pounds, which might

only indicate the equipment's upper limit.

Due to increasing pressure, concerns about the number of sturgeon fishermen and their relative success have surfaced. For that reason the Department of Fish and Game created a mandatory permit system in 1989. The permit is free and records the length of each fish, where it was caught, and the number of hours spent fishing for it.⤳

ROCK CLIMBING
CITY OF ROCKS, IDAHO

In high desert wilderness on the edge of the Snake River Plain is some of the West's most ancient stone-300-foot granite spires as old as 2.8 billion years. On this rock, climbers have etched out more than 600 routes, rated from 5.4 to 5.14a, in the 14,300-acre City of Rocks National Reserve. Upper City and Parking Lot make up the City's scenic downtown-a maze of batholiths with hundreds of one-pitch routes and occasional short second pitches to the summits. Scream Cheese (5.9), a six-bolt sport climb, is a classic route at Parking Lot. In Upper City, afternoon shade is an added bonus of the Upper Breadloaves East area; check out Urban Renewall, a one-pitch crack climb (5.11a).

Daytime fall temperatures hover in the seventies, but be prepared for nighttime lows in the thirties. City of Rocks is 75 miles southeast of Twin Falls; take Idaho 77 south outside Burley. Roadside campsites, are plentiful on the dirt road between Bath Rock and Elephant Rock, but can fill up quickly, especially on fall week-ends.⤳

THE EVERGREEN THAT ISN'T

It's a shame to look at a hillside covered with dead pine trees. You wonder what got them . . . fire, insects, disease. sometimes it's difficult to tell. And sometimes, though they look it, they're not dead at all.

Many of us can't tell one type of tree from another. There are so many different kinds. About the only thing we're sure of is that trees with leaves lose them during the winter, and trees with needles keep them year round. That's an easy rule . . . until you run across a tamarack.

The western larch, or tamarack, has needles. Most people would call it a pine tree. But it does the strangest thing in the fall. The tamarack turns orange, or brilliant yellow, then drops its needles.

Tamarack is often mixed in with ponderosa pine, Douglas fir, and lodgepole pine. In the fall the brilliant trees stand out like a scattering of glowing candles among the evergreens.

You can see tamaracks around McCall, in the Little Salmon River country, along the Clearwater River, and many places in northern Idaho.

WILD SPIRITS
by Patti Sherlock

On a rolling hill at the foot of the Lost River Range, a dapple-gray stallion lifts his muzzle to the evening breeze. The breeze brings him the scent of buttercups, sage and mountain mahogany-and something else. A warning.

The stallion wheels, squeals and nips at his mares, setting them to flight. Over the range the mares and colts race, smoothing out the furrowed ground with giant strides. Mane and tail streaming, the stallion brings up the rear so he can hurry the harem and stay between it and possible danger.

"I think most everyone likes the idea the horses are out there," said Craig Nemeth, Salmon Bureau of Land Management range conservationist. "Especially since we are controlling their numbers."

According to BLM research, horses have run wild in the Challis area since the 1870s, when white men brought horses to the area and turned them loose. Settlers gathered them during annual roundups, then trailed some to Blackfoot or other railroad stations for shipping, broke some to work, and turned some back onto the range. One year, in the 1920s, wranglers rounded up 1,000 head of horses in the Pahsimeroi Valley. Pearl Oberh's book, Between These Mountains, estimated the number of horses running free between Leodore and the Birch.

Today, after trying various numbers of horses on the range, the Salmon BLM maintains the Challis horse herd at under 200 animals. At that number, inbreeding poses no problem and the range, which in the 1970s carried several hundred more horses, shows signs of healing.

Other bands of wild horses, numbering about 200 and administered by the Boise BLM office, also run free in Idaho. The total number of horses on BLM land in the West is 37,000. Nevada has most of them, about 27,000.

The BLM gathers surplus horses in the fall, usually every other year. In the past, wranglers were contracted to collect the animals. Now, an experienced crew of BLM employees travels the West.

Those who want to adopt horses come to watch, too. A person may adopt four animals a year. The cost is $125 per horse, plus a promise to maintain it in adequate facilities.

Boise endurance rider Naomi Tyler has won national competitions with her adopted wild horse, Mustang Lady. Mustang Lady, a gray, grew up on the Owyhee wild horse range.

No road signs announce the locations of wild horse ranges. "The idea of the wild horse program is to keep them in a natural setting. No one wanted a zoo atmosphere," Nemeth said. Challis, so far from any population area, is exactly what horse protection advocates had in mind. Horses live unmolested by tourists, yet have the advantage of being monitored from a distance, to make sure they thrive.

"Winter Horses, New Meadows. All in left foreleg lead and headed for the barn." - Steve Snyder

WHO *by Steve Snyder*

*"Golden Eagle.
Out of element in
soft sugar powder
snow, learning
survival lessons,
she flew."
– Steve Snyder*

Who is happy?
Who is loving themselves?
Who is loving this planet as much as themselves?
This unfathomable galactic-earthy-body,
    spinning in space,
    surrounded by a universe,
    that is awash in a sea
    of star twinkles and winks.

The dominate world view,
    "denial of wrong,"
    regardless of consequences,
    to what, who, where, how, why, or when it hurts
    is living
    in the shadow of truth.
It is a philosophy of words,
    designed for the people condition,
    apart
    from the sustained natural balance of our planet.
Institutions of old words,
    are being taught and learned,
    absorbed unquestioned,
    by global human computer-like-brains.
Where are the individual's own words?
Where are the words of conscience
    and the words of righteousness?
What are the words of respect
    and reverence?

When will there be words
    for common sense and compassion?
Why are there no words
    for global healing,
    through wholeness of self?
Who is responsible for the word
    legacy?
The philosophy, "truth of right,"
    is grounded in planet health.
Decisions are based,
    on the survival
    of earth and human kind.
LET'S PLANET PEOPLE believe,
    in ethics, fairness and justice.
LET'S believe,
    in accountability, harmony and happiness.
LET'S believe,
    in clear-pure-bubbly water,
    clean air
    and rich soil,
    for frolicking frogs,
    hovering hummingbirds
    and baby bean stalks.
LET'S believe in singing, laughing and dancing,
    while
    we love, learn, grow, work, teach
    and
    inspire the un-aware. ✍

THE LONGING OF EAGLES

by
Robert Wrigley

No words can tell what they feel, how
mated for life they breed once a year
and no one calls it love, what preening
they do in the last light at dusk,
done for the good of the next-pure, habitual,
the sweet uncomplicated essence of instinct.
No gestures pass between them, no eloquent eye
belies a hunger not born of bad fishing,
and the annual surviving offspring blinks once
at its dead nestmate, kicked over the edge and gone.

I do not envy their flights, not climb
or dive or the hover in a hard wind,
outrigger wings gone quiveringly tense.
I do not envy what we call their play,
the swoops and feints, the talons-locked
free-fall tumble in the sun of a false spring.
I do not envy their beauty, not the keen eye
of the ornithologist, who can tell them apart.

I do not envy the air they fly through,
nor the waters that sustain them,
nor the darkness that has made of them
something rare. I do not envy their dignity.

For two weeks now I watched a single eagle
troll the canyon, and this morning
I found its mate, talons and tail-feathers removed,
a filthy hulk. I do not know if it is male or female,
but I would bet every word I love, the shot
that felled it was fired by a man. I wonder,
as he bent to his work-the hard jerks
at the feathers, the unsheathed
hatchet for the legs - I wonder
if the eyes were open, if even in death
they glared out with that fierce
dispassionate stare of the raptor,
the predator, knowing many things,
but not hatred, not need, not human love.

RAPTORS! *by Alice Koskela*

The sun hesitates just above the pines on the west side of Little Payette Lake. The water is as still as the air, reflecting perfectly the blue sky and green shoreline forest, a mirror for the stark grove of snags that rise like ruins from the lake. These barren trees, casualties of man's tampering with the boundaries of Little Payette, are the bane of boaters and human fishermen. But to a growing colony of ospreys, the graying timber columns are a perfect home.

We maneuver our boat carefully through a maze of half-submerged stumps, shading our eyes as we scan the ragged tree tops.

"There's one!" my daughter whispers, and points excitedly to a huge pile of sticks balanced high above the water on a pole-like snag. As if on cue, the big bird takes flight, making a slow, effortless circle above our heads.

"Eagle! Eagle!" cries my son, who is just two but already keen on raptors.

Our boat glides farther into this bleak but beautiful watery forest, and soon we are surrounded. There are gigantic nests in every direction: high-rise osprey architecture. A few seem dangerously close to the water, built before the lake was filled to its current irrigation capacity, close enough almost to touch as we drift past. But we are careful to keep our distance, content to count the pairs of birds who watch us warily from the rims of their stick-and-mud residences. Sometimes one will fly out to take a closer look at us, then return to the nest or a branch on a nearby snag. With binoculars we spot a few gangly fledglings, peeking over the edges of their lofty houses.

By the time we reach the eastern edge of the lake, we have counted a dozen nests, seen a score of stately birds soar overhead. We head back to the launch as the sun drops below the horizon, threading our way between dark shaggy-topped towers silhouetted in the fading light.

"Eagles!" my son murmurs happily. No one cares to confuse him, to subvert his first bird-watching rapture by correcting this minor taxonomic mistake. We are all keen on all raptors.

"Raptor" is the term used to refer to flesh-eating birds, and Idaho is a virtual raptor aerie, laying claim to a large indigenous population of predatory birds. The state boasts the 482,000-acre Snake River Birds of Prey Area, near Swan Falls Dam, including a spectacular river canyon and

habitat for hundreds of raptors of various species. Idaho also is home base for several sophisticated research projects on predatory birds, ranging from studies of local owls and ospreys to international programs for nearly-extinct tropical raptors.

In 1984 the World Center for Birds of Prey, operated by the Peregrine Fund, was established just outside of Boise. Aside from its well-known restoration efforts for the peregrine falcon in the U.S., the World Center operates programs to save endangered tropical raptors such as the Mauritius kestrel, the harpy eagle and the Teita falcon. Visitors to the World Center can view these rare birds during special tours. Each spring the Center hosts an annual Idaho Birds of Prey Festival, an event designed to increase understanding and appreciating raptors.

Despite the fact that Idaho has been well-blessed with raptors and recently, with raptor scientists, many experts believe that our new respect for birds of prey has come just in the nick of time. They worry about the future of the birds, pointing out that it is essential to provide sufficient natural habitat to ensure their permanent survival.

The Peregrine Fund and the World Center for Birds of Prey are working to undo the damage that the pesticides, poachers and an ever-shrinking natural habitat are wreaking on raptors worldwide.

Although the raptor population in Idaho continues to grow, thanks to individuals and groups supporting research and restoration programs and educational efforts, it is extremely important to maintain protection for the natural areas that support these birds of prey. The struggle to reintroduce these incredible birds into the skies of Idaho will be for naught if we leave them stranded, with no place to nest and with nothing to eat.

But now there is hope that future generations will be able to stand quietly and watch a bald eagle drop effortlessly from atop a huge evergreen, glide over a sparkling river, and dive into the water, retrieving dinner for its family.

The indescribable sense of freedom and well-being we receive from these graceful, wide-winged birds-eagles, hawks, falcons, owls, kestrels, goshawks and the like-is an integral part of life in Idaho, and well worth preserving.∽

PHILADELPHUS LEWISII

You Probably Call It Syringa

The Lewis and Clark expedition discovered, not only Idaho, but the Idaho state flower. In 1806 Captain Meriwether Lewis discovered and collected the first specimen of syringa. The shrub's scientific name, Philadelphus lewisii, recognizes that fact.

Of course, the plant wasn't new to the Indians. They had used it for generations, making soap from the leaves and arrows from the stems.

Syringa is a beautiful plant. The shrub grows from three to twelve feet high, and features large clusters of white flowers with bright yellow stamens. A hillside covered with syringa in the spring can look almost like a snowfield. It would be hard to miss a big patch of the plant, even blindfolded. Syringa gives off a strong aroma of orange. Many people call it mock orange.

You'll find syringa growing along streams and on hillsides to near 7,000 feet. It often grows along with chokecherry and serviceberry. One indicator of a large deer population is a stand of syringa that has been heavily browsed, because the animals normally prefer other foods.

Syringa, discovered by Meriwether Lewis, became Idaho's state flower in 1931. Another likely candidate for that honor might have been Clarkia, which is in the primrose family. It was also discovered along Idaho's Clearwater River, by Captain William Clark. ❦

"Porky II. Breakfast in a winter willow tree." – Steve Snyder

Dinner and a bath.

WOLVES RELEASED IN IDAHO

by Linda Kanamine

BOISE, Idaho - One hundred miles north of this thriving city in a vast, roadless, snowy wilderness, new tracks are about to be made.

Few of Idaho's 1 million residents will ever encounter the 5-inch paw prints, much less the gray wolves who'll make them, but just knowing the animals will be there has enraged and engaged an entire region.

"It's hard to believe I can actually see the day when we'll have wolves back," says a beaming Suzanne Laverty of the Wolf Education and Research Center in Ketchum.

But getting the wolves to this point has been a rocky ride, right up to the last minute.

A federal appeals court late Thursday vacated an order that had halted release of 12 Canadian gray wolves flown from Hinton, Alberta, to Great Falls, Montana. Four of the wolves are to be released in central Idaho, and the other eight in Yellowstone National Park.

In Idaho, the wolves will be released - possibly today in the snowy forests of the Frank Church-River of No Return Wilderness.

The Yellowstone wolves go to pens in the northeastern part of the park, where they will be set free next month.

And with a flick of their tails, these Canadian wolves will set in motion one of the most ambitious experiments ever to save an animal from extinction in the USA.

Much more is at stake than the mere survival of these 12 wolves and the other 18 that are expected to be released later this year.

Successes or failures will color debate over renewal of the Endangered Species Act, which is under intense criticism by Republican leaders in Congress. They argue that some measures to save plants and animals are too onerous on business and property owner.

But, without a doubt, the return of the wolf signals a new day in the West.

Renee Askins, a biologist and Wolf Fund director in Moose, Wyo., says the program finally fills a gaping void left in the region three generations ago when the wolf was intentionally eradicated by hunters.

"The wolf is the embodiment of wildness, and Yellowstone is the symbol of wild places," Askins says.

Symbolism aside, it is the people in Idaho, Wyoming and Montana who must deal with the reality of wolves roaming their forests.

West of Boise, in flat high desert terrain of Notus, rancher Brad Little is at the height of lambing season.

Hundreds of recently sheared ewes line 12-by-4-foot stalls within three long barns, most giving birth to twins. These fuzzy lambs and their mothers will begin the long walk to northern federal pastures in March, reaching the Boise National Forest just south of the wolf release site by June. And that makes for uneasy company, Little says.

Unlike Montana or Minnesota, where cattle and sheep typically stay in the same pasture areas year-round so that wolves have learned to stay away from the wellguarded herds, Idaho livestock are continually moved to new pasture.

"Wolves here have got no idea we're going to be there" says Little, whose 800 cows also graze in the national forest. "They'll get established in an area and all of a sudden we roll in with 2,000 sheep; those wolves will be pretty incensed.

Some have questioned the sense of uprooting wolves to a place where there is such controversy, coupled with threats of illegal shooting.

"We've got to look at it like it's worth it. We're hoping to establish a whole population in two new areas and these are the individuals that are going to make it happen," says Fish and Wildlife Service wolf biologist Steve Fritts.

Because wolves have been absent for so many years, not even biologists can predict exactly how the animal will behave. But the unknowns are both the attraction and the possible pitfall of the experiment.

"Where is man without the beasts? If all the beasts were gone, men would die from great loneliness of spirit, for whatever happens to the beasts also happens to the man." —Chief Seattle.

"It would be one thing if they could guarantee (wolves) will stay in the wilderness. But our concern is, we know they will migrate," says Weiser sheep rancher Margaret Soulen.

But wolf program supporters will be delighted when the arguing stops. "Now it's finally going to be in the wolves hands," Askins says.

PROJECT WOLF POPULATION

Thirty wolves, 15 going to each area, are to be released each year for the next 3-5 years. Biologists hope the population will reach about 100 in each area by 2002.

WOLVES SURVIVING EACH AREA

1995	1996	1997	1998	1999	2000	2001	2002	2003
8	14	27	45	56	68	83	101	129

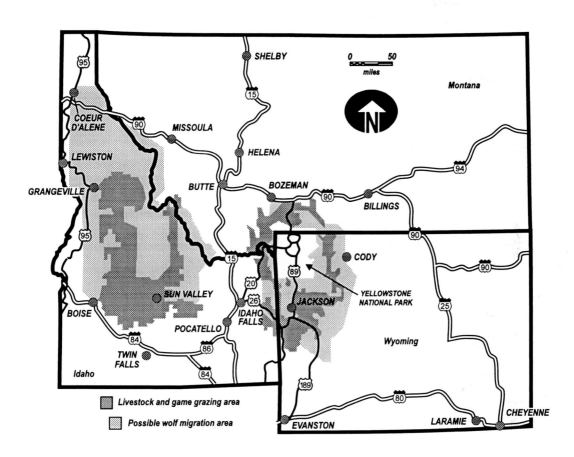

Livestock and game grazing area

Possible wolf migration area

Expected Migration

Upon release, the wolves are expected to move north toward Alberta, Canada, where they were caught. But, as they wander, they probably will find a mate and set up territories, commonly ranging 100 miles or more.

Characteristics

Length: 4.5 - 6.5 feet. Weight: 80 - 110 pounds. Height: 26 - 32 inches.

Feeding Habits

About 12 - 15 game animals per year. Can eat up to 22 pounds at one sitting, then go days, sometimes weeks, without eating.

Lifespan

7 - 10 years in the wild. 16 years in captivity.

Mortality

40% or higher for pups in the wild, 10% for adults.

Breeding Habits

Mating season starts in early January. Litter, averaging four to six pups, begin arriving mid-April to early May.

Packs

10 to 12 wolves. At age 2 - 4, wolves leave to set up new packs.

Estimate of Animals Killed by Wolves Annually in Idaho

	Population	Kills
Cattle	384,990	10
Sheep	100,713	57
Wild Game	241,400	1,650

HIGH POINTS
by Rick Baugher

The idea of cataloging a state's highest mountains is not new. Colorado's fabled "fourteeners," for example, have been recorded, publicized and climbed from almost every conceivable angle since the Hayden Survey of the 1870s made them accessible.

Idaho's highest peaks-and there are nine of them that rise over 12,000 feet-have not yet felt such a human imprint.

Here then is a glimpse of the High Nine, listed in descending order of elevation. Like siblings, they share some common traits, but each has its own unique personality. For a more detailed description, see the excellent guidebook *Exploring Idaho's Mountains* by Tom Lopez, 1990.

BORAH PEAK-elevation 12,622 feet. Lost River Range. Named for longtime U.S. Senator William E. Borah. People come from all over the country to Borah because of its "highest peak in Idaho" status. Around 300 people stand on its summit each year, making it "crowded" by Idaho standards. A few climbing routes have been forged on Borah, but there is only one sure way-the Southwest Ridge Route. As even this route has a treacherous spot, Borah is not a good mountain for beginners.

LEATHERMAN PEAK-elevation 12,230 feet. Lost River Range. Named for Henry Leatherman, an early settler and trapper in Lost River country. From this summit you can see the gruesome geology of twisted, tangled rock bands that comprise the sedimentary spine of Idaho's highest mountain range.

PEAK-elevation 12,200+ feet. Lost River Range. The PR people forgot to name Idaho's third highest mountain. In the late 1930s this hulk of a peak was called Sacajawea by Idaho author Vardis Fisher, though most climbers know it today as MT. CHURCH, after the visionary U.S. Senator who procured for the Gem State the largest tract of designated wilderness in the lower 48.

DIAMOND PEAK-elevation 12,197 feet. Lemhi Range. On clear winter days the snowy triangular slopes of this peak sparkle like facets of a diamond. When it's snow-free, 300-million/year-old coral fossils can be seen.

MT. BREITENBACH-elevation 12,140 feet. Lost River Range. Ski tracks have been observed high on this mountain.

PEAK-elevation 12,078 feet. Lost River Range. This seldom-climbed pillar of stone is a little controversial: Is it two peaks or one? The saddle between the north summit and higher south summit dips 200 feet. Mountaineering guidelines suggest 300 feet of dip and a half mile in distance to identify mountains as separate.

PEAK-elevation 12,065 feet. Lost River Range. This most hidden member of the High Nine is called MT. IDAHO or Elkhorn Peak. Most who endeavor to climb all nine save this one for last.

DONALDSON PEAK-elevation 12,023 feet. Lost River Range.

HYNDMAN PEAK-elevation 12,009 feet. Pioneer Range.

HOW SWEET IT (IDAHO) SKIS

by Claire Walter

Ever since 1936, when Averell Harriman directed the Sun Valley Lodge to be built on ranch land and the first chairlift to be strung up on a hill near Ketchum, skiers from all over America have been coming to Idaho. They have been coming for great skiing, magnificent scenery and an atmosphere of rustic comfort. Sun Valley, still one of the country's pre-eminent ski resorts, draws the overwhelming number of outlanders to Idaho.

But Idaho skiers are lucky ducks. The state boasts 18 ski areas, from Pomerelle near Albion, hard by the Utah line, to Schweitzer in Sandpoint, just 60 miles south of the Canadian border. Sun Valley may have given Idaho its half-century reputation as a top ski state, but even our smallest ski hills are substantial by other people's standards.

First among equals, of course, is Sun Valley, the country's first built-for-skiing resort, which was long in business when Aspen was just a mining ghost town and Vail a cow pasture.

Bald Mountain, one of America's classics, soars 3,400 vertical feet above the surrounding valley, and its skiable acres are also decidedly big-league. But statistics tell just part of the tale. Baldy dominates not only the landscape but also the minds and hearts of some of the country's best skiers.

It is a complex mountain, one of the few that can be skied in almost all compass directions. Baldy can be accessed from two points, Warm Springs and River Run, on the outskirts of Ketchum. Warm Springs on the north side offers skiing for everyone. Experts tackle the half-a-dozen steep runs, mostly up top, while intermediates and novices delight on a variety of runs ranging from medium-steep to wide and gentle.

The new Look-Out Express, climbing 3,144 vertical feet from the bottom of Warm Springs, has the greatest vertical of any high-speed quad in North America. The ride will take less than 10 minutes. When there are no lines (which is usually the case at Sun Valley anyway), aggressive experts riding the Look-Out Express all day will be able to ski an incredible 88,000 vertical feet in seven hours. Remember that 100,000 feet is acknowledged as a good week of heli-skiing.

Schweitzer Basin overlooking Sandpoint.

Between the top of Baldy and the expanse of Seattle Ridge are the famous Baldy Bowls, seven side by side bowls which rank among the top ski terrain in the world. Sun Valley's standards are so rigorous that these bowls are marked with modest blue squares, but at most other mountains they would sport black diamonds characterizing them as "most difficult."

Dollar mountain, the resort's smaller ski hill, has a gentle pitch and wonderful open slopes. It is staffed with members of one of the coun-try's best ski schools, making Sun Valley one of the finest places to learn how to ski.

If Bogus Basin were near Denver or Salt Lake City, its skiable acreage (2,000 acres) and frequent powder (over 100 inches a year) would make it a nationally known destination ski area. At 16 miles from Boise, it remains the biggest and one of the best day-trip mountains in America, and almost peripherally the secret preserve of canny skiers from all over the Pacific Northwest who like the snow deep, the atmosphere casual, the skiing great and the prices low.

Schweitzer Basin located 10 miles north of Sandpoint, in Idaho's Panhandle, is another huge ski area treasured by those in the know and ignored by those who have not been lucky or savvy enough to have discovered it.

Schweitzer's 2,400 vertical feet make it Idaho's second-highest skiing mountain, and its average annual snowfall of 200 inches rivals Sun Valley's and outstrips just about anything else in the state.

While there are gentle runs aplenty for small children and adult beginners, intermediate and advanced terrain accounts for four-fifths of Schweitzer's skiing. And it is the great tree skiing and magnificent basins, rilled with open bowls that make the place so special.

Grand Targhee is not technically in Idaho, but its address - Alta, Wyoming via Driggs, Idaho-is five words that speak volumes about its access as well. No matter where the state line runs and who gets the sales tax, for all practical purposes, it is more ours than theirs.

"Snow from heaven, not hoses," is the favorite slogan at Grand Targhee, a small ski resort with big snowfall-more than 500 inches

East-facing River Run is the site of Baldy's best-known expert turf. It is here that strong skiers put their leg muscles and resilience to the test on Exhibition, a steep slope with monster moguls and a chairlift carrying skiers overhead to watch the bumpers perform below. Actually, Exhibition is one of six canyons, ranging from medium-mild to super-steep. River Run also accesses handsome, super-groomed Seattle Ridge, where Sun Valley honors its most famous daughters. Gretchen's Gold is named for 1948 Olympic slalom chamipion Gretchen Fraser and Christin's Silver for 1984 Olympic silver medalist Christin Cooper.

each winter. Targhee has a minuscule bed base and no neighbors nearer than Jackson Hole, an hour away, from which it successfully tries to lure vacationers for a day of skiing. The result is no liftlines and powder that lasts and lasts.

Brundage Mountain, just north of McCall, Idaho, boasts the "driest, finest and most consistent" snow in Idaho, and proudly advertises the fact that they do not own one piece of snowmaking equipment.

The rest of Idaho's 18 ski ireas offer excellent, convenient, and uncrowded skiing for locals and visitors alike. ✍

BOGUS BASIN

by Claire Walter

Bogus Basin, just 16 miles north of Boise, essentially remains a local ski area-but what a local ski area. Its skiing exceeds that of many destination resorts, wrapping 360 degrees around one mountain and nearly three quarters of the way around another. There is a pleasant learning hill known as Deer Point, linked with the larger, infinitely more impressive terrain on Shafer Butte. Normally, great conditions prevail on 45 runs and hundreds of off-trail acres from November until well into spring.

Shafer, a greatly textured mountain, is full of major and minor ridges, drainages, headwalls and chutes. Groomed terrain comprises just a fraction of the bounty, which also includes dazzling off-trail skiing. Don't let Bogus's modest six chair, 1,800-foot vertical fool you into thinking this is small-potatoes skiing. Small potatoes brings small fry to mind, and it is worth noting that Bogus was one of the nation's pioneer ski areas in child care and ski instruction for wee ones. It remains a top family area.

There is a small, barebones slopeside condominium development, but basically, Bogus remains a busy area for locals. Groups can have a whale of a time at the resort if they're willing to amuse themselves up on the mountain, but other visitors are better off braving the 100-bend access road and staying in town. Bogus's 500 lighted acres comprise one of the biggest night-skiing operations in the Northwest, and the lights can be seen as far as downtown Boise. ✍

Nearby Bogus Basin has been a playground for Boiseans for years and years. Its square mileage is impressive, and today's lodge will soon be replaced just as this original one was years ago.

BRUNDAGE MOUNTAIN

by Claire Walter

Brundage remains one of the greatest bargains in the Rockies.

Brundage isn't just big and cheap. It's also darned good skiing by anyone's standards. The cut and groomed runs on the west-facing side of the mountain range from
steep, narrow liftlines to ballroom-wide slopes for beginning skiers. But Brundage's glory lies in the trees, where powder lingers in glades that are tight or narrow, steep or mellow, popular or hidden. This winter, Brundage is also offering snowcat powder skiing on the east side of the mountain.

This low-key family mountain is just outside of McCall, a charming town on the shore of Payette Lake. With downhill and cross-country racers on the U.S. Ski Team during seven out of the last 11 Winter Olympics, McCall is one of the towns which calls itself Ski Town USA (the other contender is Steamboat Springs, Colorado). McCall's most successful racer was Jean Saubert, who won a silver and a bronze at the 1964 Olympics, equalling the combined achievements of her better-known team-mates Billy Kidd and Jimmie Heuga, but she has since preferred to stay out of skiings limelight.

McCall is also primarily a summer resort, whose lodges and motels charge low rates. Its winter carnival over the week bridging the end of January and the beginning of February is known for immensely creative snow sculptures and a variety of special events.⋖

Burgdorff Hot Springs provides, summer or winter. Idaho has more thermal hot springs than Oregon, Washington, and British Columbia combined.

SKI AREAS IN IDAHO

Region 1

Lookout Pass
12 mi. East of Wallace on Hwy. 90
850' Vertical Drop

Schweitzer Basin
11 mi. N.W. of Sandpoint.
2,000' Vertical Drop

Silver Mountain
7 mi. South of Kellogg. 2,200' Vertical Drop

Region 2

Bald Mountain
6 mi. North of Pierce on Hwy 11.
975' Vertical Drop

Cottonwood Butte
5 mi. West of Cottonwood. 845' Vertical Drop

North South Ski Bowl
22 mi. N.E. of Potlatch. 500' Vertical Drop

Snowhaven
7 mi. South of Grangeville. 400' Vertical Drop

Region 3

Bogus Basin
16 mi. N. of Boise, Bogus Basin Rd.
1,800' Vertical Drop

Brundage
7 mi. N. of McCall; 100 mi. N. of Boise
1,600' Vertical Drop

Region 4

Magic Mountain
28 mi. S.of Hansen via I-84 Kimberly.
800' Vertical Drop

Pomerelle
Albion, 28 mi S.E. of Burley.
1,000' Vertical Drop

Region 5

Pebble Creek
Inkom, 15 mi. S.E. of Pocatello off I-15.
2,000' Vertical Drop

Region 6

Kelly Canyon
25 mi. N.E. of Idaho Falls on Hwy. 26.
938' Vertical Drop

Grand Targhee
78 mi. N.E. of Idaho Falls.
2,200' Vertical Drop

Region 7

Lost Trail
46 mi. N. of Salmon, on U.S. 93.
1,200' Vertical Drop

Soldier Mountain
12 mi. North of Fairfield - Hwy. 20.
1,400' Vertical Drop

Sun Valley
Ketchum, 80 mi. N. of Twin Falls.
3,400' Vertical Drop

Snowmobiles have 5,000 miles of groomed trails to choose from.

Idaho unBound **195**

*Cross country skiers can enjoy
renting a backcountry yurt.*

PARK N' SKI

by Paul Rawlings

Winter has arrived, and high in the Idaho mountain ranges the snow has begun to fall. Skis are being waxed and boots fitted, but not just for alpine skiing-not anymore.

For more than a decade now, cross-country skiers in the Gem State have benefited from an unusual program called Idaho Park N' Ski. Under the auspices of the State Department of Parks and Recreation, seventeen separate trail systems have been developed; in addition, four State Park Ski Areas have been created. This means that from Pocatello in the southeast to Boundary County in the panhandle, Nordic ski enthusiasts, are finding Idaho's outback to be user - friendly.

A season pass comes in the form of a windshield decal. Every vehicle must have one to use the designated trailhead parking lots.

Decals may be purchased at any of fifty different vendors throughout the state: sports shops, state park offices, Forest Service Ranger Stations, Chamber of Commerce offices, etc.

The various trail systems, which provide opportunities for skiers at all skill levels, are easily accessible for short day trips from towns throughout the state.

The most popular trail system in the program is the ten-mile loop at Lolo Pass on US-12 on the Idaho-Montana border. The region is less than an hour from Missoula and has good snow during the entire winter season due to its elevation of over 5,200 feet. The trail is groomed regularly, and skiers have access to both a warming shelter and restrooms.

Fish Creek Meadows, also in the north-central part of the state, continues to show increased use season after season.

Also in that part of the state, approximately an hour east of Moscow, skiers can find the twenty-four-mile Elk River Park N' Ski area. Scenic Elk Creek Falls provides a popular stop on this trail. Just a little further north, at Palouse Divide, beginning skiers can find eighteen miles of trail matched to their abilities.

The second most popular system of trails in the program is in the Idaho City area, where there are three separate parking areas and a total of almost thirty miles of trail. Perhaps the most dramatic skiing may be found at Banner Ridge, with its abundant challenges for the expert skier. The trail climbs 600 vertical feet in under three miles, but the hard climb is well rewarded. From the ridge, spectacular views of the Payette River Canyon stretch 2,500 feet below. Premium snow conditions and beautiful open bowls for off-trail skiing are available here, less than an hour north of the state capital.

Snow Creek a thirteen-mile trail near Bonners Ferry, offers a challenge to skiers at every level, as well as excellent views of the Selkirk Crest.

The Island Park area, just west of Yellowstone along the upper reaches of the Henry's Fork of the Snake River, was established as a part of the Park N' Ski program.

Many attractions await the skier here; among them, Harriman State Park, the wintering ground for the majestic trumpeter swan, and the nine-mile Brimstone Trail, with vista after vista overlooking the beautiful Island Park Reservoir and Buffalo River.

In the southeast corner of the state at Mink Creek, five cross-country trails have been developed. The Highland Golf Course in Pocatello has also been designated a Park N' Ski area, with fifteen miles of trail appropriate for the beginner.

In addition to the seventeen Park N' Ski areas located throughout the state, four state parks in the northern half of Idaho have public cross-country ski trails. At Farragut State Park, located on the shores of Lake Pend Oreille, the terrain is mostly flat with numerous open meadows. While Winchester State Park south of Lewiston offers a short trail excellent for beginners, the trail at Priest Lake State Park is designed for intermediate to advanced skiers. Round Lake State Park near Sandpoint follows the forested shoreline of this small lake, where ice skating is also available.

New areas will continue to be developed as need warrants, with all expansion coupled to the purchase of passes and the local generation of money and interest.

Idaho's Park N' Ski program is one of the first in the nation. Other programs currently exist only in California, Washington, Oregon, and Minnesota. A reciprocal agreement makes the pass purchased in Idaho valid in each of the other states.

Known for Mt Baldy's famous alpine runs, cross country skiers can enjoy miles and miles of carefully groomed trails in the Sun Valley area.

SIMPLY SUN VALLEY

Anyone who thinks Idaho is all about potatoes should take a closer look at Sun Valley. The skiing on Bald Mountain is as delicious as its Sawtooth Mountain setting and its romantic Hollywood history is as rich and old as the potato fields themselves.

"It's the love of the mountains and nature and space that brings everyone together here," says Judy Blumberg, former Olympic ice dancer who stars in the ice shows at the famous outdoor rink by the Sun Valley Lodge.

In Sun Valley celebs don't have to worry about keeping a low profile. Jamie Lee Curtis can sit rinkside, needlepointing, as her daughter Annie takes a lesson, and the Schwarzeneggers go out on the ice slip-sliding as a family unit.

"I've been going there forever," says Charlotte Ford, noting Sun Valley is very low-key - the kind of place where Clint Eastwood can walk down the street and not be hassled.

"A lot of Sun Valley history is there," says Lili Zanuck. "My husband (Richard) started coming here with his family when he was three years old. They took a train from L.A. to Pocatello that took two days. Then a dog sled picked them up at the station to take them to the Lodge."

Now there's the spectacular 18,000-square-foot Seattle Ridge Lodge atop a ridge crest on Bald Mountain, where floor-to-ceiling windows, cathedral ceilings and a huge "snow-free" terrace for sun-worshippers make it the most dramatic place to stay in Sun Valley.

For a day off the slopes, The Main Street Book Cafe's section on Ernest Hemingway and weekly writers readings are often what get the crowds there, while the cafe's Thai chicken pesto pizza and extensive wine selection make them stay a while. ❧

"Baldy, Sun Valley. World famous Idaho."
- Steve Snyder

200 Idaho unBound

Chapter XII
IDAHO INDOORS
Writers, Artists, Museums, Education

Carole King's
'Coming Home Ranch'.

A LITERARY HARVEST

Paul Rawlings

It could be said that Idaho's literary history began on August 12, 1805 with the notations made by the explorer Merriweather Lewis as he crossed what is now known as Lemhi Pass and tasted the cold, clear waters on the western side of the Continental Divide. First slowly, and then more and more regularly, the land and people within the Gem State's borders served to inspire poets, novelists, essayists, diarists and even script-writers. Yet most readers in our state do not think of Idaho as having produced a bumper crop of material.

Culture shows us how we feel about ourselves. It is what we do with our time, every moment we have free. Whether that moment is spent reading this book, writing a poem, or working with rocks, our culture shows our higher selves. Culture is us, revealed.

In petroglyphs on countless boulders along Weiss Bar on the Snake River — and on cliffs and under overhangs all over the state — the culture of Idaho's first people is revealed to be both simple and enigmatic. Figures of people and animals stand among symbols of unclear meaning. This art implies an ancient understanding of Time and Nature, and it helps us to better appreciate our own place in the world.

In the Nez Perce Indian museum along the river upstream from Lewiston, the elegant daily objects of the tribe are

From Ezra Pound to Vardis Fisher, Idaho has produced writers of interest and merit. And from that first entry by Merriweather Lewis to the metered lines of William Stafford, Idaho has continued to inspire creative minds to put pen to paper. Ernest Hemingway chose our state as his home. Nelle Shipman brought forth silent screen plays from the shores of our waters. Wallace Stegner mined the diaries of early residents for a great novel. Folk literature- created by men and women who were workers, citizens and seekers first and writers second- has also yielded a tremendous cache of fascinating material for readers from the Panhandle to Bear Lake.

Capital city Boise remains a cultural hub of the state, housing an art museum, children's discovery center, zoo, University, and performing arts center – all located within or adjoining Boise's impressive city parks.

Here then, to whet your appetite, are six sweet samples of fine writing by an Idahoan or about Idaho.

"... we proceeded on to the top of the dividing ridge from which I discovered immence ranges of high mountains still to the West of us with their tops partially covered with snow. I now decended the mountain about 3/4 of a mile which I found much steeper than on the opposite side, to a handsome bold runing Creek of cold Clear water. here I first tasted the water of the great Columbia river."

(Written by Merriweather Lewis on August 12, 1805 the Lewis and Clark party passed into Idaho by what is now known as Lemhi Pass. The vagaries of punctuation and spelling follow the original.)

"This river is what tawny is and loneliness, and it comes down with a wilderness of power now and then begging along a little green island with lush water grass among the rocks where I have watched it and its broken shells."

(From BY THE SNAKE RIVER by William Stafford. Award winning poet William Stafford lives in Portland, Oregon.)

"On a drizzly, rainy Friday evening we drove into Bonners Ferry. This was not rain as we had known it for years - a sudden violent deluge, over almost as quickly as it started - but a slow, gentle patter, running in rivulets down the windows and windshield, dripping from every twig and branch, gently soaking everything exposed to it. Gratefully we rolled the car windows down to admit the mingled fragrance of wet earth and fresh growing things."

"How many accept rain as a commonplace thing! Of course it rains! It has always rained. It always will rain. But such people have never lived where it forgot to rain."

The self-proclaimed "Idaho Kid", posing with his Mother in Hailey. Years later, exiled in Paris and Rome, the brilliant poet Ezra Pound would still refer to himself by this nickname.

arranged in glass cases. Because the Nez Perce lived a semi-nomadic life, they needed art that they could carry. Their bead work, leather work and weaving are sublime. The free Nez Perce believed that every object that they created needed to create its own beauty. They believed that no one could own the earth, but that we should beautify our effect on it.

The words of the Nez Perce, written down by EuroAmericans during the tragic times of the late 1800s, give the feeling that with their language, too, they improved upon nature. Chief Joseph's famous lines may sadden us: "Hear me, my chiefs ... My heart is sick and sad. From where the sun now stands, I will fight no more, forever." But at the same they inspire us with the beauty in the language.

Our culture can be demonstrated by the things we do, too. We have poet William Studebaker to thank for lines about

(From STUMP RANCH PIONEER by Nelle Portrey Davis. Published in 1942, it is a memoir of migration from the Midwest to the Panhandle of Idaho during the Dust Bowl years.)

"Do not misunderstand me, but understand me fully with reference to my affection for the land. I never said the land was mine to do with it as I chose. The one who has the right to dispose of it is the one who has created it. I claim a right to live on my land, and accord you the privilege to live on yours."

(By Thunder Traveling-to-Loftier-Mountain-Heights, or Chief Joseph, from TOUCH THE EARTH.)

"I wish I could make you feel a place like Kuna. It is a place where silence closes about you after the bustle of the train, where a soft, dry wind from great distances hums through the telephone wires and a stage road goes out of sight in one direction and a new railroad track in another. There is not a tree, nothing but sage. As moon-light unto sunlight is that desert sage to other greens. The wind has magic in it, and the air is full of birds and birdsong. Meadowlarks pipe all around us, something else - pipits? true skylarks? - rains down brief sweet showers of notes from the sky. Hawks sail far up in the blue, magpies fly along ahead, coming back now and then like ranging dogs to make sure you are not lost. Not a house, windmill, hill, only that jade-gray plain with lilac mountains on every distant horizon."

(From ANGLE OF REPOSE by Wallace Stegner The novel is based on the diaries and memoirs of Mary Hallock Foote, a successful writer and illustrator of the latter part of the nineteenth century.)

"Days of rain at just that time were a disaster. They hastened the melting of the snow but not the thawing of the ground. So at the end of three days the houses and hutches and barns and sheds of Fingerbone were like so many spilled and foundered arks. There were chickens roosting in the telephone poles and dogs swimming by in the streets. My grandmother always boasted that the floods never reached our house, but that spring, water poured over the thresholds and covered the floor to the depth of four inches, obliging us to wear boots while we did the cooking and washing up. . . If we opened or closed a door, a wave swept through the house, and chairs tottered, and bottles and pots clinked . . . After four days of rain the sun appeared in a white sky . . . The water shone more brilliantly than the sky, and while we watched, a tall elm tree fell slowly across the road. From crown to root, half of it vanished in the brilliant light."

(From HOUSEKEEPING by Marilyn Robinson. Fingerbone is a fictionalized Sandpoint, Idaho in Bonner County, where Marilyn Robinson grew up.)✍

A RELUCTANT IDAHOAN

Most Idahoans would rather live here than anywhere else. In a moment I'll tell you about a woman who desperately wanted to stay away, yet went on to popularize Idaho in illustration and story.

Mary Hallock grew up in New York, and received her education in Boston. She socialized with the elite of New England, but she fell in love with a civil engineer named Arthur Foote who had the grit of the West beneath his fingernails.

Mary Hallock Foote came West in the nation's Centennial year, 1876, but she did not

Salmon River Dick, who moved heavy rocks to make his statement about who and where he was:

I don't think I ever decided.

I just started building out of rock.

Not because there were so many

but because they were

arranged so bad.

Culture is everything, with every unimportant thing removed. In Idaho, culture has always been easy to find, whether it is in the fine tooling of a saddle's leather, or in the humor of the old Stinker Stations billboards, like the one along a waterless

come eagerly. Mrs. Foote once wrote; "No girl ever wanted less to go West with any man, or paid a man a greater compliment by doing so."

The Foote's lived in Idaho from 1883 to 1895, mostly in the Boise River Canyon near present day Lucky Peak Dam. It was a frustrating, heartbreaking time for them, but Mary made use of her hard experience. She was an illustrator for books and magazines of the era. In fact she was once called the dean of women illustrators. Encouraged by an editor to write as well, she became a popular author.

Mary Hallock Foote wrote many short stories, and a dozen novels. Much of her writing was based on her eight years in Idaho. Coeur d'Alene, Silver City, Boise, Thousand Springs, and Craters of the Moon were all settings for her stories.

In 1971 she was the subject of an enchanting story herself. Wallace Stegner's Pulitzer Prize-winning novel Angle of Repose is based on the fascinating life of Mary Hallock Foote . . . a somewhat reluctant Idahoan. ✍

VARDIS FISHER: FROM AN IDAHO BOYHOOD

by Paul Rawlings

Vardis Fisher was born near Annis, in the valley of the upper Snake, southeastern Idaho, 1895: Mormon pioneer settlers were few, the demands of this austere land many. And there seemed little room for a precocious and introverted boy who recognized early that he was more fit to read than rope, log or plow. When he completed high school shortly before WWI, his intention was to leave his home state for a college campus and then the culture of the East Coast. But the pull of the land was great; and after stints as a college professor at the University of Chicago (where he earned his PhD) and at New York University, among others, he returned to Idaho for good in 1931. He lived for 37 years thereafter in the Hagerman area, again within the sheer walls of the Snake River.

During the depression he was employed by the WPA as the director of the Federal Writers' Project in Idaho, almost single handedly writing *Idaho: A Guide in Word and Picture*.

Two early novels, *Toilers in the Hills* (1928) and *Dark Bridwell* (1931), begin the story Fisher had to tell of lonely, pioneering life; and it was continued in the brooding Antelope Hills tetralogy (1932-1936), a series of autobiographical novels. These and *Children of God*, the sweeping historical novel which depicted the birth and westward movement of the Mormon Church, created a national reputation for Fisher.

It could be argued that the frank and introspective Antelope Hills novels are the single most powerful body of work in Idaho literature. ✍

Mary Hallock Foote was the fictionalized subject of Wallace Stegner's Pulitzer Prize-winning Angle of Repose. Still relatively unknown, then and now she is unequaled as an Idaho writer and artist chronicling the West she observed.

PATRICK McMANUS
by Mitch Finley

Patrick E. McManus is one of the most successful humorists in America today. His book, *The Night the Bear Ate Goombaw*, is another in a string of bestsellers, and his monthly outdoors humor column in *Outdoor Life* has been one of that magazine's most popular features. And where does McManus get his stories? The writer attributes much of his success to the fact that he grew up in Idaho.

McManus has a shy streak when it comes to talking about himself, but, at age 55, the silver-haired humorist admits that he bases many of his stories on his rural northern Idaho childhood. "We had a little farm twenty-five miles north of Sandpoint, and I spent a lot of my time wandering the countryside. A lot of my characters and stories are based on real situations from those early years."

In fact, McManus says, most of his stories are located in Idaho. "All the stories I write about my childhood take place around Sandpoint and in the mountains of Idaho. Had I not grown up in Idaho, I would not have my orientation to the outdoors and to the fishing and hunting and camping that are so important to the humor that I write."

Growing up in Idaho, McManus says, turned him into "an environmentalist," but he can't keep a straight face as he talks about it. "I'm concerned about the environment in Idaho. Of course, when I was growing up, we didn't have any environment in Idaho, it came in years later."

The truth, McManus says, is that it was the love for fishing that he developed as a boy in northern Idaho that turned him into a philosopher. "Scholars have long known," he writes, "that fishing turns men into philosophers . . ."

"I became a philosopher at age 12, after a scant six years of fishing. One evening at supper I looked up from my supper and announced, 'I fish; therefore, I am.' Perhaps awed by this evidence of precocity in a young boy, my step-father turned to my mother and asked, 'Is there any more gravy?' Thus encouraged, I forgot about philosophy until I went off to college."

In his stories, McManus shamelessly milks a situation for laughs, even down to the names he gives his characters, and all of them are based on real-life characters and places he knew when he was growing up around Sandpoint. Crazy Eddie Muldoon, Rancid Crabtree, Birdy Thompson, Delmore Blight Grade School, Miss Deets and Miss Gooseheart (school teachers), Fat Edna, Retch Sweeney, Fenton Quagmire and Strange his boyhood hunting dog, who "had no redeeming features."

McManus finds that his stories have a universal appeal because "There may be something almost mythically universal about Idaho. People identify with the Idaho wildernesses that I write about in my stories. It may be that in the long run Idaho's wilderness will be its most important feature, over-all."

CAFE/BOOKSTORE'S POETRY SLAMS ARE HIGH-COUNTRY HIT
by Steve Crump

KETCHUM, 1995 - A pair of latecomers, tourists wearing Benetton and bemuse-ment, slide through the front door.

The third and final round of the 13th Wood River Poetry Slam has begun, and the visitors gape at the throng of locals -heavy on flannel and

---

stretch of Mountain Home desert: "No fishing within 100 yards of highway." Individual artists create cultural icons. Communities celebrate culture with ceremony and festival.

Many Idaho artists are what are known as "folk artists," practitioners of old crafts to which they add their artistry. These are quilters, carvers, sculptors, painters, weavers and musicians. The countless individual artists blend their personal visions with the collective dreams of their communities.

Idaho authors and poets seem to be writing in every hamlet and ranch house. Many of them write out of a love for Idaho — small town life, ranch life, life in the wilderness — and Idaho is better for their words. Several Idaho writers are receiving national acclaim. Idaho's women writers, in particular, have staked out new literary territory. Marilyn Robinson, Judith

denim - that surrounds them in the Main Street BookCafe.

Across the way, the nextStage Theater is disgorging yuppie playgoers, and down the road a raucous band of revelers is hanging around the telephone pole between the bank and Slaveys trading lies.

Outside Saturday night unfolds as it must in a ski town in High January. Inside, souls are bared.

Jo Ellen Collins, a 58-year-old librarian and former teacher winds up her ode to a faceless waitress in a nameless greasy spoon somewhere in the Southwest - a woman who trades in stale cigarette smoke and bad coffee, but who nurtures other dreams.

Bitsy's kitchen is spotless as Collins describes it. It is redolent of Good House-keeping and lemon and sea air.

Collins takes a seat, and the crowd murmurs its approval.

"Ten!" someone says. "At least," someone else replies.

The judges confer, and then they concur. They display their scores on hand-held cards, as if they were judging a Greg Louganis half-gainer with a twist. Collins beams. She has just won 20 bucks.

The tourists, looking confused, edge toward the door. "Private party?" the man says to a bystander in a ponytail.

"No way," he says. "Poetry."

"Poetry?" the visitor says.

"It's a slam, man."

On the occasional Saturday night since the summer of 1993, good poets and bad and many who enjoy listening to both have trooped to the hybrid bookstore and coffee house on Ketchum's main drag.

The writers are teachers and accountants and computer operators and guys who operate ski lifts some published, some not, some talented, some awful.

No matter. Just having the brass to stand and deliver imparts a certain status.

"It takes some getting used to," said Collins, who spends her days in Ketchum's Community Library transcribing oral history tapes. "But it's also quite fun."

It's a pretty rollicking place when those poets get going," said Jon Maksik, the headmaster at Ketchum-Sun Valley Community School and a past judge of the event. "Some of the poetry was good and some was not so good, but the crowd seemed to enjoy it."

Slams, which arose in the espresso joints and fem bars of Chicago and other big cities, are the direct descendants of poetry readings of the beatnik ERA, when Allen Ginsberg and William Burroughs were apt to drop by and relieve themselves of beat verse.

The crowds range from festive to boisterous, but nobody has been hooted off the stage yet.

"The hostile responses are reserved for the judges," Maksik said. "Especially if you give somebody a low score." ✍

STOPPING BY THE WOODS

by Robert Wrigley

"It must have been my fourth-grade teacher who made me memorize Frost's "Stopping By Woods on a Snowy Evening." I'm not sure anymore, though the poem is etched neatly - tattooed even - on my memory. That summer, after fourth grade I guess, I remember swinging, and I remember how the poem kept coming into my mind's ear. Two long syllables up, two more back. "Whose woods," I heard, and I was leaning back, pulling at the chains, stretching my legs outward for height; "these are," and I

leaned my shoulders into the chains and tucked my legs below me. "I think. . . I know."

The motions of that swing taught me the neat discipline of Frost's tetrameter. Sixty-four ups and backs, sixty-four swings in four impeccable quatrains. Two or three years ago, when my son was still young enough to enjoy swinging and not be embarrassed by it, I took him to a park here in Lewiston, Idaho. We could swing and look out over Tammany Canyon to the Blue Mountains of Washington and Oregon and to the low timbered, snow-belt hills known as Waha, and it all came back to me, swing after swing, line after line.

I am not at all ashamed to admit that I was drawn to the Northwest, and to Idaho, by geography. After more than twenty five years in the farm-flat Midwest, these mountains and canyons, these wild, far-falling rivers were, and are, exhilarating to me.

That afternoon as my son and I swung, side by side so that we could talk and point and see together, I was struck as I am again and again by the beauty of this irregular landscape, this dramatic unlevelness. It appeals to me, I think, for the same reasons swinging did when I was a child. It is up and down, it is rhythm on a dazzlingly vast scale. It is not the reportorial, textbook-bloodless prose of plains and plains and plains; it's the bump and clatter of Hopkins, the exuberant dance of Roethke, the heartfelt limp an eloquent stagger that goes perfectly on in Hugo.

I think we're all regional writers, that we all carry the landscape we've come to call home into the world we build with words. It is a commonplace to say so, but Ashbery's poems strike me as a kind of Gotham-personified - exciting sometimes, sometimes devoid of human features, sometimes soulless. In the same way, David Wagoner's lush music has the rain forest

---

Freeman, Mary Clearman Blew and Kim Barnes have each made contributions.

The two most famous writers often linked to Idaho are the poet Ezra Pound and the novelist and short story writer Ernest Hemingway. Novelist Vardis Fisher should be the most famous Idaho writer, and perhaps he will be someday.

Fisher grew up in the Snake River valley. He produced a mountain of literature, the best known being his novel, "Mountain Man," which became Robert Redford's film, "Jeremiah Johnson." Ezra Pound began his life in Hailey. He was a cultural elitist and it is likely he never wanted to return. But Ernest Hemingway may have faked improvement at the Mayo Clinic in Minnesota, so he could get back to Ketchum — to end his life.

Just up Trail Creek from Sun Valley, a roughhewn, bronze bust of Ernest Hemingway stands almost hidden against the

living inside it. When I write a poem, I mean for it to swing - less regularly, less liltingly than "Stopping By Woods on a Snowy Evening," perhaps; I mean for it to have the plummet and rise of the landscape around me, the humps and canyons in its consonants, the wind-driven, river-borne music in its vowels.

That's what I shoot for anyway. Dull, conversational lines bore me. They are fallow fields in depressingly vast prairies; I love mountains, canyons, violent energy. "The Harsh Country," wrote Roethke, is "the country of ourselves." Dick Hugo liked to joke that people, in their scarcity, became more valuable here. "If you meet a person," he would say, who has even one remotely redeemable characteristic, you make him a friend for life." This is a land in which people turn to and upon themselves, for lack of alternative, or for ulterior motive. The result in some cases is despair and madness; in others it is art. "That girl upstream was diced by scaling knives-/ scattered in the shack I licked her knees in. Hugo's music is schematic diagram as readable as a topographical map - harsh, powerful, and lovely.

And then there is the emptiness. It's not really like Hugo's joke, but it's not that far from it either. In Idaho, a gathering of 200 people constitutes a frighteningly large mob. There's a county in north-central Idaho - Idaho County - in which deer and elk out number people, and which would hold, with room to spare, the states of Massachusetts, Connecticut, and Rhode Island."

IDAHO CALENDAR

SANDPOINT WINTER CARNIVAL
SANDPOINT. late-January. Ten days of winter festivities and activities.

MCCALL WINTER CARNIVAL
MCCALL. early-February. Festivities include ice sculptures, snowmobile races, parades, and fireworks.

LIONEL HAMPTON JAZZ FESTIVAL
MOSCOW. late-February. Top Jazz musicians gather for a four-day festival.

DEPOT DAYS
WALLACE. Mid-May. Festival, car show, food festival and music in the streets of Wallace.

FRED MURPHY DAYS
COEUR D'ALENE. Late-May. Coeur d'Alene's kick off to summer.

ST. ANTHONY FISHERMEN'S BREAKFAST
ST. ANTHONY. late-May. An annual kick-off to the fishing season.

WESTERN DAYS
TWIN FALLS. early-June. A full week of activities including a shoot-out, barbecue, dances, chili cook-off, and a parade.

IRON HORSE ROUNDUP
TWIN FALLS. mid-June. A celebration of the railroad and a parade.

NATIONAL OLD-TIME FIDDLERS CONTEST
WEISER. mid-June. The Nation's best country fiddlers play throughout the city during the competition.

BOISE RIVER FESTIVAL
BOISE. late-June. Events include a nighttime parade, hot air balloon festival, air show, entertainment, athletic competition, and the grand finale.

TETON VALLEY HOT AIR BALLOON RACES
DRIGGS. early-July. A festival which includes 30-40 hot air balloons in a race overlooking the Grand Teton Mountains.

CLEARWATER RIVERFEST
KAMIAH. early-July. Bluegrass concert and an arts and crafts exposition.

FIRST SECURITY SUMMER OLYMPIC GAMES
POCATELLO. early-July. Summer Olympic competition for Idaho Amateur athletes.

FESTIVAL AT SANDPOINT
SANDPOINT. Summer. A summer long series of musical concerts along the shores of Lake Pend Oreille.

IDAHO SHAKESPEARE FESTIVAL
BOISE. Summer. Enjoy Shakespeare performances in an outdoor theater.

SUN VALLEY ICE SHOW
SUN VALLEY. June - early October. World-class Olympic and professional skaters participate in the only annual outdoor ice show in the country.

SUN VALLEY MUSIC FESTIVAL
SUN VALLEY. July - August. World known classical and jazz performers.

NASCAR RACING
TWIN FALLS. Summer. Exciting racing events each weekend.

---

cottonwoods. The granite crags of the Sawtooth Mountains stagger the northwestern skyline. The words on Hemingway's memorial speak for many Idaho artists, and intimate the magic of this place:

And best of all he loved the fall,
The leaves yellow on the cottonwoods,
Leaves floating on the trout streams,
And above the hills, the high blue windless skies.

OREGON TRAIL RENDEZVOUS PAGEANT

MONTPELIER. mid-July. Dutch oven cooking, music, and dancing on the Oregon Trail.

RENDEZVOUS IN THE PARK

LEWISTON. mid-July. Jazz, folk, blues, country and classical music as well as arts and crafts, children's activities, and silent movies are a part of this festival.

ROCKIN' THE TETONS MUSIC FESTIVAL

DRIGGS. mid-July. A weekend of Rock, Blues, and Reggae music.

CHIEF LOOKINGGLASS DAYS

KAMIAH. mid-August. Traditional Pow Wow of the Nez Perce Tribe including dancing and cultural activities.

BLUEGRASS FESTIVAL

DRIGGS. mid-August. Three day event highlighted by chairlift rides to a spectacular view of the Grand Teton Mountain Range and top-name musical talent.

HOT AUGUST NIGHTS

LEWISTON. mid-August. A "blast from the past" with music, dancing, and a classic and nostalgic car show and cruise.

SHOSHONE-BANNOCK INDIAN FESTIVAL

FORT HALL. mid-August. Celebration of Indian culture including traditional dress, dancing, games, and art.

COEUR D'ALENE INDIAN PILGRIMAGE

CATALDO. mid-August. "The Coming of the Black Robes" Ceremony is performed for the public.

NORTHERN ROCKIES FOLK FESTIVAL

HAILEY. mid-August. Weekend of outdoor musical entertainment.

THREE ISLAND CROSSING

GLENNS FERRY. mid-August. Celebration of the Oregon Trail's difficult crossing of the Snake River.

Over the years, Boise's Shakespeare Festival in the park has become a can't miss event for locals and tourists alike.

RODEOS

Dodge National Circuit Finals Rodeo
Pocatello mid March

Riggins Rodeo
Riggins early May

Grangeville Border Days Rodeo
Grangeville early July

Snake River Stampede
Nampa mid July

Famous Preston Night Rodeo
Preston late July

Caldwell Night Rodeo
Caldwell mid August

Cassia County Fair and Rodeo
Burley mid August

Payette County Fair and Rodeo
Payette mid August

Lewiston Roundup
Lewiston early September

Twin Falls County Fair and Rodeo
Filer early September

ART IN THE PARK
BOISE. early-September. Artist from around the country participate in this three-day event.

WAGON DAYS
KETCHUM. early-September. A celebration of the past mining history with a parade and concerts.

CLEARWATER COUNTY FAIR AND LUMBERJACK DAYS
OROFINO. mid-September. An International event which includes logging competitions, carnival, and parade.

IDAHO SPUD DAY
SHELLEY. mid-September. A country-style gala celebration of the Idaho potato.

IDAHO STATE DRAFT HORSE INTERNATIONAL
SANDPOINT. early Oct. Three days of exhibits and contests.

SUN VALLEY JAZZ JAMBORE
SUN VALLEY. mid October. Four nights of big band Jazz with bands from all over North America.

FESTIVAL OF TREES
BOISE. late-November. Kick-off to the holiday season with decorations, gifts, and holiday spirit.

WOOD RIVER VALLEY POETRY SLAM
KETCHUM. Bi-monthly Saturday nights. At the Main Street Bookcafe in Ketchum.

McCall Writers & Readers Rendezvous

Reviving a 150-year-old Idaho tradition of getting together and swapping stories, the McCall Writers & Readers Rendezvous draws Idaho literature lovers to the shores of Payette Lake. Nationally know authors, poets and publishers rub elbows with avid readers for a weekend of readings, workshops and bonhomie. Boise State University sponsors the mid-October celebration, with help from the Idaho Commission on the Arts.

Idaho communities often have their artistic specialties. Sandpoint and Hope are centers of painting and sculpture. Salmon and Challis promote Western Americana. South Central Idaho produces great cowboy poets. Unlikely Sunnyslope blows go-lightly jazz. Lewiston, Boise, Ketchum and Boise all have vibrant writing scenes. McCall's Writers & Readers Rendezvous draws together literature lovers from all over the Northwest. And, somewhere near Idaho City, Idaho writers gather at their yearly "Fandango."

Community celebrations of Idaho culture are as common as cottonwoods. Some are small and specialized, like the Porcupine Races in Council and the harmonica competition in remote Yellow Pine. Some are well known and well attended, like Art on the Green, in Coeur d'Alene; the Great Music West festival in Montpelier; the International Folk Dance Festival in

MUSEUMS

The Idaho Association of Museums invites you to . . . Discover Idaho through diverse exhibits of history, science, natural history and the fine arts. We suggest you contact any museum before you visit it to ensure that you have up-to-date hours and prices.

NORTHERN IDAHO

Bonners Ferry

Boundary County Historical Society and Museum Open May-Aug. Mon-Fri 10:30-4:30. Exhibits, photographs, and furnished displays of the history of Boundary County, Kootenai Indian artifacts. *Located at 105 Main Street.* P.O. Box 808, Bonners Ferry, ID 83805 (208) 267-7720

Coeur d'Alene Museum of North Idaho Open April 1- Oct. 31 Tue-Sat 11-5. Also July-Aug. Sun. 11-5. Exhibits depicting history of Kootenai County and surrounding area, Native Americans, naval training station; research facility; gift shop. *Located at 115 N.W. Boulevard, in front of the city park.* P.O. Box 812, Coeur d'Alene, ID 83816 (208) 664-3448

Fort Sherman Museum Open May 1-Sept 30 Tues-Sat 1-4:45. History of Fort Sherman with outdoor exhibits of logging and lumbering equipment. *Located on North Idaho College campus.* P.O. Box 812, Coeur d'Alene, ID 83816 (208) 664-3448

Coolin

Priest Lake Museum/Visitor Center Open daily Memorial Day-Labor Day 10-4. Log cabin built by CCC in 1935, exhibits on local history. P.O. Box 44, Coolin, ID 83821 (208) 443-2676

Cottonwood

St. Gertrude's Museum Open daily by appointment. Local history, Indian artifacts, Oriental art, Polly Bemis collection, religious mementos, hand-crafted textiles. *Located 2 miles SW of Cottonwood on Keuterville Road.* P.O. Box 107, Cottonwood, ID 83522-0107 (208) 962-3224 or (208) 962-7123

Harrison

Crane Historical Society Open Memorial Day-Labor Day Sat-Sun 12-4, also by appointment. Located in first house built in Harrison (1891), exhibits deal primarily with local history. P.O. Box 152, Harrison, ID 83833 (208) 689-3032

Lewiston

Lewis Clark Center for Arts and History Open daily, gallery 10-4, office 8-5; closed holidays. A gallery of rotating art and history exhibits including a Chinese Temple used in Lewiston during the late 1800's, and special events. Lewis Clark State College Centennial Memorabilia gift shop. *Located on the corner of 5th and Main.* 415 Main, Lewiston, ID 83501 (208) 799-2243

Luna House Museum Open all year Tues-Sat 9-5, closed two weeks at Christmas. Permanent and rotating exhibits depict pioneer and Nez perce artifacts, research facility, photographic reproductions available. Operated by Nez Perce County Historical Society. 306 3rd St., Lewiston, ID 83501 (208) 743-2535

Moscow

Appaloosa Museum and Heritage Center Open all year Mon-Fri 8-5, June-Aug also Sat 9-3. The Appaloosa, Idaho's state horse is a versatile horse famed for its unusual spotted markings and color. Regalia and artifacts used with the Appaloosa throughout history are on display. *Located at 5070 Hwy 8 W.* P.O. Box 8403, Moscow, ID 83843 (208) 882-5578

Latah County Historical Society Open all year Tue-Sat 1-4, closed holidays. Period rooms, changing exhibits on Latah County history. Research facility, library and photo collection at 327 E. 2nd, Tues-Fri 9-12 and 1-5. *Exhibits located in Governor McConnell House.* 110 S. Adams, Moscow, ID 83843 (208) 882-1004

Mullan

Captain John Mullan Museum Open June 1-Sept 1 Mon-Sat 12-4. Memorabilia and artifacts of Mullan and surrounding area from 1880 to present. *Located in former Liberty Theater, 231 Earle Street.* P.O. Box 677, Mullan, ID 83846 (208) 744-1461

Famous artists from the world have tried to capture Idaho's natural beauty –such as Thomas Moran's famous oil landscapes of Shoshone Falls or Mount Hayden and (now) Mount Moran.

Rexburg; the National Old Time Fiddlers' Festival, in Weiser; the Lionel Hampton Jazz Festival, in Moscow; and the enormous celebration of family and community: the Boise River Festival, in Boise.

Nationally famous Idaho rodeos include the Snake River Stampede, in Nampa; the Caldwell Night Rodeo; and the National Circuit Finals Rodeo, in Pocatello. But almost every town in Idaho seems to have its own rodeo. Buckaroo season begins every year in Riggins, in the first week in May. And because Idaho's wild rides also include kayaks, the annual Whitewater Rodeo on the Payette River showcases the state of the art in the Whitewater State.

Culture is an act of doing, not a state of being. ⌒

Murray

Sprag Pole Museum Open daily 7am-10pm. Three buildings contain mining machinery, blacksmith shop, bullet collection, woodcarvings, guns, rock collection, and Native American artifacts. *Located on Main Street in the center of town.* P.O. Box 425, Murray, ID 83874 (208) 682-3901

Orofino

Clearwater Historical Museum Open Tues-Sat 1:30-4:30, closed holidays. Exhibits include local history, mining, logging, and Native American history. Sponsored by Clearwater County Historical Society. *Located at 315 College Avenue.* P.O. Box 1454, Orofino, ID 83544 (208) 476-5033

Pierce

J. Howard Bradbury Logging Memorial Museum Open May 15-Oct 15 Thurs-Sun 12-4. The museum is located in a log cabin built in 1928 and displays memorabilia of the labors which created the economy of the area, mainly logging and mining. *Located at 101 S. Main* HC 64, Box 11, Pierce, ID 83546 (208) 464-2531 or (208) 435-4670

Sandpoint

Bonner County Historical Museum Open April-Oct Tues-Sat 10-4, Nov-March Thurs 10-4, closed holidays. History of county with emphasis on Kootenai Indians, timber, and railroad. *Located at 609 S. Ella Avenue.* P.O. Box 1063, Sandpoint, ID 83864 (208) 263-2344

Spalding

Nez Perce National Historical Park Open all year, daily 8-4:30 with extended summer hours. Exhibits, movie, programs, special events, highway wayside and auto tour explain aspects of Nez Perce Indian history and culture, Lewis and Clark Expedition, the Spalding Mission, and other Euro-American activities in Nez Perce country. *Located on Hwy 95, 8 mi. SE of Lewiston.* P.O. Box 93, Spalding, ID 83551 (208) 843-2261

Wallace

Northern Pacific Railroad Museum Open summer daily 9-7, fall/spring 9-5, winter Tues-Sat 10-3. Exhibits relate to railroad history of the Coeur d'Alene Mining District and a turn-of-the-century depot. *Located at 219 6th Street.* P.O. Box 469, Wallace, ID 83873 (208) 752-0111

Wallace District Mining Museum Open June-Aug Mon-Fri 8-7, Sat-Sun 9-6, Oct-April Mon-Fri 9-5, Sat 10-5, May and Sept Mon-Fri 8:30-6. Mining exhibits, photographs, history of area mineral production. *Located at 509 Bank Street.* P.O. Box 1167, Wallace, ID 83873 (208) 753-7151

CENTRAL & SOUTHWESTERN IDAHO

Atlanta

Atlanta Historical Society Open all year by appointment. Restored jail featuring exhibits of early Rocky Bar and city of Atlanta. P.O. Box 53, Atlanta, ID 83601

Boise

Basque Museum Open all year, Tues-Fri 10-3, Sat 11-2, closed holidays. Oldest home in Boise containing furnishings depicting the Basque people's experience in Idaho. 607 Grove Street, Boise, ID 83702 (208)343-8330

Boise Art Museum Open Tues-Fri 10-5, Sat-Sun 12-5. Featuring over 15 changing exhibits annually, the Glenn C. Janss Collection of American Realism, lectures, art classes, special events. *Located at NW entrance to Julia Davis Park.* 670 S. Julia Davis Dr., Boise, ID 83702 (208) 345-8330

The Discovery Center of Idaho Open winter Wed-Fri 9-5, Sat 10-5, Sun 12-5. Also summer Tue-Sat 10-5, Sun 12-5. Hands-on science museum for kids of all ages! *Located at 131 Myrtle.* P.O. Box 192, Boise, ID 83701 (208) 343-9895

Idaho State Historical Museum Open all year Mon-Sat 9-5, Sun 1-5. Features "The Story of Idaho" exhibit along with richly detailed interiors and exhibits which tell story of Idaho's ethnic groups, technology, and industry. *Located at NW entrance to Julia Davis Park.* 610 N. Julia Davis Dr., Boise, ID 83702 (208) 334-2120

Old Idaho Penitentiary Open daily 12-4 except State Holidays. Memorial Day-Labor Day open to 5. Walking tour and slide show interpret the history of Idaho's famous inmates, lawmen, escapes, riots, and penal scandals. Special exhibits on Idaho transportation and electricity. Located 2.5 miles SE of Capitol building, just off Warm Springs Avenue. 2445 Old Penitentiary Rd., Boise, ID 83712 (208) 334-2844

Caldwell

Orma J. Smith Museum of Natural History Open school year Mon-Fri midday, call for appointment. Extensive research collections of natural history specimens from Idaho, W U.S., and Mexico, especially Baja California. small museum shop. Also in science building H.M. Tucker Herbarium, Evans Gem and Mineral Collection, and Whittenberger Planetarium. Located on Albertson College of Idaho campus. Alberson College of Idaho, Caldwell, ID 83605 (208) 459-5507

Our Memories Museum Open Fri 10-4, Sun 1:30-4:30, and by appointment. Local history, household utensils, clothing, toys, office equipment, Victrolas, furniture, appliances and photographs. 1122 Main Street, Caldwell, ID 83605 (208) 459-1413

Cambridge

Cambridge Museum Open May 15-Sept 15 Wed-Sat 10-4, Sun 1-4, and by appointment. Local history, geology, and Native American settlement. *Located at junction of Hwys 95 & 71, 15 N. Superior Street.* P.O. Box 35, Cambridge, ID 83610 (208) 257-3485

Donnelly

Valley County Museum Open May & Sept Sun 1-5, June-Aug Sat-Sun 1-5, also by appointment. History of Valley County, features Roseberry townsite, agriculture, mining, lumber, Finnish settlement. *Located 1.5 mi. E. of town.* P.O. Box 444, Donnelly, ID 83615 (208) 325-8871 or (208) 345-1905

Emmett

Gem County Historical Society Museum Open June-Aug Sat-Sun 1-5, and by appointment. Complex of five buildings depict county heritage and industries, local Native American artifacts. *Located on corner of First and Hawthorne.* P.O. Box 312, Emmett, ID 83617 (208) 365-4340 or (208) 365-2990

Glenns Ferry

Glenns Ferry Historical Museum Open June-Sept Fri-Sat 12-5. A 1909 native stone schoolhouse with exhibits on local history, railroad memorabilia, and art work. Located at 200 W. Cleveland. P.O. Box 842, Glenns Ferry, ID 83623 No **phone**

Hagerman

Hagerman Historical Society Open Wed-Sun 11-4. Variety of exhibits including the Hagerman Fossil Horse. *Located in historic Hagerman State Bank on State Street.* P.O. Box 86, Hagerman, ID 83332 (208)837-6288

Idaho City

Boise Basin Historical Museum Open daily Memorial Day-Labor Day 11-4, also by appointment. Interpretive displays and video of Boise Basin history, emphasizing 1863-1890. Also historic village, park, mining equipment and territorial penitentiary. *Located at Wall and Montgomery Streets.* P.O. Box 358, Idaho City, ID 83631 (208)392-4550

Jerome

Jerome County Historical Society Open all year Tues-Sat 1-5. Hunt Japanese Relocation Center, history of Carey Act irrigation, county history, reading and research room. *Located at 220 N. Lincoln.* P.O. Box 50, Jerome, ID 83338

Ketchum
Community Library Association Open Mon-Sat 9-6. Research archives of local area including oral history collection. Located at 415 Spruce Ave. N. P.O. Box 2168. Ketchum, ID 83340 (208) 726-3493

Mountain Home
Elmore County Historical Society Open Fri-Sat 1:30-4:30, also by appointment. Native American and Chinese artifacts, farming tools, clothing, genealogy materials. *Located at 180 South 3rd E.* P.O. Box 204, Mtn. Home, ID 83647

Murphy
Owyhee County Historical Society Open all year Wed-Fri 10-4, summer also Sat-Sun 12-5. County history, Oregon Trail information, exhibit hall, schoolhouse, railroad depot and caboose, farm machinery, mining stamp mill, and research library. Located behind the Courthouse at 190 Basey Street. P.O. Box 67, Murphy, ID 83650 (208) 495-2319

Parma
Old Fort Boise Replica and Museum Open June-Aug Fri-Sun 1-3, and by appointment. Operated by Old Fort Boise Historical Society. *Located in Old Fort Boise park at east entrance to city.* P.O. Box 942, Parma, ID 83660 (208) 722-5138 or (208) 722-5573

Stanley
Stanley Museum Open May 15 -Sept 15 Mon-Fri 11-5, Sat-Sun 11-6. History of Stanley Basin, and Sawtooth Valley. *Located in Old Stanley Ranger Station on Hwy 75.* P.O. Box 75, Stanley, ID 83278

Twin Falls
The Herrett Museum Open all year Tues 9:30-8, Wed-Fri 9:30-4:30, Sat 1-4:30. Closed holidays. Rotating exhibits feature Idaho archeology and archaeology of Central and South America. Gallery of contemporary art. *Located at College of Southern Idaho.* 315 Falls Ave West, P.O. Box 1238, Twin Falls, ID 83303 (208) 733-9554

Twin Falls County Historical Society Open May 1-Sept 15 Mon-Fri 12-5. Antique machinery, clothing and photographs from 1800's, completely furnished pioneer house. *Located 3 miles west of town on Hwy 30.* 144 Taylor, Twin Falls, ID 83301 (208) 734-5547

Weiser
Intermountain Cultural Center and Washington County Museum Open summer Thur-Mon 12-4:30, rest of year Fri-Mon 12-4:30. Featuring artifacts and memorabilia of area Native Americans, Intermountian Institute and history of Washington County. 2295 Paddock Ave., P.O. Box 307, Weiser, ID 83672 (208) 549-0205

EASTERN IDAHO

American Falls
Massacre Rocks State Park Oregon Trail and Shoshone Indian History, living history campfire programs. Open early May-mid September, daily 9-6. *Located 1/2 mile west of I 86 off exit 28.* 3592 N. Park Lane, American Falls, ID 83211 (208) 548-2672

Arco
Craters of the Moon National Monument Visitor Center open Memorial Day-Labor Day 8-6, rest of year 8-4:30. Displays and short film describe park's lava phenomena, history, and the Earth processes creating them. *Located 18 miles SW of Arco on Hwy 93.* P.O. Box 29, Arco, ID 83213 (208) 527-3257

Ashton
Hess Heritage Museum Open by appointment, mid April-mid Oct. Restored pioneer farm of Upper Snake River Valley. Implement park, windmill, heritage home, summer kitchen, carriage house, implement barn, blacksmith shop, schoolhouse, pioneer aviation and wildlife exhibits. Located 1 mile south of Ashton and 1/4 mile west of Hwy 20 on the Fish Hatchery Road. P.O. Box 734, Ashton, ID 83420 (208) 652-7353 or (208) 356-5674

Blackfoot

Bingham County Historical Museum
Open all year Wed-Fri 1-5, and by appointment. Restored 1905 historic 15-room home with special collections of Native American relics, dolls, and World War II outfits. 190 N. Shilling Ave., Blackfoot, ID 83221 (208) 785-8065

Idaho's World Potato Exposition Open June-Sept daily 10-6, call for winter hours. Potato history, growth, harvesting, processing, nutrition, trivia, world hunger efforts. *Located off I 15 exit 93, 130 NW Main.* P.O. Box 366, Blackfoot, ID 83221 (208) 785-2517

Franklin

Idaho Pioneer Association Open May-Sept Mon-Fri 10-12 and 1-5, also by appointment. Pictures, pioneer relics. *Located on Main Street.* P.O. Box 6, Franklin, ID 83237 (208) 646-2437

Idaho Falls

Bonneville County Historical Society
Open all year Mon-Fri 10-5, sat 1-5, closed holidays. Exhibits show the area from pre-history to the atomic era, including natural history. Changing exhibits, art gallery replica 1900 town, special collections room. Museum located at 200 Eastern. P.O. Box 1784, Idaho Falls, ID 83403 (208) 522-1400

Lava Hot Springs

South Bannock County Historical Center
Open all year daily 12-5. Exhibits of South Bannock County history, new permanent exhibit, "Trails, Trapper, Trains and Travelers." Research facility with photos, documents, and artifacts. P.O. Box 387, Lava Hot Springs, ID 83246 (208) 776-5254

Mackay

Lost River Museum Open Sat-Sun 1-5, or by appointment. Local history, household utensils, mining tools, clothing, pictures. Operated by South Custer Historical Society. P.O. Box 572, Mackay, ID 83251 (208) 588-2669 or (208) 588-2597

Pocatello

Bannock County Historical Museum
Open Memorial Day-Labor Day daily 10-6, rest of year Tues-Sat 10-2. Exhibits explain the history of Pocatello and Bannock County, Native Americans, railroad history displays. P.O. Box 253, Pocatello, ID 83204 (208) 233-0434

Idaho Museum of Natural History Open all year Mon-Sat 10-6, sun 12-5. New exhibits open summer 1993, check for new hours. Exhibits depict natural history of Idaho and the Intermountain West. *Located on ISU Campus.* P.O. Box 8096, Pocatello, ID 83209 (208) 236-3168

Rexburg

Teton Flood Museum Open May-Sept Mon-Fri 10-5, June-Aug also open Sat 10-5, rest of year Mon-Fri 11-4. Teton flood exhibit, local history exhibits and library, WWII, and Idaho potato exhibits. *Located at 51 N. Center* P.O. Box 244, Rexburg, ID 83440 (208) 356-9101

Rigby

Jefferson County Historical Society
Open Mon-Fri 1-5. General memorabilia from local area. *Located in community center at 110 N. State.* P.O. Box 284, Rigby, ID 83442 (208)745-8423

Salmon

Lemhi County Historical Museum Open April-June Mon-Sat 1-5, July-Aug Mon-Sat 10-5, Sept-Oct Mon Sat 1-5. Features extraordinary Ray Edward oriental collection, local history, Native American artifacts. *Located at 210 Main Street.* P.O. Box 645, Salmon, ID 83467 (208) 756-3342

Terreton

Mud Lake Historical Society Open Thur 1-5. Local history. *Located in city building at Mud Lake.* P.O. Box 114, Terreton, ID 83450 (208) 663-4376

"YOU HAVE GATHERED THAT I LIKE IDAHO . . ."

"We stopped at a roadside restaurant and beer hall, and an old sprite waited on us, saying you just dam betcha he had what we wanted. A Sharps buffalo gun hung on the wall, and it led to talk of old times. Long ago, our ancient waiter told us, he had trailed horse herds over the divide into Montana and driven others back."

"It was branded stock," he said, grinning. "All legal, of course." He gave us a big wink then. "Oh, they'll find my marks on this country all right," he went on. "You dam betcha they'll find my marks."

Would they? The marks we found were the marks the country had left on him. It had weathered his skin and bowed his legs, and, far more important, had given him that certain cast of mind and spirit that space and nature face to face give men.

The quality perhaps can best be called resilience. It is an ability to accept what comes in a kind of life in which anything may come and many things do. The isolated Westerner, the self dependent Idahoan-and his city brother through exposure to him - more often than not learns to take it and, what's more, to make the best of it. He can dismiss misfortune with a crack. He dares nature to wipe the grin off his face.

So the quality isn't submissiveness. It is closer to defiance, and it is a triumph of the man, not over nature, but over himself. He has risen superior to self pity; he can see the humor in adversity. Best of all, he isn't posing. His reactions are unstudied and almost automatic, their origins so lost to him that, marked by country as he is, he still can think he marked the country.

If you have followed me this far, you have gathered that I like Idaho. The crystal streams. The rushing rivers. The forests. The mountains. The lakes as blue as paint. The splash of mountain ash or maple. The foam of the syringa, the state's official flower. The awesome wastes. The fruitful fields. The warm friendliness of crossroads and town. The high sky over all."

—A.B. Guthrie

PHOTOGRAPHIC CREDITS

Steve Bly - Photographer
Forty years ago, Steve left the flatlands of Kansas to work on a forestry crew in the Northwest. He specializes in travel and adventure photography. He has been recognized with awards by travel writers and outdoor journalists. His work has been featured in the New York Times and National Geographic. He maintains his home and studio adjacent to a wildlife sanctuary on the banks of the Boise River. Photos: Pages v, 59, 61, 96, 101, 115, 158, 171, 173, 179, 180, 186(bottom), 194, 195, 197.

Steven Snyder - Photographer
Steven is a Ketchum resident, and a premiere black & white photographer of the United States. He has specialized in wildlife and Idaho landscapes, and recently has become involved in promoting conservation of the earth's resources. He is a two-time winner of the "poetry slam" contest in Ketchum's Main Street BookCafe, and contributed the poem on page 182. Photos: Pages 4, 7, 181, 182, 184-185, 186(top), 219.

Idaho State Historic Society, Boise, Idaho
The entire staff of the ISHS is a model for cooperation and support for projects like this. Our sincere thanks for their professionalism and enthusiasm. Photos: Pages iii, viii, 1-8, 12, 15, 16-25, 29-31, 33, 35-41, 43-45, 47, 49, 50, 53-58, 60, 65-71, 73, 74, 76-79, 83, 85-91, 93-95, 97, 103, 105, 108,110-113, 119, 121, 124, 128, 130-133, 135-143, 146-152, 155-157, 159-164, 166-167, 169, 172, 174, 175, 177, 178, 179, 183, 190, 193, 203, 205, 209, 214.
****
Bannock County Historical Museum, Pocatello
Page 90, 109

Boise State University, Limbert Collection, Boise
Page 129

Wolf Education and Research Center, Ketchum
Page 188

The Coeur d'Alene, Coeur d'Alene
Page 13

Community Library of Ketchum
Pages 120, 126, 127, 200

James DeBoer, State College, Pennsylvania
Page 201

Tom Drougas, Ketchum
Page 130

Eastern Washington Historical Society
Page 17

Don Gill, Gooding
Page 154

Grand Targhee Ski Resort, Driggs, Idaho
Pages 107, 192

Latah County Historical Society
Page 40, 145

Steve Mitchell
Pages 75, 207

Haynes Foundation, Montana State Historical Society
Page 18

Museum of North Idaho
Photos: Page 145

Schweitzer Basin Ski Resort, Sand Point, Idaho
Pages 11, 191

Sun Valley Corporation, Sun Valley, Idaho
Page 123

The Wood River Journal, Hailey, Idaho
Pages 146, 168, 170, 196, 208

ACKNOWLEDGEMENTS

Grateful acknowledgement is made to the following for the use of their material.

"North Idaho", "Kellogg", "Lakes of the North","You Have Gathered That I Like Idaho", short excerpts from a travel piece, (c) Guthrie, A.B.

"Boundary Country", (c) Sleep, Francis

"House of the Great Spirit", (c) Bahr, Fran, *Oh! Idaho* magazine.

"Searching for the Silver Lining", (c) Bennett, Earl. *Oh Idaho* Magazine

"The Cave In" *Idaho Nuggets*, (c) Blume, Helen

"Ignace Hatchioraquasha", "Battle Near Pierre's Hole", "Andrew Henry", "Dumaris & Plante Never Return", "Bucksin Billy", "Jean Baptiste Charbonneau","Fort Henry", *Mountain Men of Idaho*, Maverick Publications, Bend, Oregon.

"Wyatt Earp in Murray", "A Sunken Treasure", "Sunshine Mine Disaster", "Our Oldest State Park", "Diamondfield Jack:Three Island Crossing", "Bruneau Dunes", "Pocatello Land Rush", "Fort Hall Liquidation Sale", "The Bonneville Flood", "Bear Lake Monster", "Sleeping in a Volcano", Arthur Hart, (c) *Snapshots of Idaho*.

From *English Creek*, pages 227-228, (c) Doig, Ivan.

"Hardhat", "Diamondfield Jack", "Blue Bucket", "Paul Bunyan", "Snake Medicine", "Hundred Dollar Jim", Fisher, Vardis, *Idaho Lore* (out-of-print).

"The Fire of 1910" Paul Mather, (c) Museum of North Idaho.

Swenson, Karen, "Coming In On Highway 12", from *Where the Morning Light's Still Blue*, University of Idaho Press.

"The Crown Jewel", (c) Margaret Fuller, *Oh Idaho* magazine.

"Idaho's Seaport", "Travel Journal" (c) London, Bill, *Oh Idaho* magazine.

Hunting the Grisly, Roosevelt, Theodore (Teddy). 1909 -out-of-print.

"Latah County Parks", Peterson, Keith, (c) Latah County Centennial.

"Indoors in Moscow", (c) McFarland, Ron. *Oh Idaho* Magazine.

"Timber", (c) Coyner, Barbara. *Oh Idaho* Magazine.

Stegner, Wallace. *Angle of Repose*, Doubleday & Co., New York.

"Pierce" from *And Five Were Hanged*, out-of-print.

Ardinger, Rick. "The Highway Home" and "Breakfast in Idaho City" , from *Where The Morning Light Is Blue*, University of Idaho Press.

"Basque Country", "Myths, Buckaroos, and Realities", (c) Preston, Scott. *Pacific Northwest* Magazine.

"Frozen Fantasies", (c) Ford, Francis W., *Oh Idaho* magazine.

"Owyhee Bones", (c) Rapp, Rodger, *Oh Idaho* magazine.

"Silver City", Baker, Bessie, (c) *Scenic Idaho*.

"Sand of Time", "In The Shadow of Yellowstone", (c) Delisio, Mario, *Oh Idaho* magazine.

"Springs Eternal", (c) Sammis, Laurie, *Oh Idaho* magazine.

"Raised in Idaho", (c) Clark, David, *Oh Idaho* magazine.

"Lyda Southard's Apple Pie", (c) Sorrels, Rosalie, *Way Out in Idaho*, Confluence Press, Lewiston.

"Minidoka's Desert Empire", "Gooding County", (c) *Scenic Idaho*.

"Healing of the Hills", Leitner, Doris, (c) *White Gold*.

"Silent City", (c) Green, Randall, *Oh Idaho* magazine.

"The Twin Falls Story", courtesy of Stan Thomas and Rock Creek Restaurant.

"Calling the Coyotes In", (c) Barnes, Kim, *Where The Morning Light is Blue*.

"Spring in Pocatello", (c) Wyndham, Harold, *Where The Morning Light Is Blue*.

"Beautiful Cache Valley", Roberts, Daniel, *Scenic Idaho* magazine.

"The Yellowstone League", (c) *Tales of Southeastern Idaho*.

"Taking Root", (c) Finnigan, Karen, *Oh Idaho* magazine.

"Jim Beckwith's Run", (c) *Mountain Men of Idaho*.

"Idaho's lava Hot Springs", (c) *Scenic Idaho* magazine.

"Butch Cassidy Hits Montpelier", Montpelier newspaper file.

"Sunrise Side of the Tetons", (c) Sherlock, Patti, *Oh Idaho* magazine.

"Idaho Falls", (c) *Scenic Idaho* magazine.

"On Going Back To Sawtooth Valley", (c) Rember, John, *Oh Idaho* magazine.

"Your Own Private Idaho", Sylvain, Rick, *Detroit Free Press*.

"How Far My House Is From Home - Going Back To Yellow Jacket", (c) Studebaker, William.

"Incident at Leadore", (c) Mcfarland, Ron, *Where The Morning Light Is Blue*.

"The Roof Of Idaho", (c) Koller, Greg, *Oh Idaho* magazine.

"Lilies of the Field-Travel Journal", Johnson, June, *Oh Idaho* magazine.

"Ghost Towns" from *Ghost Towns of Idaho*, (c) Hart, Arthur.

"Family of Families", (c) Pearson, Ridley, *Oh Idaho* magazine.

"The Miners", (c) Studebaker, Williams, *Rat lady At The Company Dump*.

"Fighting The Dragon", Carroll, Frank, *Oh Idaho* magazine.

"Claude Dallas", Idaho Centennial.

"Rodeo's Sundown", (c) Loeffelbein, Bob, *Wild West Magazine*, Cowles History Group, Leesburg, Virginia.

"Chief Joseph's Surrender", Report of the Secretary of War, 1877.

"Euzkera", (c) Purcell, Roger, *Oh Idaho* magazine.

"A Sacred Tradition", Troyer, Dianna, *Oh Idaho* magazine.

"The Railroad Comes To Moscow", Munson, Charles, *Westward To Paradise*, 1885.

"Circle of Women", (c) Barnes, Kim, *Where The Morning Light Is Blue*, University of Idaho Press.

"The Active Frontier", (c) Vanderbilt, Ann, *Oh Idaho* magazine.

"Water of Life", (c) Stilwill, Clarence, *Oh Idaho* magazine.

"Silver Creek", (c) Clark, David, *Oh Idaho* magazine.

"Denizens of the Deep", (c) Slough, Andrew, *Oh Idaho* magazine.

"Wild Spirits", (c) Sherlock, Patti, *Oh Idaho* magazine.

"Who", (c) Snyder, Steven.

"The Longing of Eagles", "Stopping By the Woods", (c) Wrigley, Robert.

"Raptors", (c) Koskela, Alize, *Oh Idaho* magazine.

"Wolves Released in Idaho", Kanamine, Linda, (c) USA Today, December 1995.

"High Points", (c) Baugher, Rick, *Oh Idaho* magazine.

"How Sweet It Skis", "Brundage Mountain", "Bogus Basin", (c) Walter, Claire, *Oh Idaho* magazine.

"Park n' Ski", "A Literary Harvest", "Vardis Fisher", (c) Rawlings, Paul, *Oh Idaho* magazine.

"Patrick McManus", (c) Finley, Mitch, *Oh Idaho* magazine.

"Cafe/Bookstore Poetry Slams", (c) Crump, Steve

Special appreciaion to Arthur Hart, past-president of the Idaho State Historical Society, author, lecturer - for stories of our ghost towns and other Idaho lore pieces.

AND THANKS TO....

Donald Stone and *Northern Lights* magazine.
Roger & Phyllis Roche.
Art Selen.
Brian, Brenda & the Main Street BookCafe staff.
Colleen Daly for the connection.

SUGGESTED READING

The Idaho State Department of Commerce & Tourism provides an excellent free state Guide & Map. *Idaho unBound* is organized to be used alongside the state material.

Idaho for the Curious, by Cort Conley is a great comprehensive roadside guide to Idaho. Over a decade old, it still is full of useful information - organized by roads and highways.

Vardis Fisher, under the grant of the Federal Writer's Project, wrote *Idaho: A Guide in Word and Picture*. This out-of-print book inspired this current work, and state antiquarian booksellers may have a rare copy -all of the libraries have it. It is still probably the best book on Idaho ever written.

Where The Morning Light Is Blue, edited by Rick Ardinger and Bill Studebaker, is a wonderful contemporary collection of essays and poetry, published by the University of Idaho Press.

A number of other useful books have been written on Idaho that are still available: Arrington's *History of Idaho* is a scholarly 2-volume set.

Special Topic Books on Idaho Subjects include:

The Sun Valley Trail Guide and *The Boise Trail Guide*, by Peak Media of Hailey, Idaho.

PROFILES

Clay Morgan - Author

Award-winning fiction writer Clay Morgan has been Idaho's Writer-in-Residence, and coordinates the acclaimed Idaho "Writers and Readers Rendezvous" held each October on Payette Lake.

Clay's *Santiago and the Drinking Party* captured national acclaim and won a Pacific Northwest Book Award. His forthcoming *Carte Rosa: A Love Story with Maps*, with renown illustrator Nick Bantock, has already received rave advance notice. A former smoke jumper himself, Clay's novel on the subject is soon to be completed.

The Boise native lives with his wife Barbara, a teacher-in-space with NASA, and their two boys in McCall.

Steve Mitchell - Editor

Editor and publisher Steve Mitchell was born in Denver, Colorado, and has lived in several regions of the U.S. In 1994 he authored an illustrated biography, *Jo Mora: Renaissance Man of the West*, and owns the Main Street BookCafe of Ketchum, Idaho. Mitchell Publishing, which Steve started in 1979, was purchased by Random House

in 1986. He is the publisher of West Bound Books, a new publishing imprint based in Ketchum.

Don Gill - Cartographer/Illustrator

Don is known for his art and his ranch life cartoons. He has illustrated a number of Baxter Black's collection of cowboy poetry and ranch stories, and recently completed the characters for a forthcoming syndicated network television cartoon series -characterized by its producers as a "cowboy Simpsons." Don and his family live in Gooding, Idaho. You might to be able to find him at home in his studio, at the Gooding feedlot, or with Denise at a state high school rodeo event.

Clark Heglar - "Oldest Man in Idaho" Stories

Otherwise known throughout Idaho as "the Oldest Man" -a series he created for the Oregon Trail celebration, Clark was born on the present site of Farragut Park in Coeur d'Alene. Raised in Pocatello, his presentations on Idaho history and folklore are popular with schools, bookstores, and various state and regional events.

INDEX

AVAILABLE NOW:

Idaho Unbound: A Scrapbook & Guide Retail Price $20.95
Order Number: 1-887504-00-3

Don Gill's ***Illustrated Maps*** are fine quality posters with enlarged images of the maps within this book. The maps are produced in 24 by 36 inch reproductions, and may be trimmed to 24 by 32 inches in desired for standard maps and frames. The retail price of each map is $20.95.

State of Idaho Map
Order Number: M951

North Idaho Map (Coeur d'Alene, Sand Point, Bonner's Ferry)
Order Number: M952

Southwest Idaho Map (Boise, McCall, Nampa, Caldwell, the Owyhee)
Order Number: M953

Central Idaho Map (Sun Valley, Ketchum, Stanley, Lost River area, Craters of the Moon, Silver Creek)
Order Number: M954

ORDER FROM:

West Bound Books, Box 753, Ketchum, Idaho 83340
By phone: Peak Media fulfillment 1-800-769-1055

Editorial & Corporate Offices: 208-788-5165
Store Returns: Peak Media 418 North River St., Hailey, ID 83333

"Oldest Man in Idaho" appearances by Clark Heglar may be booked directly with Clark at 208-726-1357.

Information on the annual Idaho Readers & Writers Rendezvous may be obtained from Boise State University at 800-632-6586 x3492.